IVOR NOVELLO

Man of the Theatre

by the same author

★

CINEMA

BRITISH FILM

SPOTLIGHT ON FILMLAND

THE NEGRO IN FILMS

PICTURE PARADE: 1949

PICTURE PARADE: 1950

THE BRITISH FILM YEARBOOK (EDITOR)

THEATRE AND BALLET

BRITISH THEATRE

THE BRITISH THEATRE YEARBOOK (EDITOR)

BRITISH BALLET

BIOGRAPHY

BETTE DAVIS

HOLLYWOOD SCAPEGOAT: THE BIOGRAPHY OF ERICH VON STROHEIM

PROFILES AND PERSONALITIES

VERSE

THE CITY IN THE SUN

LETTERS FROM LIMBO

All good wishes

IVOR NOVELLO

Man of the Theatre

by

PETER NOBLE

with a foreword by

NOËL COWARD

LONDON

THE FALCON PRESS

First published in 1951
by the Falcon Press (London) Limited
6 & 7 Crown Passage, Pall Mall,
London, S.W.1

Second edition April 1951
Third (revised) edition June 1951

Printed in Great Britain
by the C.W.S. Printing Works,
Reddish, Stockport

'I believe in the theatre; I believe in beauty in the theatre; I believe that in the theatre lies one of the roads back to sanity. I want to give the people the chance to dream again.'—*From 'Proscenium', by Ivor Novello.*

TO

MY DAUGHTER—KATINA

ACKNOWLEDGEMENTS

The author wishes to acknowledge his thanks to the following for permission to reproduce extracts from certain books and publications: Messrs. Heinemann Ltd. (*The Life I Have Loved,* by Clara Novello Davies, and *Present Indicative,* by Noël Coward); Messrs. Forbes Robertson Ltd. (*Nice Work,* by Adrian Brunel); The British Film Institute (*Index to the Work of Alfred Hitchcock,* by Peter Noble); Messrs. Methuen Ltd. (Three Plays by Ivor Novello, with an Introduction by Sir Edward Marsh); W. H. Allen Ltd. (*Theatre Royal, Drury Lane,* by W. Macqueen-Pope); World Film Publications (*Michael Balcon's Twenty-five Years in Films,* edited by Monja Danischewsky); and The Editors of *Radio Times, Everybody's, Band Wagon, The Sketch.*

The author would particularly like to thank Hartney Arthur, and the many individuals in the world of the theatre and cinema who have so willingly supplied data, lent cuttings and photographs, and in every way co-operated to make this book a fitting tribute to Novello, particularly Sir Michael Balcon, Sir Edward Marsh, Reginald Baker, Adrian Brunel, Collie Knox, Frances Rowe, Maurice Elvey, Sylvia Homewood, John Montgomery, Margot Grahame, John Counsell, Pamela Fisher, Tom Arnold, Edward Baxter, Mario Gallati, Kneale Kelley, Alec Robertson, Hilda Robinson, Margaret Heald, Dorothy Freeman, Bessie Cruft, George Freedley (Curator of the Theatre Collection of the New York Public Library), John Parker (Editor of 'Who's Who in the Theatre'), C. R. Selous Jones, Christianne Floor, Rita Cornish, and particularly Gordon Duttson, who went to endless trouble to check casts, dates, programmes and press cuttings. Without his invaluable help the book would never have been completed.

Apology: I should like to express my sincere apologies to William Newman for the error in the first impression of the book: turn to page 263 and you will see that the facts are now accurately recorded.

Contents

Illustrations

Foreword

In view of the sudden and tragic death of Ivor Novello and at the request of Noël Coward and the executors of Ivor Novello, the original foreword to this biography has been withdrawn from this, and all further editions.

A few hours after news of the death of his friend reached Noël Coward in Jamaica, the following message was received from him. It is at his request that this message is included in place of the original foreword.

Please understand and forgive me but I am too shattered by the news of Ivor Novello's death to write an estimate of his work or his personality that would do justice to either.

We have been close friends for thirty-five years and my feelings at the moment are too private and too unhappy to be put into words.

I can only say that there is a small measure of consolation in the thought that he died at the height of his triumphant career and will never know the weariness of age nor the sadness of decline.

For those who loved him there is no consolation except the memory of his charm, his humour, and his loving generosity.

His death will be a personal loss to many millions of people —this is his greatest tribute and his greatest epitaph.

NOËL COWARD

Introduction

'Novello's place in theatrical history is assured—not because of his legendary success, not just because he is a great showman, but because, in an age of mediocrity, he gave common men and women an illusion. And he made the people sing.'—*John Raymond in the 'Daily Graphic', September 25th, 1949.*

The story of Ivor Novello is simply the history of a phenomenon. Until his death he had been a stage legend for more than thirty years: a fabulously successful composer, playwright, film star and stage idol. His songs have gone round the world hundreds of times, his music is heard continually in every country on the globe, his plays are household words. There is nobody in the English-speaking world who has not heard of Ivor Novello. He was Britain's greatest genius of the musical stage. Handsome, popular, world-renowned, modest and tremendously likeable, he was essentially the same in 1951 as he was in the early 1900's, when he was just stage-struck little 'Ivor Davies', up from Cardiff with his beloved mother to see the sights of London in those glamorous years when Daly's and the Gaiety were the twin queens of the West End stage.

He remained young until he died. But for a touch of grey at the temples and a friendly line or two round the mouth and eyes, Novello still looked the same in 1951 as he did twenty years ago, at the time when he was voted England's Number One Film Star. Seeing him in the 1940's in his remarkable musical successes like *The Dancing Years, Perchance to Dream* and *King's Rhapsody,* one found it increasingly hard to believe that Ivor was born in 1893, and that he was a nationally-known celebrity during the First World War. He was a veritable Peter Pan of the stage.

Moreover, Ivor not only looked the same person, but he was the same person. Still living in the same delightful flat above the Strand Theatre in the Aldwych, he retained much the same circle of faithful friends as when—in the period 1915–19—he was an eager young composer whom everybody predicted would have 'a brilliant future': Robert Andrews, Fay Compton, Sir Edward Marsh, Phyllis Monkman, Noël Coward, Henry Kendall, etc. But if his personality and person gave not a hint that this gracious young man was in his fifties, his work had become more and more mature. Year by year his plays and music went on improving. In 1951 he had no rivals in the sphere he had triumphantly made his own.

His first theatre score was for the show *Theodore & Co.*, produced successfully at the Gaiety Theatre in 1916. Good as it undoubtedly was, it does not, could not, compare with the unforgettable scores Novello composed during the past fifteen years, music which will live as long as there are people to sing the melodies. Though he was a matinée idol and a polished and gifted actor for many years, Ivor went on the stage, it must be remembered, quite late in life. Renowned as a talented young Welsh composer and musician, he became a famous British film star in 1919, in his very first film, *The Call of the Blood,* but did not make his stage début—against the advice of many of his friends, incidentally—until he was nearly thirty. When one considers that he virtually lost a dozen years on the stage—for most young actors make their first professional appearance at about the ages of eighteen or nineteen—it seems even more remarkable that he managed to progress so swiftly to his position as one of the leading stage stars in the world, and to retain that position for a quarter of a century.

In attempting to write a book about Ivor Novello I have found myself up against a continual problem—what to leave out—for he did so much, knew so many famous people, lived such a rich, full life, contributed so greatly to the happiness of others, made such a place for himself on the English musical stage, that a really comprehensive study of his life and achievements would require several volumes. This book is, therefore, no more than a sketch for a biography. It is merely a short tribute to a great man, to chronicle his contributions to the British theatre. One cannot hope to include here all the full and fascinating details of Novello's extraordinary career, and is, indeed, bound to omit some of the tangled threads in the patchwork of his glamorous life. To some extent, what follows is simply the success story of a young man from Cardiff who rose to fame and fortune, but it must be remembered that Novello rose remarkably quickly. He was famous when he was twenty-one. Fame came suddenly—and it never really left him. Since that phenomenal song, 'Keep the Home Fires Burning', caught the public imagination in 1915, he sailed along on a fairly even keel of popularity and success, experiencing, nonetheless, some of the usual theatrical ups and downs which, in any case, mark any famous artist's progress through life. Undoubtedly Novello was lucky—and he was the first to admit it—but he had a fantastic and many-sided talent which, even without luck, would have made him famous in any age and in any country. Ivor had a gift for expressing himself, personally, dramatically and musically. In addition he had been gifted with the most devastating good looks, along with a warmth and charm of personality which made him—and I say this with sincerity—one of the best-loved men in the English theatre of the first half of the century.

Ivor Novello was acknowledged to be one of the giants of the modern English stage. His plays, his writings and his music will live for a very long time to come, and a tribute to the man, his work and his influence has been long overdue. But Novello always firmly resisted all overtures by publishers to let them bring out his memoirs, or to allow somebody to attempt a book about his exciting life. I am indeed happy that he decided to allow me to go ahead and publish his official biography a year or so before he planned to take time off from his work to start his long-promised autobiography.

Unhappily he never commenced work on his memoirs, for he died very suddenly of coronary thrombosis, three hours after the curtain had fallen on his performance as King Nikki in his play *King's Rhapsody* at the Palace Theatre. His death, on March 6th, 1951, was a tragic blow to the English theatre and to his millions of admirers. With his passing went an era. With him died a legend. There never will be, never could be another Ivor Novello, the greatest Romantic of his day. We shall never cease to mourn him, but he left us a legacy of music and happiness.

I have enjoyed writing this biographical study more than any other book I have published; I can only hope that the reader shares some of the enjoyment, and feels a little of the excitement which has gone into the chronicling of this story of a phenomenon.

In offering this volume to the public, I realize that it does not do justice one-tenth to the greatness and genuineness of the man himself, but I have written it in due humility, and can only hope that it may let loose a flood of books about the genius of the great Welshman who brought more happiness to more people through his many gifts than possibly any other man of our century.

P. N.
London, 1951.

I

Childhood in Cardiff

THE week-end of January 15th, 1893, was like most other week-ends in that peaceful year. Queen Victoria was on the throne, eighty-four-year-old Mr. Gladstone was Prime Minister and 'all was right with England'. One could advertise for a house-parlourmaid 'thoroughly experienced and a good Christian' for £18 a year, and a gentleman could buy a brougham for eighty guineas—and even a landau for a hundred. On that particular week-end there was not much news of great import. The Queen was in semi-retirement at Osborne, attended by Princess Louise and Princess Beatrice. Edward, Prince of Wales, was staying at Marlborough House, and apparently having—as usual—a very good time in London. Mr. Gladstone and his wife had attended a performance that Saturday night of *Robin Goodfellow,* with John Hare and Forbes Robertson, at the Garrick Theatre. John D. Rockefeller had given away another million dollars—this time to the University of Chicago. The London, Brighton, and South Coast Railway announced a dividend of 9¼%, and *The Times* was chock-a-block with advertisements for coachmen, footmen, butlers, grooms, cooks, parlour maids, companions, governesses, between-maids, personal maids, and under-gardeners. In the 'For Sale' columns of that august journal a house agent had seen fit to announce, 'To Be Let: a charming house in Eccleston Square—on the best side!' Yes, this was Victorian England—a 'gentleman's country'—prosperous, complacent, unexciting. Yet there were stirrings 'below stairs'. At Tower Hill on that Saturday afternoon a thousand unemployed had held a meeting to protest against the ramifications of the Poor Law, described by them as a 'legalized swindle'. Later a deputation marched to Downing Street, there to present their protest to Mr. Gladstone (who, incidentally, must have then been taking tea preparatory to departing for the theatre with his good lady in the brougham).

At Bradford, the Independent Labour Party, from which has sprung our present Labour Party, was formed; at its first conference Keir Hardie was elected President. It was a momentous day; as *The Times* commented on January 14th, 1893: 'The organization of the I.L.P. is another incident of evil omen for the Gladstonians.' The Irish were agitating for Home Rule—and were to go on doing so for the next quarter of a century. What were the main topics of conversation during that week-end? Keir Hardie and his new group of 'radicals'. Ireland and 'those troublesome Irish'. Queen Victoria and her son 'Teddy'. And the sensational World's Fair shortly to be held in Chicago.

And what of the theatre? The hits of London were Dan Leno in *Little Bo-Peep* at Drury Lane, Arthur Roberts in *Auld Lang Syne* at the Gaiety, George Alexander in *Liberty Hall* at the St. James's, and *Robin Goodfellow* at the Garrick. Two clever young actresses were making reputations for themselves at the Vaudeville in *Our Boys*; their names were May Whitty and Eva Moore. The giants of the English music-hall were Marie Lloyd, Dan Leno, Arthur Roberts, Bessie Bellwood, Wilkie Bard, and young George Robey. Arthur Sullivan's new light opera, *Haddon Hall,* was drawing crowds to the Savoy, and W. S. Penley was being acclaimed a riot in a new farce called *Charley's Aunt* at the Royalty. At the late-lamented Toole's Theatre J. L. Toole himself was starring in a new comedy *Walker, London,* by an up-and-coming young playwright called James Barrie. The great Charles Wyndham starred in *The Silent Battle,* a melodrama at the Criterion, Mr. and Mrs. Kendal were appearing together, as usual, in *A White Lie* at the Avenue, and Lewis Waller, Fred Terry and Julia Neilson formed a starry trio which packed the Haymarket nightly, in *Hypatia*. Theatrically speaking, it was quite an historic week-end. It proved to be even more historic, for on that Sunday a child was born in Cardiff who was to bring great glory to the English stage over the next half-century. The boy was Ivor Novello.

Two hours after Madame Novello Davies had given a singing lesson at Llwyn-yr-Eos (The Grove of Nightingales), Cowbridge Road, Cardiff, on the afternoon of January the 15th, her only son, David Ivor, was born. The pupil (Gwen Thomas, now the mother of film star Margot Grahame), confesses that she did not even realize that her teacher was about to become a mother!

Madame Clara was a fabulous and wonderful woman. Her son readily admitted that without her help, encouragement, and advice he would never have had all the successes he had enjoyed, nor have begun his career as a composer in such an auspicious fashion at the early age of fifteen. She played a great part in his life and her name will be found in every chapter of this book.

Born Clara Novello Davies, of pure Welsh stock (having been christened Clara Novello by her music-loving father, Jacob Davies, after her godmother, the famous Italian singer), she was brought up in a musical family. Herself an excellent singer, Clara, after her marriage to a handsome young accountant—David Davies—began to teach singing in Cardiff, eventually becoming one of the most distinguished teachers in the British Isles. David was himself very musical and fell in enthusiastically with his wife's programme of musical evenings, concerts and lessons. At that time he was a tax collector in the city; later he became head of the Glamorgan Rates Office in Cardiff City Hall. A serious, down-to-earth and sensible man, with a quiet and delightfully dry sense of humour, he provided much-needed ballast to the mad-cap musical activities of his brilliant and effervescent young wife. The family later moved to their own newly-built house at 11, Cathedral Road, Cardiff, which was their home for several years, and was to become the centre of all musical life in that city. The large house was a veritable beehive of activity, and 'pupils continuously swarmed all over the place', as Madame Novello Davies herself declares in her autobiography.*

'A few days after Ivor was born—we never called him David—although he was christened "David Ivor" after his father,' she continues, 'one of my small pupils, Ivor Morgan, son of Sir Morgan Morgan, whose wife was one of my dearest friends, hastened around to see the new baby, bringing with him a beautiful basket of flowers. "Has he had his first piano lesson yet, madame?" he very anxiously enquired.

'"Not yet, darling," I replied.

'"Good, I am so afraid he will get ahead of me," cried the dear child, running off home to practise for all he was worth.'

On seeing her baby son for the first time. Madame Clara gazed at him with something akin to horror. She beheld the most elfin face she had ever seen, with wisps of black hair seemingly glued on in places, tiny peering eyes, and the small features entirely dominated by what appeared to be an extraordinarily large nose.

'Good Heavens!' she gasped. 'It's Uncle Ebenezer come back.' (Her late-lamented uncle had possessed one of the most prominent noses in all Wales.)

'There you are, Lal. Just see what God has sent you,' chuckled David. 'He looks just like a wizened goblin. I knew you were asking far too much—and the trouble is that you can't send it back!'

Mrs. Davies cried all that day and night, and her only hope for her unfortunate child was that he might also partake of her Ebenezer's undoubted zeal for good works (her uncle being a pillar of the Salem Chapel). The next day she chided herself for her foolishness and gathered her precious bundle, 'Little Funny Face', as she called him, to her heart.

Twenty-five years later her son, Ivor, was to share with John Barrymore the possession of the title of 'The World's Most Handsome Profile'.

'When Ivor was only six weeks old,' Madame Clara

* *The Life I Have Loved* (Heinemann, 1940).

recollects, 'I had an out-of-town engagement with my Welsh Ladies' Choir, so, realizing that he must travel with me, I had him snugly tucked up, and his old nurse, Jane Thomas, proudly carried the precious bundle. A nice hot meal awaited us before the concert, and during the interval I hurried from the platform to the dressing-room, where my baby was lustily awaiting his supper, after which he went blissfully off to sleep while I resumed my baton. Ivor certainly had the full benefit of music with his meals, as I had just been directing the glorious voices of my girls and my mind was full of their melody, so that he always insists he was born in music and had it for breakfast, dinner and tea! I still remember the funny way in which he used to cry, in perfect thirds, which were not at all inharmonious to listen to!'

On the day her little boy reached the age of six months, Madame Clara was suddenly offered the greatest musical opportunity of her life. By then the famous World's Fair at Chicago, long in preparation, had reached realization, and a great World's Fair International Competition was being held to determine the finest choir in the world. Ap. Madoc, the fine bard and poet, who was representative for Wales at the Fair, invited Madame Clara to enter her choir in the competition, and it did not take her long to realize that international victory at Chicago would be a wonderful stepping-stone to greater things.

Nevertheless, the whole scheme presented many difficulties, all of which boiled down to one thing—money. Financially, to take two or three score of girls all those thousands of miles by sea and land would be a great problem. Madame Clara decided to approach Lascelles Carr, the editor of the Welsh daily newspaper, the *Western Mail.* He was highly enthusiastic about the scheme, and through his efforts, and those of his assistant, William Davies (afterwards Sir William Davies, who succeeded Lascelles Carr as editor), the necessary finance was raised by the *Western Mail.* Carr considered it essential that a Welsh choir should be represented at the World's Fair, and his vision was justified.

Her heart was full of gratitude, but it was also heavy, for

her trip to America would mean leaving her baby son. Until then she had taken him everywhere with her—to rehearsals, concerts, shopping trips—but it was simply impossible to take him with her across the sea. At last it was decided to leave Ivor in the care of his great-grandparents, William Evans and his wife; the baby could not have been in better hands, for the Evans adored Ivor and welcomed the opportunity of taking him into their home while their beloved grand-daughter and grandson were in America.

As it happened, Madame Clara and her Welsh Ladies' Choir swept on to a famous victory against the finest choral opposition the world could provide. Her Welsh girls took the prize, and also conquered the hearts of the Americans. The success of the choir made heartening news in the Welsh and English Press. Madame Clara had brought glory and honour to her native country. And that was not all; she was deluged with offers of concerts in various parts of the U.S.A., and finally her husband, who had obtained leave from his work to make the trip with her, sat down and worked out a practical tour. Because of the vastness of the continent it was impossible to fit in all the concerts they were asked to give, but a most enjoyable tour of the East Coast of the U.S.A. was made before setting sail for Southampton.

There the choir received a rousing civic reception. Later, at Cardiff Station, ten thousand people gathered to pay tribute, and Clara and David were surrounded by a cheering mass of proud and happy Celts.

'This civic reception, however, all seemed as nothing to me,' she declared, 'in my desire to get home and hold my baby in my arms again. I rushed into my house and up to the nursery. There was my precious in his nurse's arms. My heart was like to burst with emotion, and I stretched my arms out to take him, but he just clung tightly to her with a stranglehold around her neck, and howled when I tried to take him away. I tried again, but was kicked furiously for my pains, while he screamed the louder. Downstairs reporters were flocking in, but I refused to see them. I was weeping. My return home had been an anti-climax. I dried my eyes, smiled my most charming smile, and eventually wheedled him into coming into my arms, where, worn out with crying, he finally fell asleep. I sat there holding him tightly to me for many hours, not daring to move in case he should wake and want to leave me.'

From that moment onwards Ivor hardly left his mother, and until the day of her death they remained devoted to each other, with Madame Clara doing everything possible to further the career of her talented son. Ivor owed everything to her, as he was the first to declare, and it is therefore fitting that the opening chapter of this book should pay tribute to a remarkable and wonderful woman, whose death in 1943 was a great loss to music.

On the very day that she celebrated Ivor's first birthday, some months after her return from the U.S.A., Madame Clara was asked to give a Command Performance before Queen Victoria at Osborne. The Queen had heard from her harpist, John Thomas, who had been present at Chicago, of the enormous success of the Welsh Ladies' Choir, and was very much interested in hearing them. That was the first of several appearances before Her Majesty, and resulted in the choir being known henceforth as 'The Royal Welsh Ladies' Choir', and in making Madame Clara Novello Davies one of the most famous names in the musical profession, and a national celebrity into the bargain.

Small wonder that Ivor became a musician and composer. He was born to the sound of scales and arpeggios, for, as he recalled, 'my mother seemed to be teaching the whole of South Wales to sing'. He grew up with a love of every kind of music; it was his entire background. Little Ivor was in close and constant touch with all the celebrated prima donnas, actresses, instrumentalists and conductors of the late 1890's and early 1900's, for his mother knew them all. Madame Novello Davies' closest friend was that fabulous singer, Clara Butt; it was during a visit to the house in Cardiff that Clara became engaged to Kennerley Rumford, and at their wedding the sallow-faced, handsome little boy, known as 'Ivor Davies', was one of their pages, dressed in a white satin suit (in which, although he was subsequently sick all over it, he admitted, 'I rather fancied myself at the time').

During his mother's lessons Ivor and his nurse often sat on a rug in one corner of the studio. 'One day,' Madame Clara relates, 'I was having rather a difficult time with a pupil of mine who could not seem to get an exercise. If we repeated it once, we did it twenty-five times. I was almost in despair when Ivor, a little tot in a pinafore, toddled over and, looking up at me with a serious expression, said, "Mammy, may *I* try it?" I was a little surprised and somewhat nonplussed. The situation was truly an embarrassing one, and more so when Ivor did the same exercise perfectly in his piping voice. You won't believe it, but my pupil saw the idea and did the exercise after him without a single mistake.'

Among the other famous figures who visited Ivor's home during those exciting childhood days in Cardiff were actors like Julia Neilson, Fred Terry and Lily Hanbury, that brilliant contralto Kirkby Lunn, Ben Ffrangcon Davies, and the incomparable Adelina Patti. Ivor was only three years old when his mother persuaded him to sing in public at a party given for her by Clara Butt and Ffrangcon Davies the night before she sailed with her choir to New York for the second time, there to give seventy triumphant concerts.

On the journey home from the U.S.A. the choir gave a concert aboard ship. Back in Chicago Madame Clara had been most impressed with the conducting of a slim young man who was taking the orchestra through a rehearsal before the Welsh Ladies' Choir was itself due to rehearse. She had never known his name, although she had vainly tried to discover it on several subsequent occasions, but at the ship's concert, while her choir was singing, she suddenly noticed this same young man standing at the back of the hall. Afterwards he came and shook her warmly by the hand, congratulating her upon her wonderful choir, and introduced himself as Landon Ronald. If ever two congenial spirits met it was at that moment, and they were to remain close friends throughout the years. When Ivor was four years old the child was taken on his knee by Landon Ronald, then passing through Cardiff on his way to Merthyr Tydfil. Ivor looked the famous conductor straight in the face and said: 'What a nice long nose you have.' At this Ronald replied: 'You have a fairly long nose yourself, young man!'

When Ivor was only six, Clara Butt stood the boy up on a chair and taught him to sing 'Abide With Me', while at the age of eight Ivor even sang a duet with the great Patti herself. (The duet was hardly operatic, however, being the verse and chorus of 'If You Were Just the Sort of Fellow', a popular song made famous by Gertie Millar and George Grossmith in *Our Miss Gibbs*.) He became one of his mother's hardest-worked pupils, endlessly studying singing and the piano and practising scales for hours daily. He loved the piano, and before long became quite an accomplished child, his *pièce de résistance* at his mother's musical soirées being 'Poor Wandering One', from *The Pirates of Penzance*, which he invariably sang at the top of his voice, with 'Hear Ye, Israel' as an encore—and, let me add, accompanying himself at the piano!

Madame Clara became so famous and so much in demand as a singing teacher that during the late 1890's she began to extend her activities to London. Once a week she used to come up to London, take a room at the late-lamented Hotel Cecil, or stay with her friend Clara Butt at Hyde Park Mansions, teach there all day, leave for Bristol the same night, teach at Bristol all that day, and then make the journey back to Cardiff. Occasionally, as a special treat during his school holidays, Ivor was allowed to accompany his mother to London, and it was during one of these visits that he saw his first West End play, *English Nell*, at the Prince of Wales' Theatre, in which the late, great Marie Tempest, as Nell Gwynne, made her début in a 'straight' role.* Ivor confessed that he remembered very little about that wonderful artist because he was concentrating on watching for the appearance

* The very first play he saw was *Secrets of the Harem* in Cardiff, which he remembers as 'one of the most blood-curdling, appalling, and horrifying melodramas ever produced'. He went at the age of five, with one of the maids, while his mother was away in London, and it gave him recurrent nightmares for years.

of his friend Lily Hanbury, his mother's first London pupil, who was playing the second feminine lead. In the play Lily had to sing 'Early One Morning', which had been taught her by Madame Clara, and the little boy had to be hurriedly shushed when the actress began her song, for he exclaimed in peculiarly piercing tones, 'Ma'am taught her that at the Hotel Cecil!' Apart from this, the excitement of seeing a play which was not merely a pantomime (up to then almost the entire extent of his playgoing experiences in Cardiff) gave him such palpitations that he had to be taken back to the hotel before the final curtain.

The boy loved it all so much, however, palpitations or no palpitations, that he begged to be taken again next night, but as his mother had to go home to attend to her Welsh pupils this was not possible. To make up for it, she took him to Hamley's, in Regent Street, and bought him a fully-equipped toy theatre. That started the germ inside him which was to grow into an all-conquering love of the theatre—any and every kind of theatre.*

This toy theatre became an obsession with Ivor. When he wasn't at school or taking music lessons he was busily working as impresario, scene painter, composer, author and star. He painted and designed the scenery, wrote the plays himself, dressed up all the little dolls who played the various characters, spoke all the dialogue himself and sang all the songs. In fact, as Ivor declared, 'I was the most pronounced type of actor-manager at the early age of eight. He also made a profit, because every pupil who came into Madame Clara's for a lesson—and sometimes there were as many as thirty a day—were all roped in to see Ivor's latest production. For this he charged an admission of one penny, and all profits were ploughed back into further productions for his beloved toy theatre. And when he was not busy with his theatre, or at school, he was working hard at piano lessons and also having singing tuition from his mother. He simply adored the

* At the age of twelve Ivor pawned a family heirloom, a valuable set of calf-bound works of William Shakespeare, in order to attend every performance of the 1905 Gilbert & Sullivan season in Cardiff.

stage and wanted desperately to act. As Ivor's mother wrote:

'I was dividing my teaching activities between Cardiff, Bristol and London at that time (as well as earlier), and Ivor would plead to come and see me off. At times when I would be starting for the Metropolis I could not bear to see his sad face, and just before the train was flagged he would be bundled in beside me, so happy, although often quite unsuitably dressed; and once in our hurried exit from home I found him London-bound with only one shoe on. It had not been noticeable in the dark of the cab.

'When visiting my London studio he took full opportunity of indulging his growing passion for the theatre, and, unknown to me, would borrow half a crown at times from a maid and find his way by bus to the theatres he fancied most, often the Theatre Royal, Drury Lane. There he would climb the gallery stairs, a tiny mite but filled with a mighty purpose. And as he sat entranced in a world of make-believe which was wholly real to him, sharing the tenseness of the crowd in that vast auditorium, the excited little fellow felt the first dawning of his own future success. As he told me in later years, the thought flashed into his mind in childhood: "Some day I am going to make a play with music, a great big play, and be in it myself on that stage."

'Ivor was methodical in his theatre-going as a child, and before his father would put him in the train for London, when he was visiting me there for a week's holiday, he would be sure to provide himself with a London newspaper which gave full theatrical menus. Spreading it open at the theatre advertisements he would place it on the floor of the carriage and, kneeling over it, would pencil what seemed to be the most attractive shows. His great sorrow was that matinees were confined to Wednesdays and Saturdays then. All his pocket-money was spent on the theatre, augmented by what he could borrow. When I revealed to Ivor that acting was an art I had no intention of turning his thoughts towards a stage career. Music was to be his *forte* in my opinion, and from his earliest days he had studied the piano. But a knowledge of acting was also necessary to fulfil my greatest ambition for him, which was that he should be a composer and conductor of English or Welsh operas.'

In 1903 Ivor entered the National Eisteddfod at Aberystwyth, appearing on the programme as 'Ivor Cardiff'. The reason for this anonymity was that Madame Clara's pupils, 'those foreigners from the South', had several times carried off all the prizes at the northern Eisteddfod, and so there was virtually a ban on her pupils henceforth. She knew that she could not enter her son under his own name as there would be unavoidable prejudice. As she anticipated, the ten-year-old, unknown boy with the big dark eyes and the pale face was a sensation. He quickly sang his way through to the finals, and at length his singing of a Bach aria brought him the coveted First Prize.

John Thomas, King Edward VII's harpist (and formerly harpist to Queen Victoria), in presenting the prize, told the audience: 'You have been listening to an angel singing.'

The next morning the villagers discovered who 'Ivor Cardiff' really was, and they were justifiably annoyed that Madame Clara had pulled it off again.

In the local paper that week appeared a twenty-line poem dedicated to 'Ivor Davies' by a poet who signed himself 'Idris'. Since Ivor treasured this verse, his very first Press cutting, and therefore one which occupied an honoured place in his scrapbooks, I reproduce it here: —

Before the mighty crowd he stood,
And sang with all his little heart,
Like to a bird within a wood,
From sorrow far apart.

Upon each note his hearers hung,
(For childhood has a magic power),
As the sweet strains were heavenwards flung,
Unfetter'd in that hour.

And bosoms fluttered in the throng,
And many an eye was glistening wet,
Such magic lingered in the song—
Who heard will ne'er forget.

Press on, dear lad! The sacred flame
Of harmony within you glows,
Your mother's and your grandsire's fame
Full many a Welshman knows.

Be yours the gift to pass along
When voices of to-day are dumb,
That Wales may be a land of song,
Down the long years to come.

★

In her book Ivor's mother also recalls that she could never remember any real naughtiness in the boy, nor destructiveness of any kind. Neither had he any of the childish cruelties sometimes found in small boys. He was a gentle little soul, often up to mischief, but if it harmed anyone it hurt only himself. He was devoted to his mother and father, and although he was not treated as a child (he grew up in the happy Bohemian atmosphere of artists, and was therefore a little old for his age), he never became precocious or sophisticated in the worst senses of the words. He was quite shy, obviously a dreamer, and had great, thoughtful brown eyes and a delicate skin. From his youngest days Ivor had the privilege of knowing the world's greatest artists, singers of world-renown; he grew to be a friendly, lovable, highly-intelligent and thoughtful boy with whom everyone who visited the house immediately fell in love. Maids literally fought with each other for the privilege of taking him out for walks, and people turned in the street to look at the pretty and beautifully-dressed young man as he strolled proudly along, holding his nursemaid's hand in his.

On the rare occasions when Ivor was naughty or mischievous his mother punished him by standing him in a corner of her studio. Sometimes she would be so busy with her pupils during lessons that she would forget the small boy in the corner, so that he stood there, perhaps for an hour or two, waiting patiently for his mother to come along and 'unpunish him', as he called it. Ivor's own particular corner, Madame Clara points out, must have been apparent to all, as he had a habit of whiling away monotony by licking at the paint. Why he did not succumb to extensive paint-poisoning at a very early age is one of the mysteries she never unravelled.

Because of the continual comings and goings at 11, Cathedral Road, Ivor never felt the usual loneliness of an only child. To keep him company his mother had adopted a young singer and called her 'Marie Novello', but he never forgot his own little sister, who had died nine years before he was born, and of whom he had only heard his parents speak.

Most Sundays, after chapel, where his mother was a tireless and enthusiastic organist for more than thirty years, Ivor would visit his sister's grave, a bedraggled posy in his hand. On returning home he would explain to Lizzie, his devoted nurse: 'I have just been to my dear little sister's grave', and his eyes would swell with tears. (Ivor later said that this 'little sister act' was his first dramatic role!)

Madame Clara writes:—

'I escaped the usual question put to mothers by their offspring at an early age. Ivor never once asked in childish curiosity: "Where did I come from?" His fancy already provided the answer, and to many a visitor he told the following:—

'"One morning, when Mam was very busy giving lessons, a most important gentleman came to our front door carrying a huge big box from Queen Victoria. He was all dressed in a beautiful uniform of red, and had on a blue hat with a white feather. Mamsie couldn't leave the studio, so he walked right in and laid the box on the piano, saying: 'For you, Madame', and went out backwards. There was a letter on top, written in gold ink, and here's what it said:—

'Dear Madame:

I think it was very kind of you to let me hear your lovely choir singing at Osborne, and I hope you will like this nice present I am sending you with my fondest love.

The Queen.'

'"When Mamsie hurried to open the big box she found

it was all lined with red, white, and blue cotton-wool, and there in the very middle was ME, lying!"'

As his mother declares: 'Lying was the operative, if albeit unkind, word in this case.'

The boy had a quick brain and a remarkable imagination. He loved the piano, and even as a tiny tot he would strum out little tunes, obviously derivative from his practice pieces, but in some cases quite original little songs, one or two of which he was to develop into published successes some years later. His first school was a private academy in Cardiff, run by a Mrs. and Miss de Saulez. Here he quickly seized the opportunity of being in the school plays which were put on every season, for he continued to adore the theatre. The first play in which he was to appear was called *Robin and His Merry Men,* and the little boy was obviously delighted with his doublet, hose and other accoutrements. The great day arrived, and Ivor, all dressed up, went in the morning to the final rehearsal. He came home soon afterwards, quite distressed. 'Miss de Saulez says we cannot put on the play to-day unless the weather improves', he exclaimed. All day he kept looking out of the window for the sun, but it refused to shine, and his mother at last persuaded him to take off his grand clothes and put on more everyday attire. Next morning, to his great glee, the sun shone brightly, and he flew off to the school, carrying his costume with him. Alas! although Ivor may have thought his part quite important, he discovered, to his disappointment, that the play had been given on the previous day after all—and he had never even been missed.

However, Christmas came, and with it a school pantomime, *Aladdin,* in which he had a part. His mother waited with fluttering heart for the first appearance of her boy on the stage. Ivor played the role of a singing page at the emperor's court, and came on to the stage looking quite at home in his pretty trappings. To everyone's surprise, however, instead of singing the number that he had rehearsed, he saucily gave Gertie Millar's 'Keep Off the Grass', the song he fancied most at the moment. Singing a Gertie Millar song to a hushed Emperor's Court of the Orient must have seemed slightly incongruous—but the emperor beamed his delight, all was well, and the audience enjoyed the unexpected tit-bit.

When Ivor was twelve his mother gave him his first gramophone, an old Edison-Bell model with cylindrical records. It became the delight of his life. When he was not tinkering on the piano he was listening over and over again to the voices of Caruso, Galli-Curci and Tetrazinni. Small wonder that the boy showed such an aptitude for music; he was literally absorbed in it from birth.

He left the de Saulez school to study at Gloucester, where for a time he lived in the charming home of Mrs. Arthur Sly, a great friend of his mother's. Madame Clara was undertaking more and more work, various tours with the choir, and many journeys to London, and her fear of her little boy 'running wild' in her many absences prompted her to find a temporary home for him, where, with no studio and pupils to distract him, he might reap the benefits of a more conventional home for a period, and—what was more important—a more conventional education. At first Ivor missed the glamour and excitement of the studio, the pupils and the visiting celebrities, but he soon settled down, and the fact that he saw 'Mam' once or twice every week compensated somewhat for his being away from Cardiff.

Madame Clara had deliberately planned this temporary separation, as she wanted him to be used to being away from his mother and his home. She had set her heart on his obtaining a singing scholarship at Magdalen College, Oxford, when he was ten years old, and meantime she hoped he would begin to adapt himself to a more independent existence. Adelina Patti had put this idea into Madame Clara's mind when Ivor first sang to her in her dressing-room at the theatre.

'Why, that is *my* voice,' she exclaimed in delighted surprise.

Later Patti and Ivor's mother had discussed what would be best for him, considering what an exceptional boy-soprano voice he possessed, and they had decided that a scholarship

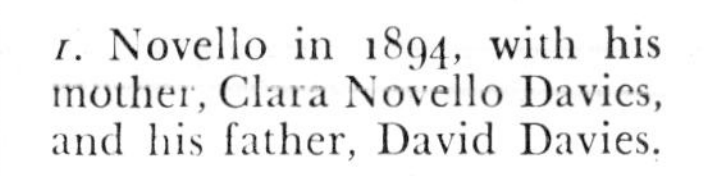

1. Novello in 1894, with his mother, Clara Novello Davies, and his father, David Davies.

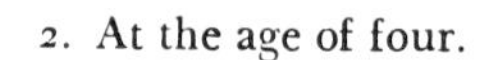

2. At the age of four.

3. As soloist of the famou choir at Magdalen Colleg School, Oxford, 1906.

4. At twenty-one—a flying officer in the Royal Naval Air Service, and the composer of 'Keep the Home Fires Burning'.

to Magdalen School would be ideal, especially as Madame Clara hoped that Ivor would devote himself to music in later life, either as a singer, composer or conductor.

Gradually the boy became less homesick at Gloucester, and, indeed, fell in love for the second time. The first girl he had been enamoured of was a certain Winnie Holland, a fellow-pupil at his first school in Cardiff. His second sweetheart was Winifred Selous Hodges, daughter of Mrs. Selous Hodges, who stayed at Longford House in Gloucester. Dorothy and Ivor had the same tutor at Mrs. Arthur Sly's house, and they became inseparable. Longford House saw the boy frequently, and it was here that he played his very first speaking part on any stage. A small but very beautiful private theatre was attached to the great house, and on its small stage a juvenile amateur production of Sheridan's *The School for Scandal* was put on, with the ten-year-old Ivor playing Sir Peter Teazle, with his beloved Winifred as Lady Teazle. He was an unqualified success, and definitely made up his mind to be an actor.

*

Ivor's voice—he was really a most remarkable boy-soprano—had improved over the years. Through constant propinquity with music he knew most of the great operatic arias, and at the drop of a hat would burst into the Jewel Song from *Faust,* the Polonaise in *Mignon,* or even Handel's 'He Shall Feed His Flock'. He became a wonderful little singer, and, indeed, it was through his voice that Ivor managed to be educated at the celebrated Magdalen College School. His mother persisted in her ambition for her son to sing in the choir of this school, which, under the direction of Dr. Varley Roberts, had become probably the most famous church choir in Britain. It consisted of sixteen carefully-picked choir boys, and any boy who was lucky enough to obtain entry into it also received a scholarship which gave him free schooling for as long as his voice lasted. This free education was most important to the Davies', as Madame Clara's earnings as a singing teacher fluctuated considerably, and she had lately launched out into renting a house in Sutherland Avenue, Maida Vale, London, for resident pupils, where she taught for three days a week. The large outlay, coupled with her fares back and forward from Cardiff to London, meant that the family's finances would have been strained to their utmost with the addition of Ivor's school fees. So it was fortunate for everyone that the child, with his lovely voice and remarkable musical knowledge, finally won a scholarship into this famous choir in 1903. He was even luckier when, in his first term, he was given all the solos to sing, as the existing solo boy's voice had just broken. 'Ivor Davies' was an immediate success, and for nearly five years sang solo with the choir, while his musical education was further increased, ranging from Bach, Beethoven, Mozart and Mendelssohn to the lesser-known but nonetheless delightful Victorian church music and folk songs.

'I suppose I must have been just an extremely average schoolboy', he recalled. 'I have a school group of the period in which it is impossible to pick me out from sixty other scrubby little faces. The only difference was that I *was* the solo boy, and therefore privileges came my way, such as ten-bob tips from old ladies who had heard the last solo boy and the one before that, and thought I was better—hence the ten-bob; singing grace in hall before celebration dinners; and being allowed to fill my stomach with rare and unaccustomed delights. I remember carrying my mortar-board full of raspberries and red currants over the bridge at ten o'clock one night, while legs of chicken stuck shyly out of my Eton trousers-pockets, all of which resulted in a dormitory feast of horrifying proportions.'

Ivor loved music, and understood it. His whole childhood had been steeped in it. In adolescence he decided that he would like to become a musician of some kind, preferably a singer or pianist, although he still cherished secret thoughts about being an actor. During the summer holidays, from the age of twelve onwards, he used to act as accompanist to the Royal Welsh Ladies' Choir on various of their tours, and eventually he grew into a most accomplished and gifted pianist as well as an exceptional vocalist.

On one occasion when the leading soprano of the choir was suddenly taken ill before a concert, young Ivor left the piano and deputized for her, without previous rehearsal, singing 'Angels Ever Bright and Fair' with absolute perfection and to the immense delight of the audience, who were enchanted by the voice of the little boy in the Eton collar. He had an amazingly lovely voice; it is a great pity that he never recorded it at the time. After it broke he hardly ever sang again, and certainly never professionally.

Of this period he declared: 'I think I must have been a dreadfully conceited little boy. Perhaps it was my fault. Perhaps it was the fault of those who let their enthusiasm run away with them in their congratulations. I am told now that my singing then was exceptional, that it was "quite the thing" in Oxford musical circles in 1905 and 1906 to go and hear "the solo boy at Magdalen". Heaven knows, there is no conceit in talking about a thing that is irrevocably gone. It is like losing a precious instrument that can never be replaced, and the tragedy of the boy-soprano whose voice suddenly breaks is indeed a very great one. My voice, happily, lasted longer than most boys' voices; in fact, I was sixteen and a half before it broke. Like so many other things that have happened to me, it occurred dramatically.

'It was the last night of term, and I was to sing the solo "O for the Wings of a Dove" in Mendelssohn's *Hear My Prayer,* and the college chapel was packed. Of all anthems this was my favourite, and, incidentally, it is the greatest tax on a boy's voice. I am told by those who were present that I had never sung it better. Dr. Varley Roberts told me after chapel, in his strong Yorkshire accent, "Eh, boy, you will be singing for me like that when you are twenty!" I was feeling particularly happy and pleased with myself that evening, but the next morning I woke up with a slight feeling of a sore throat. I found I couldn't speak at all, and decided I must have a bad cold. When the matron heard me trying to speak she rushed me to the doctor, who, taking one look at my throat, reported rather casually, never dreaming that he was to me a public executioner, "That's all right, my boy, your voice has broken".

'I looked at him in stunned silence. "But, doctor," I stammered, "it can't be! I sang last night. I was good. They all said so." I was getting desperate. My eyes pleaded with him. Again he repeated, and this time he was quite kindly, "Sorry, Davies, your voice has broken. There is simply nothing to be done about it". And that was that. I just did not know how I got out of the room. I remember rushing down to the playing fields, lying in the long grass, and sobbing as if I had lost everything that was dear to me. The only thing that cheered me up was a voice inside me which said, "This is ridiculous. You knew it had to come. Isn't it better that the last time you sang was the best you had sung in the whole of your choirboy career?" And that was the end of Oxford and my career as a star boy-soprano. It took me quite a while to get over it. Looking back now, of course, it seems a lot of bother over nothing very much, but it was for me, at that time, the great tragic crisis of my young life.'

Many years later, when Ivor had devised, written, composed and starred in a series of successful musical plays at Drury Lane, he was asked several times why he did not give himself singing as well as acting roles. He invariably replied: 'My singing voice finished at the age of sixteen and a half. Now it's like the croak of a rather tired bullfrog, and I would not dream of asking an audience to pay to hear me. How much more pleasant it is, in any case, always to be asked: "Why don't you sing in your shows?" than "Why *do* you?"'

2

Adolescence in London

Ivor's parents could not really afford to send him to the University, and the question of what the boy was to choose as a profession now he had left school was one which kept the family in a constant state of quandary. A friend of Mr. Davies' had promised to give Ivor a 'nice job' sitting up at a desk in a shipping office at Cardiff docks, but he strongly protested. His mother was against this also, and finally the good-natured David shrugged his shoulders and gave in. The boy affirmed passionately that he wanted a career in music. He was not quite sure just what he wanted to do, although he knew that he wanted to have some connection with the musical world. He would still continue to act as accompanist to his mother's choir at concerts, but he really wanted to become a composer and conductor.

At the age of fifteen he had already taken to writing songs, and in between composing ballads and small pieces he had begun to study harmony, the organ, theory and counterpoint with Dr. Herbert Brewer, the organist at Gloucester Cathedral. The old doctor confessed later that he had never had a lazier pupil in all his years of teaching. Constantly, and at length, he assured the boy that although he seemed to have undeniable musical talent, it would never develop until he stopped 'gadding about' and really started working. In between periods of 'gadding about', collecting autographs of celebrities who visited Cardiff, writing little playlets, studying under Dr. Brewer, as well as Lewis Prout of London—

and, of course, his mother—and scheming to live in London (where he could be in closer touch with the theatre), Ivor had his first small success. He had sent dozens of compositions to Arthur Boosey, the famous London music publisher, and one of these songs was finally accepted for publication. Called 'Spring of the Year', it was a waltz song to which he had composed both the music and the lyrics, and was the first composition to be published under the name of 'Ivor Novello', as he now called himself professionally. Through his mother's influence it was eventually sung in London for the first time at no less a place than the Albert Hall. The singer was Evangeline Florence, a friend and former pupil of Madame Clara's, and Ivor, as a schoolboy in an Eton collar, accompanied her on the piano. This, coupled with the fact that he had written the song, at the age of sixteen, was thought to be—by Ivor at least—most appealing. Sad to say, 'Spring of the Year' suffered a very poor reception, and there was barely sufficient applause to take Miss Florence and a rather dejected little Ivor off the platform. As if that were not bad enough, the singer, in none too sweet a mood, turned on the boy and hissed under her breath: 'I couldn't hear a note you played!'

This initial failure did not dampen the boy's spirits. He continued to write ballads and to send them to Arthur Boosey. Two or three more of his songs were published, and the boy began to realize that he might have a future in music. Some of his songs—particularly 'The Little Damosel' (first sung at the Albert Hall in 1910)—really did catch on, and were sung by almost every soprano in the country, including that genius Galli-Curci. To have his songs sung by the great Galli-Curci! Ivor could hardly believe it. Madame Clara was quietly jubilant, by this time realising that she and David had been justified in giving the boy his 'musical head' as it were. She always 'knew' Ivor was talented, but now her secret hopes and ambitions for her son seemed to be on the verge of fruition. Madame Clara was justifiably happy. Her favourite pupil was 'making his name'.

By now she had become quite a 'name' herself in London

musical circles, and was one of the leading lights behind the Sunday League Concert Society, which arranged regular celebrity concerts at the Albert Hall and elsewhere. Many of her pupils had become well-known concert artists and instrumentalists; some of them wrote to me, when it became known that I was writing a book about Novello, to tell me how Madame Clara had helped them in their careers and what a truly wonderful woman she was. Kneale Kelley, for example (now music director to the municipalities of Eastbourne and Scarborough, and guest conductor to the B.B.C. Symphony Orchestra), told me of the following incident:—

'At the age of nineteen I was trying, with the usual difficulty, to make my name as a solo violinist, and had "knocked-on-the-door" of the Sunday League Concert Society, as they had much activity in those days, but not with much success. I happened to be playing solos at a concert, and a very gracious lady, quite unknown to me, approached me after the concert and was most complimentary, and assured me that she would help me in any way she could.

'The courage of youth immediately prompted me to take advantage of this kind offer, and I asked for a letter of introduction and recommendation to the Sunday League.

'This was immediately granted me by her, and so armed I once more attacked the powers-that-be, and thus became a very regular artist at their concerts, entirely due to the kindness of Madame Novello Davies, the mother of Ivor.'

At the age of sixteen Ivor sang opposite Thelma Kaye (later to be the first Mrs. Ronald Colman) on the stage at the New Theatre, Cardiff, in a production of the Cardiff Amateur Operatic Society, a musical comedy called *The Pigeon House,* composed and produced by the Earl of Yarmouth. The boy had a good stage presence, and his voice was really superb. Later he planned to produce his own light opera, *The Fickle Jade,* for this society, but, alas! nothing ever came of this, although his operetta, of which he wrote the complete libretto, lyrics and music, gained second place in a national contest organised by Chappell's, the music publishers. For a boy of sixteen Ivor Novello was not doing at all badly. He continued to scribble lyrics to his own music, and gradually managed to get his songs performed on more and more concert platforms. Nevertheless, when Ivor finally left Dr. Brewer, on his seventeenth birthday, the good doctor pronounced him 'pretty well hopeless', declaring: 'You have no future in music.'

Various of Ivor's compositions—including another success called 'Slumber Trees'—were sung and played almost every other Saturday at the famous London Ballad Concerts held at the Albert Hall, and the boy soon began to be quite a celebrity. In Cardiff he was dubbed 'The Welsh Prodigy', and his fame started to spread. Feverishly he composed further songs, the royalties on which brought him in a tiny income. Nevertheless, tiny as it was, the income was enough to justify Ivor's proposal that he should join his mother in London and study music there. At that time Madame Clara was still spending three days of every week in London, and had now given up the Maida Vale house in order to take a little flat in Bond Street, five doors away from Chappell's. Ivor, who had spent many happy holidays at the Maida Vale house, begged to be allowed to go and live with her in Bond Street, in order to be near the world of music and theatre.

Eventually his parents assented, and soon after he was seventeen the boy was at last allowed to leave Cardiff for good, and come to live in London. (At week-ends Ivor and his mother usually returned home, as it was impossible for Mr. Davies to give up his official position and move to London himself.) The flat was tiny, but it had a charming Bohemian atmosphere, and the boy was happy and excited. To live in London had always been his ambition; now he felt that nothing would hold him back. The piano in the flat was continually playing, pupils streamed in and out at all hours of the day, and there was literally never a dull moment. Occasionally musical or theatrical celebrities would stop by to take tea with Madame Clara, and Ivor would be proudly introduced to them as 'my composer son'.

Madame Clara often took him with her to concerts and musical gatherings. One day she received an invitation to attend a musical soirée at the Lambeth Palace, and she took her son along with her. In front of an audience of bishops, clerics and dear old ladies, Ivor was 'trotted out' to play his own latest composition. He shyly obliged, and played two or three of his songs, when suddenly, in one of those sudden silences which unaccountably occur in every gathering a rather deaf old lady was heard to declare: 'How well he plays! I *do* love those old songs!' Ivor flushed and longed for the floor to swallow him up. But he passed the incident off with a smile, and became the young lion of the party.

By now Ivor had grown into an extremely good-looking young man, with a shock of raven-black hair and big brown eyes, the beauty of which were accentuated by the paleness of his face. He was sensitive and still somewhat shy, even though he had already met hundreds of people and many famous celebrities during his young life. (Later on Novello developed a gregariousness which he possessed until his death, but that quality of shyness also prevailed, making his personality all the more appealing.)

*

Ivor's thoughts were constantly turned towards the stage. Even at fifteen he had wanted to be an actor, but this ambition was looked upon with the greatest disfavour, not only by his parents, but by all his friends and acquaintances. However, ambition apart, he still continued to work and learn, learn and work, at being a good composer. He was still earning a modest income from his songs, and he persisted at his piano, composing songs and ballads, several of which continued to be sung at concerts in London and elsewhere. At seventeen he was a remarkably mature young man, and extremely successful for one so young. But he still hankered to act. Madame Clara knew this, and it worried her quite a lot.

'Music is your life. You have the making of a very fine composer. Don't spoil your chances by yearning after the precarious life of an actor.' That is what she told him time and time again. But Ivor persisted in his stage ambitions.

One day, without telling his mother, he went with a friend to an audition at Daly's Theatre for a job as a chorus singer in a tour of *The Count of Luxembourg*. He knew the manager at Daly's, Merlin Morgan, who recommended him to the producer, and when Ivor sang one of his own songs at the piano he was promptly given the job. The boy was jubilant. Happily he hurried home and broke the news to his mother. Strangely enough, she took it all very calmly, and Ivor was a little surprised—and somewhat apprehensive—at her apparent acceptance of his decision to go against her wishes. As the days went by, however, and he had not heard from Daly's, he began to wonder whether she had not been rather too calm. After four weeks without a word, he at last became suspicious and wrote a note to Merlin Morgan asking when he would be called to the first rehearsal. For the next two mornings he tip-toed down to the letter-box before his mother was awake to see what the post had brought. On the second morning there, sure enough, was a card from Daly's Theatre. It bore the fatal message: 'As you have not attended rehearsals, we have very reluctantly been compelled to fill your place."

Ivor was frantic. He stormed into his mother's room, woke her up, and poured forth a storm of reproaches. Madame Clara, unruffled, smiled up from her pillow. 'Darling,' she exclaimed, 'do you seriously believe that going on tour in the chorus of a musical comedy is of more value to you than your career as a composer? And,' she continued, 'do you think I'm going to watch you ruin your life as a musician?'

'I hate my damned music. I want to go on the stage,' cried Ivor unhappily.

'Quite, darling,' responded his mother; 'you probably will one day. But this is definitely *not* the way to start. One day you'll see I'm right."

At the time he did not see her point, because he felt that once on the stage he would have been learning his job, playing small parts, getting the 'feel' of an audience, obtaining valuable experience in theatres all over the country—serving his apprenticeship, in fact, for a stage career. And later on he felt that it was a mistake to accede to her wishes, for his stage debut was thus delayed for several years. It is true, of course, that the war intervened, and it is quite likely that he would not have been acting at all for some five years during the war, but he always regretted losing that early theatrical training. On the other hand, he admitted that his mother was, as always, probably quite right. In his life he had found that, however bitter one's disappointment may be about things happening or not happening, in the end it 'always turned out for the best'—a cliché, but, like most clichés, basically true. But to return to 1910. Here he was, a handsome youth of nearly eighteen, with just enough pocket-money to make himself independent. He was theatre-mad. Every penny he earned or could borrow from his mother was spent on seats for the theatre—in the gallery, in the pit, and (when he was particularly well-off) in the stalls. In those exciting pre-war days Ivor haunted Daly's and the Gaiety. He had seen *The Merry Widow,* with the enchanting Lily Elsie as Sonia, no less than twenty-seven times when he was a schoolboy on holiday from Oxford, so it can be imagined just how he revelled in the theatre when he was at last free to go any day or evening. He worshipped Lily Elsie and Gertie Millar; to him they were simply the most glamorous creatures in the world. Although realizing that, in retrospect, everyone and everything seemed to take on a thousand per cent of added glamour, he felt certain that there had never really been a more glamorous and exciting period in the London theatre than in the early 1900's, leading up to the outbreak of war.

'In those days,' Novello remembered, 'we really cared what happened to the heroine of a musical comedy, particularly if it was at Daly's, riddled with flashing uniforms and the broken-hearted heroine sobbing herself into a frenzy in the second act and imploring her lover to "dance with me now for the last time" before she collapsed to the never-too-often repeated strains of the latest waltz tune by Lehar, Leo Fall, or Oscar Strauss. I saw various Daly's musicals dozens of times each. There was, I believe, a gentleman who saw *The Merry*

Widow every night during its fantastic run, except on those nights when Lily Elsie was not playing. Incidentally, this brings me to the subject of understudies. In the U.S.A. there is no such thing as an understudy to the star. If the star is ill the show is cancelled. The star knows this, and subsequently seems to be immune from all the ills the flesh is usually heir to! Never in all the times I have been to the theatre in the U.S.A. have I not seen the star I had paid to see. But I'd hate to think of the times in England when, as a small boy or young man, I went, all unsuspecting, to Daly's or the Gaiety, and instead of my glittering adored goddesses Lily Elsie or Gertie Millar floating on to the stage, there arrived a good—but generally dull—understudy. What a disappointment! What an agonized "Oh-h-h!" went up from the audience. How the evening suddenly seemed to lose its magic. There is one thing to be said for films—whenever you see a film it is always played by the original artists.'

When the Davies', mother and son, were living in Bond Street, Madame Clara also rented a studio in George Street, Hanover Square, where she now taught a large number of pupils all day long. She had first taken the studio in 1906, when her friend Daniel Mayer opened new premises at 13, George Street, in connection with his concert—and later theatrical—agency. Her studio and her flat were almost back to back, with windows facing each other. When meals were ready in the flat, Ivor would wave a red scarf wildly from the window and mother would fly round, all furs and veils, for her lunch, rest for half an hour, and then rush back to the studio (where her next-door neighbour was the celebrated Edouard de Reszke). Invariably she would teach from 9.30 in the morning until 8.30 at night, with a short break for food. At one period no less than twenty-seven girls from the chorus of *The Dollar Princess* at Daly's were all studying with her at the same time. Their lessons were paid for by George Edwardes, the famous 'Gaiety George', who knew that leading ladies were few and far between, and did everything possible to foster new talent.

And while his mother worked hard at teaching, Ivor worked

no less hard at composing. He completed a revised version of his first really lengthy effort, the musical comedy called *The Fickle Jade,* but it was, he admitted, 'based apparently on every musical comedy I had ever seen'. Unhappily this, his very first musical play, was turned down by every management who read it, and Ivor eventually consigned it to the bottom drawer, Curiously enough, although it was a very adolescent effort, one of the tunes in it was subsequently used by Ivor many years later as the Skating Waltz in *Glamorous Night,* the first of his famous Drury Lane musicals, and James Agate, who did not care very much for musical plays, told Novello that this was the tune he liked best in the show.

In any case, the new version of *The Fickle Jade* was only a part of Ivor's output, for he continued to write dozens of ballads for the Saturday afternoon series of concerts at the Albert Hall, for many of which he acted as accompanist to the various prima donnas who were good enough to sing his compositions. (One of the other young rival composers, who brought their songs along to the Albert Hall under their arms, and proudly played piano accompaniments when their songs were sung, was Eric Coates. He and Ivor became great friends, and remained so until Ivor's death) Novello was still only eighteen when he had the supreme thrill of hearing one of his songs performed to an orchestral accompaniment. It was a setting of 'O God Our Help in Ages Past', and was beautifully sung at the Crystal Palace by the great Australian contralto, Ada Crossley. To hear one's music played by an orchestra for the first time is, Ivor declared, one of the greatest of all emotions, and that day took its place in his memories as one of the most exciting days in his life. All the morning he sat in the concert hall listening to the orchestra rehearsing. Everything he had heard in his mind for the past months came out into the open for the first time, magically played by the various instruments. It was a great experience. At the performance of his work in the afternoon he took a bow in a hired morning suit slightly too large for him, and a few people in the front row giggled. But the boy was above giggles. He was walking on air. Although he afterwards heard his music played by orchestras all over the world, in concert halls and theatres, and on the radio, gramophone, and films, Ivor never forgot that first wonderful day at the Crystal Palace. The first signs of the genius that he undoubtedly possessed were given to that Sunday afternoon audience in South London in 1910.

*

The year 1911 was an historic one for Ivor, for it was then that he made his first trip to America—and this at the age of eighteen. Following on the successful Festival of Empire, which was held at the Crystal Palace that year—and to which he had contributed some very promising music—it was proposed to repeat the great pageant in some of the larger cities of Canada. It was also proposed, much to the boy's surprise and delight, that he should write the music for the entire pageant. There would be no remuneration, but every expense would be paid, and it would mean a six months' stay in Canada and the U.S.A. Ivor, of course, was immensely thrilled and jumped at the idea. Under the most ideal conditions he saw Montreal, Quebec, Toronto and Winnipeg, during which time he worked on his music, attended preliminary meetings with city dignitaries, and revelled in the wonders and wonderful sights of an entirely new continent. He finished up with a three months' visit to New York, during which time the organizers of the pageant were trying to obtain financial support for its presentation in that great city after it had opened in Toronto. Unfortunately they failed to get the required capital, and, strangely enough, the pageant never saw the light of day either in Canada or America. Preparations and conferences took place daily, and Ivor wrote masses of music, but the whole thing at length fell through, and the organizers and sponsors were forced to return to London with their mission unaccomplished. After the gradual disappointment of not having his music played in the pageant had worn off, Novello delighted in the life in a new continent, in the sights of these wonderful new cities—and especially in New York.

New York staggered him with its beauty, excitement and glamour. Fortunately he stayed in the same apartment house as Ricardo Martin, then one of the principal tenors at the Metropolitan Opera House, and Martin and his wife took the British boy under their protective wing, giving him the freedom of their apartment and, what was even more delightful, the freedom of the Metropolitan Opera House. Ivor was to be seen there night after night, and simply revelled in the singing and performances of all the great names of that time. There was Caruso, in his absolute prime; thrilling Geraldine Farrar, the first operatic singer the boy had seen who could also act as well as any dramatic actress he had ever seen; the incomparable Scotti, Mary Garden; and Toscanini, conducting four nights a week. *Tristan and Isolde,* which he saw for the first time, left him completely exhausted. Novello was in heaven. To hear Caruso. To see Toscanini. To meet Mary Garden. It was all like a dream come true. The boy became part of the musical theatrical life of New York; he went everywhere, saw everything. Life was one continual round of excitement. He went to parties, and was introduced by Ricardo Martin as 'the brilliant young composer from London'. He met all kinds of celebrities; some of them remained so for years. At a party given by Mrs. Benjamin Guinness he met Nellie Melba, talked with the great Caruso, and also met for the first time Constance Collier, later to become one of his greatest friends and to collaborate with him on two famous plays. At this same party he danced the tango with that great singer Lina Cavalieri, who remained in his memory as the most flawlessly beautiful person he ever saw.

In her autobiography, *Harlequinade,* published in 1929, Miss Collier tells of their meeting. 'I remember', she writes, 'one night at a party in New York given by Mrs. Benjamin Guinness, in her Washington Square house, after my performance in John Masefield's *Nan,* I met a dark-haired young man, very good-looking and with charming manners. I talked to him for a moment casually, and then turned to talk to someone else. Some instinct should have told me that years afterwards we should be comrades, and work and struggle in the theatre and eventually achieve success; that we should write plays together and produce them in spite of all opposition. But at that first meeting we didn't impress each other much, or meet again until years after. That was how I first met Ivor Novello.'

Every night, when he was not at the opera, Ivor was at the theatre. The New York theatre season of 1911 was a particularly brilliant one; he saw Mary Pickford, exquisite as a little blind girl, in a play called *The Good Little Devil*; Jane Cowl in her first success, *Within the Law*; the first night of Edward Sheldon's *Romance,* in which that wonderful creature Doris Keane captured New York overnight; Billie Burke, one of the most beautiful girls ever seen on the Broadway stage (and who appeared in Novello's *The Truth Game* in New York twenty years later), in *Mind-the-Paint Girl*; and many others. These were just the outstanding memories of his first trip to New York, the theatre experiences he remembered most vividly. He resolved to return to the U.S.A. as soon as possible—but this time as a *real* celebrity.

One of the now-famous men whom Ivor met when he first came to live in London was a youngster called Alec Robertson. Now, of course, he is one of the best-known broadcasters on music in such programmes as 'Music Magazine', and has written several books on the great composers. At the time he met Ivor he was an inveterate theatregoer and concertgoer, and had met the Welsh boy at a Sunday League Concert where one of Ivor's songs, 'In the Shadows', had been featured quite successfully. The two ambitious young men became firm friends, and Novello valued Robertson's opinions very highly, since the latter knew many people in the London musical world and numbered several well-known composers and musicians among his personal friends.

When Ivor was in New York working on the Great Festival of Empire, to be produced in Chicago, he wrote to Robertson as follows:—

'I am very anxious for "In the Clouds", my new song, to become popular, and the only way for it to become so is for

5. His first film, *Call of the Blood,* Italy, 1919.

6. Co-starring with Gladys Cooper in the film version of *The Bohemian Girl,* London, 1921.

7. With Nina Vanna in Adrian Brunel's production of the film *The Man Without Desire,* Germany, 1923.

8. For D. W. Griffith he co-starred with Mae Marsh in *The White Rose,* made in Hollywood in 1923.

it to be played everywhere. So I want you, whenever you possibly can, to ask the orchestras at tea-places and restaurants for it, and ask people you and I know very well to go and do likewise. I would love to come home and find "In the Clouds" almost as popular as "In the Shadows" was. I feel sure it can be done.'

As Robertson comments, 'Considering how deservedly famous Novello was for nearly forty years, this letter is a charming and touching reminder of his youthful ambitions.'

During the last few weeks of Ivor's visit to New York he acquired a small shaggy mongrel who answered to the name of Wudge. Actually Ivor called her 'Little Damosel', after his first successful published song, but somehow she became 'Wudge' and would answer to no other name. Wudge was to play a most important part in Novello's life. He had booked a passage on the *Empress of Ireland,* which was to take him from Ontario, Canada, to Southampton, and he intended taking Wudge back with him to England as he had grown very fond of her. On the very morning that he was due to sail, Ivor suddenly found that Wudge was missing from the apartment and nobody seemed to know where she was. It was almost sailing time and still she had not appeared. Ivor had always been a very gentle and emotional person, and he had formed such an attachment to Wudge that he was determined to stay in Ontario until he found her. Consequently he cancelled his passage on the *Empress of Ireland,* transferring it to the next homeward-bound liner. Two days later the whole world was aghast at the news that the ship had been rammed during a thick fog and had sunk with a loss of 950 lives! Wudge, by the way, turned up at the back door of Ivor's apartment on the following morning. That dog probably saved his life.

On his return, after being away in Canada and the U.S.A. for eleven months, Ivor threw himself into the task of writing songs and musical comedies. He was determined to make his way in the London musical and theatrical world. However, with the exception of 'The Little Damosel', he never seemed to strike a popular success. Looking back, he felt that the trouble might have been that he was a little bit too highbrow for the popular ballad success, and not nearly highbrow enough to be accepted as a serious musician. In any case the months flew by, and although he went through intermittent bouts of tiring and extensive work he often felt that he was simply getting nowhere. He was naturally inclined to be lazy, however, and his mother often reminded him that he had not yet achieved anything of importance.

'Darling,' she used to say to him, 'do you realize that if you died to-morrow it would not make the slightest difference to the world?' As the boy felt that this might apply to ninety-nine per cent of the human race, he didn't take her remark too seriously. Nevertheless he instituted a more serious phase of activity, working rigorously day after day, and sending dozens of songs weekly to various London music publishers. Many of these were returned by the following post, and even those which were published became only moderately successful. Ivor was inclined to be depressed, and felt he needed a change of atmosphere. While he was away in the U.S.A. Madame Clara had moved into a more expensive flat in Hanover Square, but the move was becoming too costly for her. She had won the reputation of being the best singing teacher in the country, but although her teaching was continuing unabated, her pupils were apparently reluctant to pay for their lessons. Eventually she found she was teaching for seven hours at least every day and getting precious little financial remuneration. So in 1913, when the war clouds were already gathering, Madame Clara moved out of expensive Hanover Square and took a flat in Aldwych, and also a modest bungalow in Biggin Hill, Kent, where she continued to give lessons to those pupils enthusiastic enough to make the journey. (She was at this time advocating singing lessons in the open air as being most beneficial to the lungs and to the development of tone and timbre.) Attached to the bungalow was a stationary caravan in which Ivor, who had eagerly gone with her in the search for 'inspiration', would work tirelessly, trying to finish at least a dozen musical comedy ideas that he had started and re-started since first coming to London in 1910.

The flat which Madame Clara took, on the top floor of 11, Aldwych, became a famous flat, one of the theatrical landmarks of London, in fact, for Ivor continued to live there until his death. Atop the Strand Theatre, it had an unassuming entrance and a creaky little lift. But Ivor and his mother fell in love with it on sight, and a wonderfully happy period of creative activity commenced here. Ivor's father retired from the Glamorgan Council in 1913 and joined his wife and their son in the Aldwych flat, where he lived until his death in 1931. A genial, ruddy-faced man with a shock of thick, grey hair, and his dry sense of humour always predominant in his attractive personality, he joined enthusiastically in all his family's musical and theatrical activities, still acting as a kind of ballast to the high spirits and sudden bursts of madness occasioned by his brilliant wife and even more brilliant son. There were times when gentle David Davies must have sat in the window of 'The Flat' (as everyone in the Theatre called it), puffing at his pipe, and thinking to himself: 'How did I come to have such a clever son? How is it that a modest official in Cardiff suddenly finds himself the father of one of the most famous and talented young men in the world? Anyway, no matter how it all came about, I think I rather like it. He has always been a wonderful son to me, and I am very proud to be living with him in London and to share some part of his enormous success and popularity.'

One of the tragedies of Novello's life was that his father died quite suddenly while he was in Hollywood, so that he could not be at home to comfort his mother. He hurried home to London as soon as he could get free of his film contract, but No. 11, Aldwych, seemed a different place without his Dad. In his play *Proscenium* Ivor modelled one of his characters on his beloved father, and himself played the part. Because the character was based on someone he knew and loved so well, Ivor's performance was a tremendous success. Nearly twenty years after David's death, Ivor played both himself and his father in a radio adaptation of his mother's autobiography, *The Life I Have Loved,* which told of Madame's Clara's triumphant progress from being a humble organist in a Cardiff chapel to becoming one of the most celebrated teachers of singing in the world.

3

'Keep the Home Fires Burning'

'By 1915 a change came over the songs of the British soldiers. They began to sing a new and haunting melody, the first of all the songs specially written for the war to gain universal popularity. Composed by a brilliant young man, Ivor Novello, this song, "Keep the Home Fires Burning", has become the Battle Hymn of the Great War.'—*'Daily Mail', December 1st, 1915.*

NOVELLO was obviously destined for fame, and when he was twenty-one it came suddenly and without any warning.

By 1914 the young composer had created quite a small reputation in musical circles with such songs as 'Up There', 'Blue Eyes', 'Why Hurry, Little River?', 'Not Really', 'The Valley', and a song cycle called 'Songs of Syria', which became something of a *succès d'estime*. To some of these he also wrote the words, although several of the lyrics were provided by such well-known musical personalities of the time as John Yorke Bailey, Edward Teschemacher and Canon Scott. Several concerts were given of Novello's compositions, a typical success being one at the Æolian Hall on June 13th, 1913, the programme of which I have before me. It consisted of a dozen of his songs played and sung by a group of Clara Novello Davies' well-known pupils and other famous instrumentalists and singers of the day, such as Sybil Vane, Marie Novello (his adopted sister), Sara Melita, Winifred Lewis,

Charles Mott, Arthur Strike, James Hay and Ulick Brown. (Other composers whose work was included in this concert, along with Novello's compositions, were Handel, Weber, Liszt, Verdi, Brahms, Donizetti and Massenet—distinguished company to say the least!)

The war everyone had been expecting broke out at last, in August 1914, at the time when Ivor and his mother were living in Biggin Hill, and for the first few months of this disastrous war they stayed in their little country retreat and waited to see what would happen. Ivor took it for granted that, sooner or later, he should have to join up, like everybody else. He decided that when he was called up he would join the Royal Naval Air Force, since there seemed to him something rather romantic about fighting in the air. It must be remembered that the initial year or so of the First World War was surrounded with certain aura of romance and patriotism. Thousands of eager young Englishmen joined the Forces 'to teach the Kaiser a lesson'. London was the exciting hub of patriotic activity, and a uniform meant Open Sesame everywhere. The boys in khaki and blue went off to France with the cries of encouragement of enthusiastic crowds ringing in their ears. It was exciting, melodramatic and—in retrospect—rather sad. But, in the first year at least, the war 'against German militarism', as it was called, was certainly a 'popular' war.

In the midst of all this excitement something happened which was to change the entire course of Ivor Novello's life. That was the composing of one song, just one simple, patriotic melody. But it made the young man famous overnight and earned him a fortune. And no wonder; the song was 'Keep the Home Fires Burning', destined to become, with 'Tipperary' and 'Pack Up Your Troubles', the most popular marching song of the British Army during those four long years of war. This is how it came to be written. Ivor had continued unabated with his compositions during Autumn 1914, but his mother, herself frantically busy, was continually urging him to try his hand at a patriotic song.

'But, darling,' Ivor pleaded with her, 'there are so many.

Nobody wants patriotic songs any more. They want to get away from it. They want to be cheered up.'

'All right, dear,' she replied, 'if that's the way you feel about it, I shall write one myself.'

And write one she did. It was called 'Keep the Flag A'Flying'. Ivor privately considered that the song was pretty awful, and he declared that it was mainly with the idea of preventing her song being published that he decided he would sit down and write one of his own. He worked for hours on end, finally finishing what he considered to be a good tune eminently suitable for the type of song he had in mind. But who could write the words? He had from time to time set the lyrics for his own compositions, but on this occasion he felt that he needed a fresh brain—someone, perhaps, with a more lyrical and poetic approach. Then he remembered that a very old friend of his mother's, Lena Guilbert Ford, an American poet, who had lived all her life in England (and was later to be tragically killed during a Zeppelin raid on London), had often said she wished young Ivor would set some of her lyrics to music. On impulse he rang her up and told her what he had in mind. She came along to the flat later in the day, and the young man played her his tune on the piano. Miss Ford seemed quite pleased with it, but, strangely enough, Ivor found that he did not like it himself as much as he thought he did. He banged around on the piano for half an hour, improvising around his theme. Suddenly, and he felt it must have been inspiration, he cried out: 'No, that's not the tune I want. *This* is the tune!' Straightaway he played an entire chorus of 'Keep the Home Fires Burning', including most of the words of the chorus, which he sang at the top of his voice—except the last phrase, which he hummed. Lena was delighted. 'That's a wonderful phrase', she exclaimed. '"Keep the Home Fires Burning." I like that. It's good.' Ivor, now exhausted but happy, told her excitedly that he thought this tune might be 'it'.

'Don't bother to use the words I've just sung', he exclaimed, 'but keep in that line "Keep the Home Fires Burning"—it's just right. I believe it's really good.'

'You bet it's good, and I'm going straight home now to write the complete lyric', responded Miss Ford.

Ivor played his tune to her over and over again while she jotted down notes in an enormous notebook which she invariably carried around with her. Finally off she went to her own flat, and two hours later she rang up, saying, 'I've got it, and I've also got a wonderful last line to the chorus—"Turn the dark clouds inside out till the boys come home"'. She then dictated over the telephone the entire words of the first verse and chorus. Excitedly Ivor took them all down on his blotting pad, then flew to the piano, set the verse to music, wrote the entire song out in an hour, and the whole thing was complete. One of the truly great popular songs of the past half-century was born.

Ivor himself told me, 'That's the true story of how it all happened. As in the case of other successes, people have tried to prove that (1) I never wrote the song at all; (2) It was my father who wrote it; (3) My mother had had a share in composing the music; (4) The song would have been no good without the words; (5) The words would have been nowhere without the tune; (6) It was based on an old German folk tune; (7) It was a dreadful song anyway. So now I affirm once and for all that, whether you like it or not, I did compose "Keep the Home Fires Burning"; I invented that phrase, and I shall be grateful to it all my life. Not only did this success give me the nucleus of a certain financial security that was to last for years, but it gave me a prominence that undoubtedly called valuable attention to my work, and to me as a personality. I am intensely grateful to that song. And when anybody ever says to me: "Doesn't it make you sick to hear it?" I reply, "It is difficult to be sick when you are on your knees"'. (It is interesting to note that the song which Novello originally composed as a great patriotic work, and which he rejected in favour of his final version, was later sung by José Collins in *Our Nell,* a musical based on the life of Nell Gwynne, produced at the Gaiety in 1924.)

Since 'Keep the Home Fires Burning' (or 'Till the Boys Come Home', as it was officially titled) swept Britain in those hectic war-time years there have been many legends about it. The first was that it made Novello into a millionaire overnight, and, secondly, that he disposed of it for a song, 'thereby proving that exchange is no robbery'. Actually, Novello steered a middle course. He received a royalty on every copy sold, and in those pre-radio days, when people bought far more copies of sheet music than they do now, this assured him of a comfortable income which was spread over five years. Then, just when the sale was slackening in Europe, America made an appearance on the war scene and the sale began all over again in the U.S.A. 'Keep the Home Fires Burning' earned about £15,000 for Novello, whereas to-day, given the same circumstances, it would probably earn less than £500.

Through the medium of this one song the composer made friends all over the world. Letters poured in to him from soldiers and their wives expressing gratitude to him for the inspiration which lay behind the song, and years afterwards, when he had become a successful actor, playwright and composer, he was still known to millions as the man who composed 'Keep the Home Fires Burning' when he was only twenty-one.

John McCormick told Ivor during the war that he himself earned the sum of £20,000 from his gramophone recordings of 'Keep the Home Fires Burning', which were sold all over the world. At least six prominent singers reminded him every time they met him that he, or she, was the first to sing the song in public. What actually happened was that a little Welsh girl called Sybil Vane, a pupil of Madame Clara's, was engaged by the Sunday League to sing at a concert at the Alhambra Theatre, Leicester Square (where the Odeon Cinema now stands), with Ivor to accompany her. In the first part of the programme she sang an operatic aria and in the second part a group of songs, one of which was to be 'Till the Boys Come Home'. It was billed in the programme as 'First Performance of a New Song, Accompanied by the Composer'. After Sybil had finished its first verse and chorus, she repeated the latter, and as she started the first line of the repeat chorus Ivor could have sworn that he could hear some of the audience singing. Sybil then went on to sing the second verse, and as she started the refrain 'Keep the Home Fires Burning' they both heard—and this time there was no question of illusion—the audience joining in without any hesitation or faltering. By the time they had finished the repeat chorus the whole house was singing as if they had known the song all their lives, and the military band on the stage hastily improvised an accompaniment. It is not exaggerating to say that the people in the audience went crazy with enthusiasm, partly because they liked the catchy tune and partly because they were delighted with their own singing. Sybil and Ivor simply could not get off the stage. They had to repeat the chorus no less than eight times before the audience allowed the rest of the programme to continue. Ivor's father was standing at the side of the stage with tears rolling down his face; unfortunately, Madame Clara was at home in bed with a cold, so could not witness her son's first real big public triumph. Mr. Davies hugged Ivor, and Ivor hugged Sybil, and Sybil hugged the conductor of the military band. In fact, everybody hugged anybody within an arm's reach. Ivor, in all the confusion and noise, with people cheering and shouting for encores, realized that here, at the Alhambra, on a Sunday night in the autumn of 1914, something very exciting, very unexpected and very wonderful had happened.

On the following day Ascherberg, Hopwood and Crewe,* the publishers of the song, were inundated with singers anxious to perform it, and by the public who wanted to buy copies. It was still known as 'Till the Boys Come Home', but after Ivor had visited France later in the year with the Lena Ashwell Concert Party, and introduced the song to the troops themselves, it was finally launched on its phenomenal career under the name by which it became world-famous, the name the public themselves had given to the song they loved. 'Keep the Home Fires Burning', as Ivor readily admitted, was not in any sense a masterpiece. It was not great music, nor

* The song was actually rejected by Boosey's, Novello's own publishers, to whom it was first sent, but Novello had faith in his work and refused to change a line of it. Ascherberg's were finally prevailed upon to take it; it quickly ran into six languages. and subsequently sold scores of thousands of copies all over the world.

was the lyric specially inspiring. But it had an instantaneous appeal to the emotion. It was exactly 'right' for its period. It had a musical form which was easily learned, and it had a message of hope which appealed both to those who were fighting and those who were waiting at home. Whatever the reasons for its colossal success, however, Novello could only continue to be grateful for the accident which brought him fame and fortune at such an early age.

The song has continued to be a popular national song, and was widely revived during the Second World War, when it was sung wherever British soldiers gathered.

In foreign countries there still lingers the belief that 'Keep the Home Fires Burning' is one of our national anthems. Basil Dean tells the story of a party of entertainers in France in 1940, playing to the troops, who were acclaimed when they entered a café by the patrons. In their honour the French men and women stood up and sang, not 'God Save the King', but 'Home Fires', while the slightly bewildered English artists, taking their cue, stood to attention!

After the young man had taken part in over seventy concerts in the war areas in France he applied for and received a commission in the Royal Naval Air Service, and, as a Flight Sub-Lieutenant, was drafted to the Crystal Palace for training. Although he loathed the whole idea of regimentation of any kind, he at least, as he remembered, became extremely fit and ruddy-faced'. From the Crystal Palace he was transferred to Chingford, where, as he would have told you with a smile, for many months he battled hopelessly with the science of aviation and navigation (in company with another young actor-pilot, Henry Kendall). A couple of crashes put him out of action as regards active service, however, but they did not save him from the ensuing drudgery of office routine at the Air Ministry, work about which he knew nothing and cared even less. The months wore on. It was now 1916, and Novello had tended to neglect his work as a composer. He had managed to get one song into *The Bing Boys Are Here,* with George Robey and Violet Loraine, at the Alhambra, but he decided to make a real effort to write the complete score of a show, and in his spare time in the evenings, and on occasional leave, he sat at the piano for hours on end trying to compose something new and different. Certain of the songs were excellent, but he did not try to get them published as he did not think the time was propitious for romantic melodies. Finally, through a meeting with the celebrated George Grossmith, the young man was invited to work on the score of *Theodore and Co.,* a musical comedy which was being prepared to follow the enormously successful *To-night's the Night* at the Gaiety Theatre. After discussions with Grossmith and his partner, Edward Laurillard, Ivor was taken by the latter to the Gaiety Theatre one evening while *To-night's the Night* was running, and as they stood at the back of the dress circle Laurillard turned to the composer and pointed to a little fellow on the stage, exclaiming, 'That's the boy we have to look after in the next show'. The little fellow on the stage, who was convulsing the audience with his husky voice and fish-like countenance, was a youngster called Leslie Henson. He consolidated his reputation in *Theodore & Co.,* and has never looked back.

Ivor's music, however, was almost not heard at all.

One day, while on his way to a conference before rehearsals, Ivor left the score of *Theodore & Co.* in a taxi-cab. Frantically he phoned the police from the Gaiety stage door, and the call went out to all taxi-cab drivers. But the score never turned up, and Ivor was forced to work for three days and nights completely re-writing the score from memory. It had originally taken him three months to compose, and had a first act finale which was forty pages long! The loss was almost a disaster. 'The manuscript has never turned up to this day', Ivor told me a few months before he died.

The book of the new show was by H. M. Harwood and George Grossmith (based on a rattling French farce by Messieurs Nancey and Armont), and the cast included Leslie Henson, Austin Melford, Davy Burnaby, Robert Nainby, Julia James, Joyce Barbour and Mercia Swinburne. It was just another pleasantly successful Gaiety musical which had a long run during the war years, but it takes its place in theatrical history because it was the first London musical comedy in which the music of Ivor Novello was really heard, the first of his memorable series of stage hits which continued until 1951.

Ivor had an intense admiration for Leslie Henson; he considered him one of the truly great English comedians of the century, and a most lovable and generous person into the bargain. They met during rehearsals, immediately liked each other, and remained friends ever since. Ivor also got to know and like Gladys Gunn, the daughter of the famous Gaiety beauty, Hilda Corral. Gladys later married Leslie Henson (their marriage was subsequently dissolved after several years), but at the time of *Theodore & Co.* she was, as Ivor remembered, 'a chorus girl with no qualifications at all for being on the stage'. Ivor went on: 'Gladys could not sing, she could not dance and she could not act. She wasn't even very much to look at. But there *was* something—a most endearing personality and appreciation of humour such as I have seldom, if ever, met; a cockney wit, combined with Irish charm, which has kept her the enchanting personality she has been all these years.'

When Ivor first met the irrepressible Gladys she had been in the chorus of the London Hippodrome for two years, and was then in the chorus at the Vaudeville Theatre, under Charlot. He used to tell an amusing story about her. A few years after *Theodore & Co.* had opened, Ivor, by that time great friends with Gladys, was writing the music for *The Golden Moth* at the Adelphi. He sent a card to Gladys reminding her that they were holding the chorus audition. (This was before she had married Leslie, when she was a very hard-working chorus girl, quite often out of a job.) The next day she rang Ivor up on the telephone. 'Oh, duckie,' she exclaimed, 'they won't want me to sing, will they?' 'No, dear,' replied Ivor, 'they won't want you to sing.' 'But, duckie, won't they want me to dance?' 'No, dear, they won't want you to dance.' 'But what *do* they want me to do?' 'You just come down and you'll see,' Ivor replied.

And down she came. Ivor greeted her and introduced her

to the producers. All seemed to be going well when suddenly, while Ivor happened to be looking the other way, someone asked Gladys to sing a scale. To his horror Novello heard a little tremulous pipe go up. It was Gladys attempting to sing. Heads were shaken in all directions. There was a sudden silence as Gladys finished. 'That's fine,' exclaimed Ivor, with a note of uncertain bravado in his voice.

'It isn't fine at all,' said the producers. 'We want girls who can sing. I am afraid that she is "out".'

Ivor was nonplussed. He looked weakly at Gladys, and Gladys, in desperation, looked up into the flies. 'All right,' Novello exclaimed, 'if she is "out", then so is my music.' (This was pure bluff, as he had signed his contract and all the music was written and approved.) At first they all thought the young man was joking, but when he began gathering up his hat and coat to leave the theatre they realized that, after all, one chorus girl more or less wasn't going to make much difference to the show. So Gladys opened in *The Golden Moth,* and now relates that every time Ivor went away from England during the run of the show she trembled in her shoes for fear of receiving her notice! But she didn't get it. She was far too popular, far too much of a personality, far too talented, in her own strange whimsical fashion. After her marriage to Leslie in 1926 she retired from the stage for seven years, reappearing in Noel Coward's *Design for Living* when it opened in New York. Since then she has successfully acted in many New York and London productions, being associated for some years with the production of plays by Emlyn Williams. Gladys Henson is now a very popular and successful film actress, and certainly one of our most brilliant players in her own particular *genre.*

Theodore & Co. opened on September 16th, 1916, and ran for eighteen months at the Gaiety. It started Novello off on his career as a successful composer of musical plays, even though, as he confessed, the big hit of the show, '365 Days', was composed by Jerome Kern.* In the meantime, 'Till the

* Two of Novello's own hits from *Theodore & Co. were* 'Every Little Girl Can Teach Me Something New' and 'My Friend John'.

Boys Come Home' (or 'Keep the Home Fires Burning' as people preferred to call it) was still being sung wherever there was a group of British soldiers. It was sung at recruiting meetings, at concerts, by soldiers on leave and in the trenches, and by their wives and sweethearts at home. The phrase 'Keep the home fires burning' was incorporated into the English language. It appeared daily in the newspapers, cartoons were drawn around it, and, in fact, by the time the war was over nobody in the English-speaking world had not heard the phrase or did not know the name of the composer.

In another letter to his friend Alec Robertson, written in 1915, Ivor notes: ' "Till the Boys Come Home" is now heard everywhere, I am glad to say. One hears it whistled in the streets all the time, in all the restaurants, between the acts in the theatres, and even on the barrel organs. So, as you can imagine, I am doing very well. I drew a cheque for £235 last month, and before Christmas I expect to make about £1,000! Just think of that!'

Going on to talk about what he called 'real music', young Novello declared: 'In some moods I like Debussy better than anyone, but usually Puccini rules me.'

Ivor followed it up with other patriotic ballads like 'Laddie in Khaki' and 'When the Great Day Comes', and although these did not duplicate the fabulous success of 'Till the Boys Come Home', they were, nevertheless, continually played and sung all over England. The words and music of the latter were published in full in publications like the *Daily Mail,* the *Evening News,* the *Daily Sketch,* the *Stage, Tit-Bits,* and *Answers,* and literally scores of newspaper magazine articles were written about the twenty-one-year-old Welshman whose composition had caught the imagination of the world. He was a much-lionized celebrity, interviewed by newspapers and magazines, invited to speak at meetings, to appear at concerts, to open bazaars, to address recruits. He was photographed by the *Tatler,* the *Star,* the *Daily Sketch,* and the *Evening News,* in his caravan in the Kentish hills, in his London flat, in Trafalgar Square with the pigeons, in Hyde Park with his dog, at home with his pet kitten, in uniform as a young flying lieutenant, with his mother at home in their Aldwych flat, and even with a South Wales choir singing his song in the Welsh hills! His profile became one of the most celebrated in the country. He received thousands of congratulatory letters. Lady Beerbohm Tree, for example, wrote to him: 'It must be a great pride to you to see the soldiers delight in your music. That half-glad, wistful song haunts one wherever one goes, and it will echo all over the world.'

★

'Till the Boys Come Home' was first introduced in New York during the latter part of December, 1915, at a Sunday concert at the Century Theatre by John Bardsley, a well-known tenor, late of the Covent Garden Opera Company. Then it was sung every night for one week at the Metropolitan Opera House, Philadelphia, and during the next few months it 'caught on' all over the U.S.A. In countries like New Zealand, where it was introduced at the Great Exhibition by Anna Novello, cousin of the composer, it created a similar sensation. In Canada it even rivalled 'The Maple Leaf' as the marching song of the Candian troops. 'Sensation' was hardly the word to describe its success. Charles Granville, the American tenor, even sang it for the inmates of Sing Sing Prison at Christmas, 1915; they were most enthusiastic, and clamoured to be taught the chorus! 'Till the Boys Come Home' was, however, more than just a song. It became a symbol of the Allied cause against German Imperialism. It rallied men to the colours; it was used everywhere as a propaganda medium. And it got results. In the early part of 1916 it was sung and played during the screening of British war films all over the United States, and the stirring melody, plus the impact of those flickering newsreels taken on the war fronts, was, to a remarkable extent, responsible for the wave of pro-Allied feeling which swept the U.S.A. and eventually led to its entry into the war. The *New York Tribune* published the words and music of the song in its issue of August 22nd, 1915, and other newspapers all over the U.S.A.

followed suit. It swept America as it had swept Europe, and, with the beloved 'Tipperary', became the battle hymn of the Allied armies.

Indicative of its popularity with the English people was that during the first Christmas of its publication no less than twenty-four famous pantomime principal boys made it the theme song of their shows—from Dorothy Ward at the Grand Theatre, Leeds, to Sybil Arundale of the Princes Theatre, Bristol, and from Winifred Roma at the Theatre Royal, Glasgow, to Pearl Grey at the Theatre Royal, Edinburgh. The *Daily Mail* printed the words and music right across its front page for the *second* time in December, 1915, and during the remainder of the war years Novello's song continued to increase in popularity, while he himself enjoyed a reputation as a 'boy wonder' which was to last until he was more than thirty years old.

★

Ivor's flat in the Aldwych, above the Strand Theatre and opposite the Gaiety, became one of the most famous flats in London, but, as Novello himself wrote in an article for the *Sunday Graphic*: 'It has got a dreadful entrance and a strange, creaking little lift—but I would not live anywhere else for the world. I have a rooted objection to chromium-plated fittings and commissionaires, penthouses, and all the things which make a modern luxury flat more like a high-class incubator than a real home. In the case of Number Eleven, never has a place changed itself so drastically and so often. I have gone through every period of decoration. When I first lived here my mother's bedroom was white and pink, with enormous pink roses round the dado. The drawing-room was decorated in a neat little scheme of grey and mauve, with a hideous, and I fancy insanitary, method of lighting. This consisted of a series of revolting arty-crafty jars placed round the dado, each jar containing an electric light which did nothing but show up the stains on the ceiling and give people black circles under their eyes. The end of that lighting scheme was spectacular. During a party we all took a dislike to the jars, threw apples at them, broke the lot and fused the lights in the entire building!

'The dining-room was brown and yellow, and my bed-sitting-room was described as "wine-red and dove-grey". What it really was was crushed strawberry and fog-coloured felt. I couldn't afford a carpet, but later, when I began to make money, I began to change the decoration of the flat. During the war my mother crossed and re-crossed the Atlantic seven times, and it was during one of her trips to the U.S.A. that I turned her bedroom into a baronial hall, the baronial part consisting of bad brass and lincrusta wallpaper disguised to look like oak panelling. My own bedroom became "Arabian Nights-cum-Wembley Exhibition-cum-Oriental Tea Rooms", with gold wallpaper and a purple dado and a black carpet. Being next to the kitchen it suffered a great disadvantage—the strong smell of kippers, which lasted from early morning until well into the afternoon, unless I opened all the windows. That décor didn't last long, I am glad to say. During my own absence the drawing-room was transferred into a kind of lacquer box, with all the worst kinds of Indian lamps, and the sitting-room was later changed from oak to orange, of a colour so brilliant that it seemed that one had plunged into the heart of a poached egg. I hated this, and later had it covered with gold paint, which faded almost immediately to a rich jaundice. I suppose all young people with a bit of money to spend get these fantastic ideas of decoration. I went through my "bright" period long ago, and now my taste has sobered down. My flat, greatly altered since I moved into it in 1913, can now breathe in peace with the knowledge that its pale wood walls and unobtrusive, comfortable, chunky, furniture look as though they are permanencies.'

*

While *Theodore & Co.* was running at the Gaiety, Ivor, still an Air Force Officer, helped to compose the music for the musical comedy, *See-Saw,* at the Comedy, which starred Winnie Melville, Ivy Tresmand and that wonderful artist, Phyllis Monkman, and was later asked to collaborate with actor-composer Guy Le Feuvre on the music of a light operetta called *Arlette*, produced at the Shaftesbury. The cast of this show included Winifred Barnes, Adrah Fair, Stanley Lupino and Joseph Coyne, a link with the 'dear old days of Daly's', when Joe Coyne, one of the most universally beloved figures in theatreland, sang and danced with Ivor's adored Lily Elsie.

Lily Elsie! What a wonderful creature she was—and still is.* What memories of an era she conjures up. Ivor had been her adoring fan ever since he first saw her, and at last he succeeded in meeting her. And where? Of all places, it was at Number 10, Downing Street! The war was still on, and Ivor was still a lieutenant in the Royal Naval Air Force when suddenly he had what he thought was a brainwave. Why not persuade Lily Elsie—who had retired in 1911 at the age of twenty-four—to return to the stage and appear in something he had written, the proceeds to go to various war charities? Accordingly he approached Mr. Asquith's daughter, Elizabeth, who was extremely kind and promised that she would write to Miss Elsie, at that time married and living in her castle in Scotland. Novello had completed the libretto and most of the music of an operetta which he decided to call *The Argentine Widow*, and this was the production in which he hoped that Lily Elsie would make her long-awaited return to the stage. For several days Ivor waited anxiously for a call from Miss Asquith, and finally she rang and told him that Lily Elsie had replied to her saying she would be quite prepared to make appearances for charity if the proposed vehicle suited her. Elizabeth Asquith had then suggested that Miss Elsie should meet Mr. Novello for tea at 10, Downing Street, so that he could play her the music and tell her something about the story. Ivor was jubilant and thanked Miss Asquith profusely. It is difficult to convey what this projected meeting meant to him. He hardly knew how he got through the days that intervened. It was to be something more than just meeting a woman of talent, charm, grace and beauty—it

* Lily Elsie and Ivor were two of the distinguished guests at a Foyle's Literary Luncheon held in January 1950 to mark the publication of W. Macqueen-Pope's history of the Gaiety Theatre.

was a chance to recapture, as he hoped, those thrilling pre-war days when he first made his acquaintance with the London theatre, and when he had spent so many exciting evenings at the Gaiety.

At last the great day came. Ivor arrived early, and had the joy of meeting Mrs. Asquith for the first time. She was about to set forth on a journey up North, and was darting about the room giving final instructions and dashing occasionally into the next room, where she was having high-tea with some friends. If Ivor had not been expecting his idol he would have regarded meeting that phenomenally attractive woman as an event of the greatest importance, but his mind was mainly on Lily Elsie. He could hardly believe that he, who had waited hours and hours outside stage doors for a mere glimpse of this lovely creature, he who had collected dozens of postcards depicting her in all her stage roles, and had, in fact, pasted an entire wall of his bedroom with photographs of her, was actually going to meet Lily Elsie in the flesh—and in the house of the Prime Minister. When the footman announced 'Mrs. Ian Bullough' Ivor's heart started pounding madly. When they were introduced he stammered out a conventional greeting, but soon she had put him at his ease. As Ivor remembered, the thing that made Lily Elsie the adored figure she was was her extreme feminity. To him she seemed to arouse all the very spirit of man's chivalry. She made him want to ride in the lists for her, to throw his cloak down for her to walk over, to sacrifice himself for just a smile. He was hot and excited—and not a little confused. In addition he suddenly had an attack of hiccups, but everyone pretended not to notice. As Miss Elsie sat there in the Prime Minister's drawing-room, sipping her tea and looking like a perfect dream, in a lovely sable coat, the hiccuping young man did not even dare to broach the subject in hand for fear he would have to take his eyes off her. However, it was broached eventually, and the great lady promised that she would indeed read Novello's play. At the same time she suggested that he should play some of the music to her. And that was where the trouble started.

The moment Novello—still hiccuping violently—had diffidently touched the piano keyboard a regimental band struck up in the Horse Guards' Parade. It was apparently marching round the Parade, and when it receded round from the back of 10, Downing Street, a faint tinkle of music could be heard from the piano, but when it approached the house again not a note could be distinguished. And then Mrs. Asquith took a hand. At the sound of the waltz tune Ivor was playing she flew into the room and danced gracefully and persistently round the piano, round the chairs, round the tables. But over and above everything came the solid brassy uproar of the regimental band. It became pandemonium. Ivor stopped playing. Everything had gone wrong. It had turned into a sort of Mad Hatter's tea party.

'This is awful. Here goes my chance. Lily Elsie is not even listening', he thought to himself. He looked over to where she was sitting and saw that she was convulsed with silent but unmistakable giggles. At once the young man felt relieved. 'Thank heavens,' he thought, 'she is a human being with a sense of humour, and this fantastic meeting is not to be the end of everything. I know I shall see her again, and then I shall play my music to her without interruption.' (As it happened, she played opposite Ivor a dozen years later in *The Truth Game,* one of his most successful plays.)

Lily Elsie rose to go, and she flashed Ivor a look that said quite clearly, 'You poor boy! Never mind, I'll listen to it all again some day, but not now'. With good-byes all round she was suddenly gone—and the dream went with her. That look of hers did mean something, however, for a few months later she suddenly wrote to Ivor inviting him to come and see her. To his further delight she asked him to play for her at a series of charity concerts, and their appearances together at such concerts, in aid of every kind of worthy object, became quite a feature of the war-time years. He was even allowed to sing duets with her. To sing duets with the famous Sonia of *The Merry Widow,* London's pre-war darling! When that happened Ivor Novello felt he had really achieved something. To him that was more important than all the songs he had

ever written. He never forgot those wonderful, exciting days, nor the incomparable 'Elsie', as she always preferred to be called by her friends.

★

The war years in London were distinguished by alternate moods of gaiety and depression. The theatre flourished as never before, *Chu Chin Chow* began its phenomenal run, and people flocked to every kind of show, and parties afterwards, as a relief from the tedium of a war-time existence. People reverted to the herd instinct, believing that if disaster came it was better to die in company than alone. Thus parties flourished, and through them all ran a strain of hectic gaiety. Many were held in Ivor's Aldwych flat, which had gradually become the rendezvous for most of theatrical London during his leave periods. His particular friends included Fay Compton, Beatrice Lillie, Phyllis Monkman, Gertrude Lawrence, Ethel Baird, Gladys Gunn, George Grossmith, Viola Tree, Billie Carleton, Robert Andrews (his closest friend for thirty-five years), Seymour Hicks, Leslie Henson, Laurette Taylor, Jack Buchanan, Sir Edward Marsh, Phyllis and Zena Dare, Keneth Kent, Noël Coward and Henry Kendall. With the latter Ivor had spent a riotous few months being taught to fly at Chingford, and their friendship was always flavoured with the happy-go-lucky feeling of 'Let's have a good time to-day, for to-morrow we may crash' which most members of the Air Force felt at one time or another during the war years. Keneth Kent remained one of Ivor's friends since they first met at Harrogate when Novello was fifteen, during the time that their respective mothers were taking the cure. They instantly disliked each other, and began by fighting like young demons. They stayed friends, however, for more than forty years.

The gay parties continued unabated during the war years and afterwards. Ivor and his friends were just an excited group of youngsters, talented, undisciplined and gay—with only one point of view: where was the party and how late could they stay up? Everybody went to those parties, invited and uninvited. Nobody cared. The days of gatecrashing had

not arrived; in those days there weren't any gates. War broke down all kinds of barriers, and Ivor made many friends in those hectic times to whom he remained devoted since then—Phyllis Monkman, Henry Kendall, Gertrude Lawrence and Noël Coward among them.

His flat, when he was on leave, was always crammed with people—every stage celebrity in London—though, of course, many were not celebrities then. Supper would be ordered from the Savoy; even an orchestra would sometimes be engaged. Heifetz once played there. Maggie Teyte sang (and once, some years later, Paul Robeson sat on the floor and sang Negro spirituals). The Dolly Sisters danced. Mrs. Pat Campbell recited, and burlesque dramas were improvised and enacted by Fay Compton, Beatrice Lillie, Bobbie Andrews, Nelson Keys, Noël Coward, Constance Collier, Leslie Henson and others, with Ivor playing the incidental music on the piano and hissing instructions from the 'wings'.

From midnight until 2 a.m.—the actors' time of relaxation—was when most of the parties were held. And what parties they were! The guests varied from night to night, but there was always a 'hard core', as it were, of Ivor's most devoted friends, who would always help to prepare everything and make things go with a swing. Viola Tree, for example, or Bobbie Andrews, or Noël Coward. Noël came to all of them. In his teens—as he was then—he was just a young actor with a burning ambition to write plays. He was continually writing funny sketches, some of which were performed by Ivor's guests. He was excellent company; his conversation was always full of fun and he was surprisingly knowledgeable and sophisticated for one so young. He had been friends with Ivor since the middle of the war.

In the first volume of his autobiograhy* Coward tells of his meeting with Ivor: —

'I first met Ivor Novello outside the Midland Hotel, Manchester, when he was introduced to me by Robert Andrews. It was 1916, and I was acting at the Gaiety, Manchester, in *Wild Heather,* in which I played Helen Haye's son.

* *Present Indicative* (Heinemann, 1937).

I had not seen Bobbie Andrews since we were boy actors in the dear old romantic days of Savoy parties and teas in Lyons' Corner House. He introduced me to Ivor, and we stood there chatting while I tried to adjust my mind to the shock. My illusion of this romantic, handsome youth who had composed "Keep the Home Fires Burning" drooped and died and lay in the gutter between the tram-lines and the kerb. The reason for this was that I had caught him in a completely "off" moment. He was not sitting at a grand piano. He was not in naval uniform. The eager Galahad expression which distinguished every photograph of him was lacking. His face was yellow, and he had omitted to shave owing to a morning rehearsal. He was wearing an old overcoat with an Astrakhan collar and a degraded brown hat, and if he had suddenly produced a violin from somewhere and played the "Barcarole" from *The Tales of Hoffman* I should have given him threepence from sheer pity.

'They walked along to the stage door of the Gaiety with me, and Ivor asked me to come over to the Prince's Theatre when I had finished my performance to see the last act of his musical comedy *Arlette,* which was playing there before opening in London. I remember very little about *Arlette* except the score, which was charming. Winifred Barnes was in it and Joseph Coyne, and the plot was Ruritanian.

'Afterwards we had tea in Ivor's rooms at the Midland Hotel, and he shaved and changed into a dinner-jacket for a company supper party. I envied thoroughly everything about him. His looks, his personality, his assured position, his dinner clothes, his bedroom and bath, and, above all, the supper party. I pictured him sipping champagne and laughing gaily, warm in the conviction that he was adored by everybody at the table. I envied the easy intimacy with which he referred to Winifred Barnes as "Betty" and Joseph Coyne (my hero of *The Quaker Girl*) as "Joe". I don't think honestly that there was any meanness in my envy. I didn't begrudge him his glamorous life. Nobody who knew Ivor for five minutes could ever begrudge him anything. I just felt suddenly conscious of the long way I had to go before I could break into the magic atmosphere in which he moved and breathed with such nonchalance. In bed that night in my combined room I devoured minced haddock on toast with a certain distaste. A sense of frustration oppressed me.'

★

Three of the people Novello met during the war years and just after, and whose friendship endured, were Viola Tree, Sir Edward Marsh, and Constance Collier. Each was destined to be of singular importance in his life.

His first sight of Viola Tree was in the first year of the war, in the doorway of her house in Welbeck Street; Ivor had gone there to visit Ellen Tuckfield, a charming and attractive young musician who was Viola's 'P.G.', occupying the top floor of the house. From this first unexpected meeting grew a devoted friendship. Viola, as Novello declared, had more entertainment value to the square inch than anyone he had met before or since. In all the years he had given parties or 'small romps' as he called them, Viola's presence at these had been not only desirable but essential. She was a vivid, fresh personality, had exquisite natural taste, great knowledge of pictures and music, and had lived a varied and exciting life. Sir Herbert Tree, her famous father, put her into leading parts when she was sixteen, and then sent her to Italy to study opera. She returned to become an actress on the London stage (Mrs. Patrick Campbell once said of her: 'She brings the outdoors indoors'), wrote books, was an actress-manager, an expert journalist, a serious heroine in straight plays and even a knockabout comedienne in musical comedies and revues.

It was Viola who introduced Ivor to Sir Edward Marsh. In late 1915 she had invited the young man to her box to see Lily Elsie, then making her return to the stage in *Mavourneen* at His Majesty's Theatre. Ivor had already seen the play on the first night from the heights of the upper circle, but he welcomed the idea of seeing his beautiful Elsie from the stage box.

'I hope you don't mind, but I've got an awfully nice man, Eddie Marsh, coming.'

'But no, Viola, please', Ivor pleaded. 'He might not like Elsie, and if he doesn't I should insult him. Please put him somewhere else.'

Viola was slightly nonplussed, but she understood completely, knowing Ivor's obsession with Lily Elsie, and found Sir Edward Marsh a seat in the stalls. At the end of the first act, when Ivor was sitting enraptured, a man found his way from the stalls to the front of the box.

'Ivor, this is Eddie Marsh; Eddie, this is Ivor Novello, who wrote "Keep the Home Fires Burning",' introduced Viola. A look of absolute blankness came over Mr. Marsh's face. 'I'm sorry', he stammered, 'Keep the what?' 'What! You've never heard of it!' Viola cried. (At that time 'Home Fires' was being hummed, whistled and barrel-organed all over London. Every military band played it in the park, every concert featured it, every soldier and most civilians knew it by heart. In fact, as Ivor confessed, 'You simply could not get away from it if you tried'.)

'No, I am afraid I just don't know it', replied Eddie, reluctantly, embarrassedly, but firmly.

'Oh, Eddie, da-da-da- da-da-da-,' she hummed the tune a trifle anxiously. Eddie's face lit up. 'Oh, yes, of course—but I didn't know it was called that!'

The tension evaporated slightly, and when Marsh went on to say 'Isn't Lily Elsie superb?' Ivor practically lifted him into the box. Since that time Eddie Marsh was friend, advisor, critic, and a most cultured and delightful companion. Ivor owed him a great debt. 'From my point of view,' he told me, 'it is absolutely impossible to put into words my gratitude to Eddie for his deep, abiding, and patient friendship, and equally impossible to describe the vistas he opened up for me of taste and appreciation of painting and poetry.'

The war continued. Things were going better for the Allies, especially after the entry of the U.S.A. into the war against German militarism. America's declaration of war, belated thought it was, stirred and encouraged the Allies; all the setbacks, disasters and tragedies were forgotten, and each month seemed to bring the end of the war nearer. By now

Ivor had been discharged from active service in the Air Force and was working in London at the Air Ministry. He hated clerical work, and tried hard to get back into some kind of active service, but the two crashes he had had in 1916 had convinced the authorities that he would never make an airman, and he was told that he was 'doing his bit' where he was. The only good thing about this monotonous office job was that it gave Ivor his evenings off in London, and he was able to see his friends, go to theatres, live at home and continue to give his delightful parties.

The job at the Air Ministry also meant that Ivor could continue with his composing in his spare time. After the fabulous success of 'Keep the Home Fires Burning' he had been so involved with Air Force training and routine that for months on end he had not put pen to paper nor touched a piano. In April 1916 he had contributed that one song to *The Bing Boys Are Here,* and six months later he worked on *Theodore & Co.,* the show which really established his name as a composer for the theatre. This he soon followed with *See-Saw, Arlette,* and *Tabs,* all three of which were successes. *Theodore & Co.* ran for 503 performances at the Gaiety, and *See-Saw* 154 at the Comedy. *Arlette* opened at the Shaftesbury on September 6th, 1917, and ran for 260 performances, while *Tabs,* the new revue featuring Beatrice Lilli at the Vaudeville, completed a quartet of first-rate West End shows all featuring Novello compositions. *Tabs* really consolidated his reputation. In addition the young man had contributed a few distinctive songs to the score of *A Southern Maid,* in which José Collins again made a big personal success after her three-year run in Frederick Lonsdale's *The Maid of the Mountains.* The music of the latter was, of course, composed by Harold Fraser Simpson, who also composed the bulk of the music of *A Southern Maid.* That show opened in Manchester in December 1917, and was subsequently produced at Daly's in 1920. José Collins had always been a great admirer of young Ivor's work, and it was through her influence that his songs were included in her show. She helped his career considerably; later Ivor was to collaborate again with Fraser Simpson on the score of *Our Nell,* in which José starred at the Gaiety.

Life went on. The theatre prospered, and amidst all the forced gaiety which is always part of the background to a war the parties and gay gatherings continued. Several of Ivor's friends had by now joined the services, and during their various leaves happy reunions would take place. Noël Coward had joined the Army, after making a fleeting appearance at the Garrick in *Saving Grace* at the end of 1917. As a rather uphappy raw recruit of eighteen he would come up to London on leave, ring Ivor up at the Air Ministry, and the two of them would go out to lunch and talk avidly about the theatre. Ivor, of course, had become a stage celebrity by that time. Apart from the remarkable and unforgettable 'Keep the Home Fires Burning' he had half a dozen important West End shows to his credit—and all this at twenty-five! Everyone said that he had a great future as a composer. Coward, with three more years to go before he was to write his first play, *I'll Leave It To You,* admired Ivor tremendously, and spent as much time as possible in the famous Aldwych flat.

'I saw a lot of Ivor and Bobbie and Glady's Gunn', recounts Noël in his *Present Indicative*: 'And one day in 1918 Ivor gave me a dress-circle seat for the opening matinee of *Tabs,* his new review at the Vaudeville, in which Beatrice Lillie was the leading lady and Gertrude Lawrence was understudying her.

'In his flat there was a delicious atmosphere of slight quarrels and gossiping. Everyone drank a lot of tea and discussed what Charlot had said, and what Fay (Compton) had said, and how Eddie (Marsh) thought it was marvellous anyway. This would have to be changed and that would certainly have to be changed. The whole conversation swirled around all the topics I loved best, occasionally enhanced but never interrupted by peculiar noises from the next room, in which Madame Novello Davies gave interminable singing lessons to small Welsh women in grey clothes.'

In 1918 Ivor received a letter from Lloyd Williams, a boy with whom he had studied music in Cardiff, and who had been one of his mother's protégés. Lloyd was a man of about Ivor's age, who had served in the Army during most of the

war years. He wrote to Ivor telling him that he was among the first group of soldiers to enter the Holy Land, and that as the men crossed the border they spontaneously broke into 'Keep the Home Fires Burning'. Ivor was touched to hear this from Williams, and they continued to correspond until the war was over.

In 1919, when Lloyd was demobilized, Ivor met him and liked him at once. He later asked him if he would be interested in looking after his business interests. Lloyd Williams accepted eagerly, and was henceforth Novello's right-hand man from 1919 until he was taken ill with a heart-attack in 1945. 'Lloydie', as he was known to everybody in the theatre, was a wonderful character with a tremendous sense of humour, full of mischief, yet reliable and extremely clever at handling all Ivor's difficult business activities, like contracts, copyright, radio performances, recordings and so on. Ivor missed him terribly, for not only was he a devoted friend, but he smoothed away all the minor difficulties which made Novello's life complicated when he was trying to write or compose. Ivor never ceased regretting the loss of 'Lloydie', who died in August 1948.

During the last August of the war, after three years in the Air Force, Ivor was sent to Sweden on a propaganda mission. He was asked by Ernst Rolf, the Swedish entertainer and impresario, to bring out a small party of representative young English artists to combat the influence of the German cabaret that was all the rage in Stockholm. The mission was entirely successful, and Ivor loved every minute of his two months' stay in the Swedish capital, but the trip was responsible for one of the greatest disappointments of his life. On November 11th, 1918, the Armistice was declared, at the time when Ivor and his four companions were sitting in a small hotel bedroom in Stockholm. While London was going mad with excitement, and all Ivor's friends were holding joyous celebrations, he just sat and cried—because it all seemed so far away. A feeling of relief and great happiness intermingled with his tears of disappointment as he stood at his bedroom window gazing out at the Swedish newsboys crying out the

wonderful news. Yes, that was a wonderful—but a very saddening—moment.

When Ivor returned to London a week later he was greeted with news of the death of his friend, that lovely actress Billie Carleton. The tragedy had a sobering effect on Novello's little group, and Billie's passing left a gap which was never quite filled. But life must go on—and here he was, immediately after the war, demobilized, young, successful, with lots of friends, and quite a nice little bank balance—for with all his parties and gay life he had still managed to save about £5,000 from the proceeds of 'Keep the Home Fires Burning'. Novello was happy—on the surface at least. Yet underneath he experienced an uncomfortable feeling that he was not getting anywhere. It was all very well, he thought, to be liked and quite well known, and to have an easy, gay time—but what was his future going to be? He decided to talk it over with his mother—always his guide, friend and mentor, always the one who saw things most clearly. She suggested that perhaps they ought to go away for a little while, maybe to America for a visit. She, in any case, was returning to her New York home, which she had established in 1916. Ivor agreed. Deciding that a trip like that would blow the war cobwebs away and prepare him for a bout of new work in London, he booked passages for America. The party consisted of Madame Clara, Robert Andrews, singer Fay Evelyn and Ivor himself, thoroughly excited at the prospect, like a child opening a birthday present.

4

His First Film

THE plan was to stay a month in New York, and Ivor took with him £500, which he considered would cover the expenses of the stay. As it transpired, they all stayed five months, and he had to send back home for money no less than four times. But, whatever it cost him, the trip was worth every penny. He was in love with New York—that glittering city of enchantment—and he simply could not get enough of it. In five months he went to a hundred and sixty plays, saw innumerable films and attended two concerts every Sunday.

After England during the war years, the exciting, sparkling American city came as a wonderful change of atmosphere and environment. Through his mother, Ivor (and Bobbie) met dozens of famous American stage celebrities. They went to scores of parties and theatre gatherings, gave several parties themselves in Madame Clara's studio, and luxuriated in a new life of ease and pleasure. The Broadway stage particularly fascinated the ever stage-struck Ivor. He saw John and Lionel Barrymore in *The Jest,* Fay Bainter in *East Is West,* George M. Cohan in *A Prince There Was* (one of Cohan's least-successful plays, but one which was distinguished by the personality and performance of that inimitable comedian), Percy Marmont in *The Invisible Foe,* by Walter Hackett, Lowell Sherman and Janet Beecher in *The Woman in Room 13,* the great John Barrymore again in Tolstoy's *Redemption,* the unforgettable and tragic Jeanne Eagels in

Daddies, Charles Coburn in *The Better 'Ole* (an English importation), and *Up in Mabel's Room,* that perennial American farce. He met—and adored at once—his mother's dear friend Clifton Webb, and laughed uproariously at Webb's antics in *Listen Lester,* a musical staged at the Knickerbocker Theatre. Webb continued to be one of Ivor's good friends ever since.

And there were others. Famous plays. Infamous plays. Successes. Failures. Revivals. Ivor saw them all—or as many as he could cram in during five months. He saw the original production of *Lightnin',* which Will Rogers was later to make into a well-beloved film, *Good Morning, Judge,* a musical based on Pinero's farce *The Magistrate,* Ernest Truex in *Please Get Married,* the first presentation in New York of Shaw's one-act comedy *Augustus Does His Bit,* and *The Royal Vagabond,* a musical play in which Dorothy Dickson and Carl Hyson stopped the show with a magnificent dance number. (This was two years before the lovely Dorothy conquered London in *Sally.*) And he saw Richard Dix in *I Love You,* Charlie Ruggles in *Tumble In,* and *Scandals of 1919,* with Ann Pennington, the very first of the famous George White's Scandals. There were many more, but the above shows are those which Ivor remembered best.

It was all new and exciting. Ivor saw all the great names of the New York stage, and met many of them. While he was there Mary Ellis, a beautiful young newcomer in her 'teens, was appearing in her first roles at the Metropolitan Opera House. (Sixteen years later she was to be the star of Novello's first big musical play, *Glamorous Night,* at Drury Lane.) He met the fabulous Barrymores, adored them, went to matinees with Clifton Webb and Bobbie Andrews, and renewed his friendship with several of the people who had been so kind to him on his first visit. The five months simply melted away; the holiday passed in a flash, and soon Ivor was obliged to think seriously about going home.

The New York holiday, if it could be called that, had one effect at least. He had left England as a potentially brilliant but lazy young man, with only vague stirrings of uneasiness

9. As the Young Pretender in the film *Bonnie Prince Charlie,* with Gladys Cooper as Flora Macdonald. While appearing in this they were also co-starring on the London stage in *Enter Kiki,* Novello's fourth stage appearance since his debut in 1921.

10. As Pierre Boucheron in his first play, *The Rat* (1925), which was afterwards made into a successful film. Novello starred in three 'Rat' films for Michael Balcon.

as to what was going to become of him, but he started back from America with the most insane craving for work, work, work, of any and every description. He had made up his mind that he was going to be 'someone'. He was going 'to matter'. In his mother's words, 'At that time Ivor seemed changed. He really looked as if he were going to conquer the world'.

In that spirit they sailed home. Then Fate accordingly dropped a gold brick right into the young man's lap. Half-way across the Atlantic he had the surprise of his life—a cable from Angus McLeod, of the London firm of Daniel Mayer, Ivor's theatrical agents, asking him if he would consider acting in a film! This was right out of the blue with a vengeance. Ivor had not only never acted in a film before, but he had never acted at all (except as a schoolboy amateur). He had certainly been connected with the theatre as a composer for quite a few years, and all his friends were of the theatre—but the fact remained that, although he had wanted to be an actor ever since making the abortive attempt to join the chorus of the tour of *The Count of Luxembourg* in 1910, he had never actually, as they say, 'set foot on the boards'. Hastily he consulted his mother and Bobbie Andrews, his two chief advisers. They were even more surprised than he was, but urged him to accept anyway; and finally Novello excitedly cabled back 'Yes'.

Directly he arrived in London he was greeted by McLeod and rushed over to Paris to meet Louis Mercanton, the French director, who wanted to take a look at him before any contracts were signed. Apparently Mercanton had been shown a photograph of the young composer in the Daniel Mayer office, and since he was looking for an Englishman with something of a 'name'—and who might conceivably have had a Sicilian grandmother—the director decided that Ivor was the 'type' he wanted.

'But he's a composer!' expostulated Rudolph Mayer.

'If he's at all receptive we'll soon knock that out of him!' was Mercanton's reply.

Naturally the chosen actor, who was to be virtually the star of the film *The Call of the Blood* (from the best-selling novel by Robert Hichens), had to be responsive to direction. Over luncheon in a little restaurant off the Champs Elysées, Mercanton, after a two-hour discussion, at length decided that young Novello—composer or no composer—would not only be responsive, but seemed to be completely ideal for the part.

★

Within a few days Ivor signed a contract to co-star in the picture with Phyllis Neilson-Terry, and was whisked off to Taormina, that lovely village in Sicily where most of the filming was to take place. He took to film acting as if he had been acting in the movies all his life; he was a 'find'. He threw himself into his work, learned all he could, and spent an altogether delightful month in Sicily. (Even the fact that he developed blood-poisoning in his foot from walking on the jagged rocks did not spoil it for him.) The boy put himself completely in Mercanton's hands, trusting in Providence —and the camera—that it would 'look all right'. As it turned out, he acted like a veteran and photographed like an Adonis. He was, without any question at all, an absolutely 'natural' actor, with an easy style in which his lack of training and technique were not apparent. However, his first film almost ended in disaster. The villain engaged by Mercanton was an old actor from a Sicilian theatre group famous for the realism of its performances. In one scene, having found out that Ivor had betrayed his daughter (played by Desdemona Mazza), he was supposed to spring out from behind the rocks, hurtle down upon the unsuspecting boy, strangle him, and throw his body into the sea. The Sicilian played the part with such realism that it took two men to drag him off the unfortunate Novello. (Ivor ruefully recalls that literally inches of make-up were used in the next shots to cover the marks of the fingers on his throat.) After the shots, when the boy was still lying unconscious on the ground, the Sicilian burst into floods of remorseful tears for having so far forgotten himself as to half-kill his 'caro Novello'. The most saddening aspect of the whole incident was that the scenes of the strangling were completely ineffective and had to be done again. The next time the veteran actor knew exactly what he was doing, and, of course, the scene was infinitely better. This raises some fascinating points about acting technique—Stanislavsky method versus Coquelin method—which, I am afraid, there is no space to go into here.

Four weeks in Sicily were followed by three weeks in Rome. Unluckily for the producers, the studio workers in Rome decided to have a strike in the middle of the production. This, of course, was fortunate for Novello, for it left him and Phyllis free to see Rome and Venice for the first time. He adored Italy, and regarded filming as 'one long holiday'. At length, however, the studios were ready, the scenes were completed, the last shot was put 'in the can', and Ivor returned to London. For months he waited in suspense, but he need not have worried. To everyone's surprise—including Novello's—*The Call of the Blood,* when shown some months later, turned out to be a very big success. The newspapers were full of praise. One of the critics wrote: 'Director Mercanton can even make the rocks act'. Robert Andrews was heard to remark slyly: 'That's nothing. He can even make Ivor act!' But Novello did not agree with him. When he saw the film he thought he looked awful, and acted worse. He was thoroughly ashamed of himself, realizing only too well how much he still had to learn in the art of acting. He did not like himself in the film one bit, but filmgoers apparently disagreed with him. The movie magazines began receiving letters about Ivor Novello, 'the new screen lover', and articles appeared about him in every kind of cinema journal. Overnight Ivor suddenly became a 'film name', to his absolute astonishment. Even Madame Clara, that indomitable creature of unbounded optimism, was slightly taken aback by her son's sensational film début.

Louis Mercanton was vastly impressed with his new 'discovery'. This talented director had worked in England, France and Hollywood, and had directed the great Sarah Bernhardt herself in *Queen Elizabeth,* a film made as far back as 1911. He subsequently worked for various British, French and American companies, making *The Call of the Blood* for

Stoll, a leading British concern. Both Mercanton and Stoll were eager to sign Novello for further pictures, and the director made plans to bring him to France for *Miarka,* a film in which the great Rèjane was to appear.

Shortly after returning from Sicily, Ivor met Constance Collier at the Three Arts Ball at Covent Garden Opera House. His friend Fay Compton suggested that she and Ivor should share a box with Constance, who had recently come back from America, after successfully playing on Broadway in *Peter Ibbetson* and *An Ideal Husband.* Novello was delighted with the idea as he had always admired her (although he had met her only once—and extremely casually —in New York). In that evening at Covent Garden Ivor met two women who subsequently played important parts in his personal and professional life. One was, of course, Constance Collier; they liked each other at once, and were close friends for thirty years. The other was Gladys Cooper.

As the boy chatted with Constance and Fay in their box, a voice called up from the floor below: 'Hello, Constance!' He looked down and found himself staring into the lovely face of Gladys Cooper. Constance introduced them from the box, and Ivor, greatly daring, asked Gladys to dance with him. She assented, and somehow or other he found himself on the floor, dancing happily with the great star whom he had admired so much for many years. He was thrilled, and his excitement lasted all the evening. For two hours they danced together. A photographer rushed up: 'Oh, Miss Cooper, will you and Mr. Novello pose for a photograph?'

Ivor completely unselfconscious, replied 'Of course'. But not so Gladys. 'Yes,' she cried, but get somebody else to be photographed with us. Look, there's Owen Nares over there —we'll make a threesome!' Ivor once told me: 'I still have that photograph taken at Covent Garden—Gladys looking very lovely in an apparently Turkish costume, Nares in evening dress, and myself in Georgian brocade with a white wig, grinning broadly, obviously pleased with myself and englamoured by my exalted companions.'

Gladys was to be a great influence in Ivor's life (though

he subsequently acted with her in a play which was to prove almost a disaster). So was Constance Collier, who not only acted as a kind of Mother Confessor, but helped and advised him during the uphill and most difficult period of his acting career. She was the influence behind his having his first play produced, and that meeting at Covent Garden resulted in many other things. Ivor later appeared in a film of *The Bohemian Girl* with both Gladys and Constance as his co-stars, and a few years later he was to make his stage name as the star of a play written by Constance and himself.

While making *The Call of the Blood* Ivor was still busily working on his music. He followed up the shows *Arlette* and *A Southern Maid* by collaborating on the score of *Who's Hooper* (with W. H. Berry, Cicely Debenham, Robert Michaelis and Marjorie Gordon), which opened at the Adelphi on September 13th, 1919, and ran for 350 performances. It was during this run that Novello was first presented to King George V, who was present at the performance on November 13th. The King complimented the young composer on his songs in the show, adding a few warm words on 'Keep the Home Fires Burning', which he insisted 'was the best song the war years had produced'.

Then came Ivor's second film, *Miarka,* which was quickly followed by *Carnival,* after which he composed the complete score of *The Golden Moth,* which also starred W. H. Berry and Cicely Debenham at the Adelphi, and collaborated on the score of *A to Z,* which opened at the Prince of Wales on October 11th, 1921, and ran for 450 performances! * But he was still not satisfied. He not only combined the careers of popular film-star and extremely popular composer of musical shows, but he still continued to hanker after a career as a stage actor. Although he had starred in three pictures, he had never appeared on the stage. He had great ambitions in this direction, for he had always been completely and overwhelmingly stage-struck, but although he knew literally

* One of the greatest revue successes of the 1920's, *A to Z* featured Beatrice Lillie, Jack Buchanan, Gertrude Lawrence, Phyllis Monkman, Teddy Gerard, Maisie Gay and many other famous names.

everybody in the theatre, and everyone respected his talents, no one offered him a job on the stage. Ivor, however, persisted in his ambitions, and shortly after *A to Z* opened he told Noël Coward that he would not rest until he had made a reputation as a stage actor as well as a film-star.

'Stick to the films, Ivor,' warned Noël. 'You will be much better on the screen than on the stage. You've got a real film profile.'

But Novello would not listen, and at length, through the intervention of his friend Madge Titheradge, he made his stage début* at the Ambassadors Theatre on November 3rd, 1921, playing Armand Duval in H. M. Harwood's production of *Deburau,* in which he had a five-minute scene with Madge Titheradge herself. (Robert Loraine, Jeanne de Casalis and Leslie Banks were the other leading members of the cast.) For *Deburau* Novello received £15 a week, somewhat of a climb-down from the £100 a week he was getting for *Carnival,* and the £200 he received for *The Bohemian Girl,* but he was delighted to be 'treading the boards' at last.

Neither the play nor Ivor's performance caused any great stir in the English theatre, but after the run of *Debureau* (limited though it was) he experienced less difficulty in getting further parts. In *The Yellow Jacket,* written and produced by Benrimo at the Kingsway in March 1922, he was engaged to play the Chinese hero, Wu Hoo Git, and confessed 'I adored the part, though I was not very good'. His third stage role was Javier, a handsome Spanish boy, in *Spanish Lovers,* also produced by Benrimo, which followed *The Yellow Jacket* at the Kingsway, and he received a set of excellent notices from the London critics for his performance in this play. By this time Novello was becoming accepted as a stage 'name' as well

* Actually in 1914 Ivor had made a brief appearance in a revue at the Little Theatre called *As It Used To Be,* starring Stafford Hilliard and produced by Bertram Forsyth. In one scene Novello acted the part of Mozart, and in addition to playing 'Drink To Me Only With Thine Eyes' on the harpsichord he had two lines to speak. He admitted that he could hardly be described as a success, and since he was engaged at £4 a week, but did not receive any salary—the show closed after a week—he could not call his appearance a truly 'professional stage début'.

as a film star—and not only by the critics. During the short run of *Spanish Lovers* he first noticed—almost incredulously —people standing outside the stage door—waiting for him. They pressed presents and autograph books on him. They flocked around him. They adored him. They were his admirers, his stage-door 'fans'. At last he had 'arrived' in the theatre; and he was supremely happy.

Novello had an extraordinary career. Between 1920 and 1930 he literally had four separate professions: film-star, actor-manager on the stage, composer and successful playwright. When he made his first appearance on the stage he had already been famous for half a dozen years as the composer of 'Keep the Home Fires Burning' and many other songs, and as a brilliant stage composer. He had also starred in his first film, his initial acting job—and been successful at it—and although he was a novice as far as stage technique was concerned, by 1922 Ivor Novello was already a cinema celebrity of national—indeed, one might even say world—renown.

When one considers what an internationally-famous actor he became, the star of a score of films and twice as many plays, it seems all the more remarkable that this young man did not set foot on any stage until he was nearly twenty-nine years old. So great was his reputation for more than thirty-five years that one imagines that Novello must have gone into the theatre as a child, and so built up a big reputation in his twenties. The fact that he had no theatrical training of any kind, and did not make his first stage appearance until a dozen years after all his contemporaries, makes Novello's success story even more extraordinary than it is.

5

To the U.S.A. for D. W. Griffith

LOUIS MERCANTON, as I previously noted, had been so excited by Novello's screen début in *The Call of the Blood* that he had prepared another picture to follow it immediately. In 1920 he signed Ivor to co-star with the great French actress Réjane in *Miarka: The Daughter of the Bear,* by Jean Richepin (who also played a leading role in the film). The story of an old gypsy woman and her granddaughter, Miarka, who become involved with a squire and his nephew, the film was made entirely in France, with Novello the only English actor in the cast. Desdemona Mazza, the heroine of *The Call of the Blood,* played Miarka, with Mme. Réjane giving a truly brilliant performance as the old gypsy woman, her grandmother.

The film marked Réjane's last appearance in public. Then a frail old lady, with great burning eyes, she bore little resemblance to the beautiful, commanding, glittering presence who had had all Paris at her feet. In *Miarka* she had to act a death scene; she played it marvellously. Perhaps she had a presentiment, for she said to Novello, 'This is just a dress rehearsal'. Two weeks after the film was completed the incomparable Réjane was dead.

That fine actor, Charles Vanel, still active in French films to-day, completed the cast. The film was released in England at the end of 1920, and Ivor again received excellent notices for his second screen vehicle. The *Kinematograph Weekly* of November 11th, 1920, for example, recommended the film 'because of the names of Mercanton and Novello'.

At the end of the year Ivor was engaged on his third picture, *Carnival,* made by the old London Films, a leading British film company of that time, with Matheson Lang and Hilda Bayley repeating their stage successes, and Novello as the young lover. *Carnival* was mainly a starring vehicle for Matheson Lang, who made the most of a wonderful sequence in which he played Othello in real life as well as on the stage: the setting of the story was in Venice, and Ivor spent an enchanting holiday in Italy making location sequences. When released in March 1921, *Carnival* added to the young man's reputation. Both Mr. Lang and Miss Bayley already enjoyed the high esteem of the critics, but Novello, comparatively unknown, was acclaimed for his subtle portrayal of the youthful seducer in a lavishly-produced film which became the biggest success of any British film until then. Ivor's performance led to an immediate offer from Harley Knoles, the American director of *Carnival,* to appear with Gladys Cooper in his next production, a film version of that popular operetta, *The Bohemian Girl,* which was to be made in England and on the Continent. (*Carnival,* by the way, was re-made ten years afterwards as a sound film, again with Matheson Lang as the elderly cuckold, but with Chili Bouchier as his erring wife. The producers were anxious for Ivor to repeat the role he had made famous in the silent version, but at the time of production Novello was in Hollywood under contract to M.G.M., and the American actor, Joseph Schildkraut, finally played it instead. As Ivor commented: 'Schildkraut, long one of my favourites, is such a brilliant actor that I was rather pleased at being replaced by him. Indeed, I thought, flattery could not go higher.')

The production of *The Bohemian Girl* was a constant delight for Ivor. It co-starred him with his adored Gladys Cooper, who played the role of the nobleman's daughter kidnapped by a band of gypsies, and Constance Collier was also playing a prominent part. He himself, as a young aristocrat who joins the gypsy band and falls in love with Gladys, was ideally suited in looks and temperament to the role, and scored a resounding success. The picture also featured C. Aubrey Smith and Gibb McLaughlin, and was distinguished also by the fact that in it the great Ellen Terry made her first appearance on the screen. To act with both Réjane and Ellen Terry was surely the height of ambition? At any rate Ivor thought so, and continually congratulated himself on his good fortune. His film career certainly seemed to be progressing in leaps and bounds, and every new picture brought him further fame and popularity and increased his following.

Harley Knoles, director of *Carnival, The Bohemian Girl* and other British silent films, directed films in America before coming to England, including an interesting version of Sir James Barrie's play, *Shall We Join the Ladies?* (under the title *Half An Hour*). Knoles was a genial person, but was somehow not at home in British studios, nor fully cognisant of production methods in this country. So confused did he become at one stage in the making of *The Bohemian Girl* that Ivor, to everyone's amusement, dubbed him 'Hardly Knows'—and the name stuck until the picture was finished. Nevertheless, Ivor and Knoles (who laughed when he heard his nickname) remained great friends; indeed, it was difficult not to be friendly with the sympathetic Novello. From his childhood days he had developed a sense of kindness and sincerity which gave him a charm all his own. He was completely lovable in every sense of the word. During the writing of this book I have had the pleasure of interviewing and meeting dozens of contemporary stage and screen celebrities, and everyone has spoken of him as a real human being, a friend in need, and, 'without doubt, the kindest man in the English theatre'.

As Constance Collier, for instance, says in her book, *Harlequinade*: 'I shall always be indebted to Ivor. When I was appearing with him in *The Bohemian Girl* it was a great struggle for me to finish the picture. The shock of my husband's death had been too great, and I became gradually worse in health. Ivor's kindness to me through that time was remarkable. We became firm friends—and have always remained so. He was young and attractive, and the whole world sought him; yet he found time to entertain me when I must have been a nuisance to everybody. I was terribly morbid, and even my sense of humour seemed to have left me. Ivor sang and played for me, and tried to make me laugh. I will never forget his kindness in those difficult days, and many times since.'

In her autobiography, *The Maid of the Mountains* (published in 1932), José Collins also has many pleasant things to say about him.

'At the Gaiety,' she writes, 'I had two great friends who frequently came to see me and invariably arrived together. They were Noël Coward and Ivor Novello. In those days Noël was still a struggling young actor-author of about twenty-three, while Ivor had by then made a name for himself both on the stage and films, as well as having composed "Keep the Home Fires Burning" almost before he had left the nursery, and later, several of my own most popular numbers at both Daly's and the Gaiety. Ivor has remained the same unspoiled boy. He has a kind of Peter Pan quality about him which makes him especially lovable. I don't think he will ever grow up.

'Ivor's flat was just across the road from the Gaiety, and he and Noël used to arrive at my flat in time for lunch or tea. After lunch we used to switch on my big wireless and spend hours, we three, tuning in to stations all over Europe and the U.S.A. When "Uncle Caractacus" sang in the Children's Hour on the wireless, Ivor and Noël used to go to the piano and do an impersonation. Noël sang while Ivor played. They are both mimics and both screamingly funny.

'Since then we have drifted our respective ways, but I still see Ivor from time to time. He is still just the same boyish person that I have known for some years.'

★

While Ivor was appearing in *Spanish Lovers* in the summer of 1922 he heard that the great American director, D. W. Griffith, had arrived in London for the presentation of his latest film, *Orphans of the Storm*. Novello was most anxious to meet Griffith, not particularly because he ever expected to work in one of his pictures, but because he appreciated so much the great man's achievements in the cinema. He had seen *The Birth of a Nation* and *Intolerance* several times over, and wished very much to have the pleasure of meeting and talking to him. One night, as luck would have it, he found himself next to Griffith's table at the Savoy, and several times he almost got up from his chair to go over and introduce himself to the American. He just could not bring himself to do this, but on the way out to make a telephone call Novello passed Hannen Swaffer, who was sitting alone at a table by the wall, the usual cigarette drooping from the corner of his mouth. Ivor had no cause to like Swaffer, for this critic had been most unkind to him when reviewing his appearances as a stage actor. He was therefore quite prepared to brush past Hannen's table without even glancing down at the critic when Swaffer beckoned him with his finger. Ivor bent over.

'D. W. Griffith wants to meet you,' the famous journalist declared, and went on: 'I told him you were Ivor Novello, but he said that that makes no difference to him! Why not give him a ring?'

Ivor was nonplussed for the moment, not knowing whether to take Swaffer seriously. Nevertheless he thanked him, and the next morning phoned the Savoy, where Griffith was staying, and made an appointment to see the director. At this meeting Griffith, who told Ivor that he had been struck on the previous evening by his resemblance to Richard Barthelmess, strode up and down the room, looking this way and that at the young actor's face, fixing him with his magnetic eyes and telling him time and time again that if Novello ever came to America to work for Griffith he would have to work hard—harder than he had ever worked before. Ivor, both surprised and excited, assured Griffith that he would be quite prepared to work twenty-four hours a day—if it ever meant being in a Griffith film.

'I will send you a cablegram if and when I have the right

part for you,' promised Griffith. And that was how matters stood when Novello signed the contract to appear in Adrian Brunel's film, *The Man Without Desire,* later on that year. Then, quite suddenly, out of the blue, when Novello had made all arrangements to go to Italy with Brunel, a cablegram came from New York from D. W. Griffith asking Novello if he would like to sign a contract with him, the first picture under the agreement to be *The White Rose,* in which he would co-star with Mae Marsh and Carole Dempster. The film was to be made in the U.S.A. in the early part of 1923.

To star in a Griffith picture! It was almost too good to be true. Since the Brunel production would be finished soon after Christmas, Ivor immediately cabled back his acceptance. Although a youthful veteran of four British films—and just then completing his fifth starring vehicle—he was greatly honoured at being put under contract by D. W. Griffith to star in an American picture. His rise to screen fame had certainly been both dramatic and meteoric. Understandably, it was in high spirits that he sailed with Brunel and the company for the Mediterranean.

This time he would be going back to the U.S.A. as a film star, and he had never looked forward to anything so much in his life. *The Man Without Desire,* an excellent film as it turned out, was made in an atmosphere of great good humour and high anticipation.

Adrian Brunel, the celebrated British film director and author, writes in his autobiography*: 'Ivor had agreed to come in with us at a nominal salary, even though he was awaiting a call to go to America for D. W. Griffith. He was already becoming well known as a film "name", since he had played in films for Louis Mercanton and others. The problem was to find someone as beautiful as Ivor to play opposite him. I was all for taking a chance with a newcomer, and fate brought to me a young Russian girl named Nina Yarsikova (which we later changed to Nina Vanna).'

As Brunel goes on to relate, the film was produced in Italy. With him Ivor brought his devoted friend and secretary,

* *Nice Work* (Forbes Robertson, 1949).

'Lloydie', who was also given a small part in the film. The picture was made in and around Venice, and finished off in the Joe May Studios at Weissennsee, Berlin. As by this time Novello had signed his contract to make the film for Griffith, Brunel and the others were obliged to work every night and day, with only a few hours' break for sleep.

The Man Without Desire, written by a clever young screen-writer, Frank Fowell,* from an original story by Monckton Hoffe, was completed after a number of production ups-and-downs. Following a week or so at Weissennsee, the unit had to move over to the Max Lander Studios in Neukoln, ending up at the Lixi Studios at Weissennsee. There were many other difficulties before the picture was at length finished, but the last shot was successfully dispatched in time to allow Ivor to get to Hamburg and catch his boat to New York.

Some time later, in the early part of 1923, Brunel showed an incomplete edited version of the picture to Ivor—back from America—Nina, Constance Collier, and the film's backers. They were all agreed that it was a most excellent and unusual film, pictorially very beautiful because of the Venetian settings and delightful photography, and distinguished by Novello's fine performance. It was distributed by a new company, Novello-Atlas Distributors, which had also acquired for distribution *Ow'd Bob* and two other pictures directed by Brunel, *Lovers in Araby* and *Moors and Minarets.* British post-war film production was then in a very bad way, and Novello-Atlas found it difficult to keep afloat because of the time-lag between renting the picture and obtaining the money owing on its exhibition, usually about a year to eighteen months after the trade show. In order to help the firm through the bad patch, Novello wrote a frankly-commercial film story which he called *The Rat,* and offered it to Brunel at a percentage, with his own services as star at less than a quarter of his usual salary. Adrian, however, could not get a penny towards the finance of *The Rat.* He tried to

* Now Publicity Manager for Metro-Goldwyn-Mayer Pictures in London.

sub-let it to Gaumont, but they were not interested. Nor was anyone else. Brunel and Ivor were therefore forced to give up the idea of making the story as a picture, although later it was turned into a successful play and afterwards into a highly successful film—as we shall see.

In any case, we are anticipating. When Ivor left Hamburg and arrived in New York he was amazed to discover that he was received as a visiting celebrity. The Griffith Organization had released the story of his contract to the American Press, and dozens of reporters were waiting to meet him on landing. He was treated as the great new star from England, and for a week or two was in a daze, but was not so pleased to discover that he was being referred to everywhere as 'the most handsome actor in England'. The *New York Morning Telegraph* reported: 'Griffith has secured the signature of Ivor Novello, said to be the handsomest star in England', and all the other American papers featured stories on the looks of the new British star who had been chosen by Griffith out of all the male stars on both sides of the Atlantic. Eventually Novello was able to live down the publicity stories about his good looks, and to convince the American Press that he could also act.

Since Ivor's trip with his mother to New York in 1919 Madame Clara had made this city her second home. In fact, she had previously established a school in New York as far back as 1916, and spent six months of every year there. Madame Clara loved America, and the American musical world knew her as one of the finest teachers of singing in Europe or the U.S.A. Consequently she was able to operate a studio and salon in New York, to which came the finest opera singers from the Metropolitan Opera House and elsewhere. Indeed, in the 1920's Madame Clara Novello Davies became the 'vogue' in New York.* She was busy and celebrated, and travelled back and forth from New York to

* Among the scores of famous theatrical personalities who studied in New York with Madame Novello Davies were Jeanne Eagels, Dorothy Dickson, Hope Hampton, Mary Ellis, Ilka Chase, Edmund Goulding, Turner Layton and Allan Jones.

London several times a year. Her flat on West 67th Street became a famous salon to which came all the leading American theatre and musical personalities. When Ivor sailed to New York in December, 1922, his mother was waiting to meet him and to instal him in splendour in her comfortable apartment.

On the occasion of his 1919 visit to New York Ivor had been quite unknown in the U.S.A. except as the youthful composer of 'Keep the Home Fires Burning', and had gone the round of the new Broadway plays just like any sightseer. In 1923, when he stayed in New York before going down to Florida for D. W. Griffith, he was a genuine celebrity, interviewed daily by all the New York newspapers (who described him variously as 'the British Adonis', 'the Valentino of England', and 'the Welsh Genius'). According to the *Detroit News,* Novello shared with Richard Barthelmess and Ramon Novarro the honour of being the chief contender for the cinematic throne then occupied by Rudolph Valentino. There was no doubt that Novello made a spectacular hit with the American Press. The New York *Evening Telegram* featured a full page of photographs of him in his famous stage and screen roles, quoting him as saying, 'Please don't write me up as the handsomest man in England. Everybody I've met since I've been in New York insists on tacking that unwarranted description on to me, and I was never more embarrassed in my life. Promise me you'll cut out all that rot in your article!' The report went on: 'Throughout the informal Press reception the much-photographed Novello was totally without affectation. He was just a good-natured young man, anxious to please, whom you could not help liking at first sight. He was sincere in his ambition to achieve a name for himself in the U.S.A., and he certainly seemed sincere in his aversion to being described as the handsomest man in England.'

What helped considerably to make Ivor so well received in New York was the fact that by the time he had arrived in the U.S.A. two of his films had become Broadway successes —*Gypsy Passion* (the American title of *Call of the Blood*) and

11. His most famous silent film part, the title role in *The Lodger,* directed by Alfred Hitchcock in 1926 and one of the greatest British films ever produced.

12. As Benvenuto Cellini in the play *The Firebrand,* Wyndham's, 1926.

The Bohemian Girl. As the New York *Evening Mail* declared (February 5th, 1923): 'Ivor Novello gives every indication of becoming another Valentino. He is not only one of the best-looking men on the screen to-day, but also a finished actor. He plays the role of the Polish patriot who joins the gypsy band and falls in love with the kidnapped Bohemian girl with admirable dignity and restraint.'

The *New York Times* said: 'In this faithful adaptation of William Balfe's opera, Ivor Novello and Gladys Cooper distinguish themselves.' The *New York American,* in reviewing the picture at length, described Ivor as 'an excellent exponent of the romantic school of film acting'.

Paul Gallico,* in the *New York News,* gave as his opinion: 'Mr. Novello is as attractive as they make 'em, and Mr. Griffith is some picker. Novello looks a little like Conway Tearle, a little like Ramon Novarro, and a little like Richard Barthelmess. He is natural and has no annoying mannerisms. A couple of years under good direction should see him the great idol of the movie fans.' Every New York newspaper was similarly enthusiastic. The *New York Telegraph* described Ivor as 'a Greek God who is both handsome and an intelligent actor', while the *New York Tribune* went into ecstasies about 'the most gorgeous profile to be seen on the screen since Francis X. Bushman'. Novello really conquered the New York newspapers, and they apparently took to him completely for his sincerity, modesty and genuine charm.

Within a month Ivor had become quite a famous young man all over the U.S.A.; the Griffith Organization had seen to that. The *New York Review* described him in a leading article as 'the most popular screen star in Europe next to Pola Negri', and every newspaper in the States carried the story of his supposed engagement to Gladys Cooper, who arrived in New York, so the newspapers said, to marry Novello, following her anticipated divorce from H. J. Buckmaster. For some time Ivor and Gladys were seen everywhere together, and became one of the most-photographed couples in the

* Now the distinguished New York correspondent of the London *Sunday Graphic.*

U.S.A. The *New York American* of January 12th, 1923, headed its front-page story 'Will Love Find A Way?' and went on to point out: 'Griffith, to whom Novello is under contract, is not in agreement with his star marrying until the film *The White Rose* is completed.' 'Will Gladys Cooper marry Novello?' was asked by dozens of film magazines, and thousands of words were spilled on the controversy: Should a screen idol disappoint his thousands of film fans by getting married at the height of his fame?

Both Gladys and Ivor were embarrassed by the barrage of publicity—especially as she was not yet divorced. A little thing like that did not, however, worry the American Press.

The upshot of the whole thing, of course, was that their film *The Bohemian Girl* became one of the most popular English movies ever to be shown in the U.S.A.—even though Gladys returned to England some months later without having married Ivor. She was one of the many famous beauties with whom Novello's name was linked during the next twenty years —Benita Hume* was another—but Novello would never talk about the various entanglements of his romantic life, preferring discretion on this subject.

★

By the spring Gladys had left the U.S.A., and Ivor was involved in the production of *The White Rose* at Miami, Florida. A story of the Old South, it co-starred Ivor, Mae Marsh, and Carole Dempster in a large cast which included Neil Hamilton, Lucille La Verne, and Porter Strong. By the summer of that year Ivor had been 'taken up' by the American movie magazines, *Photoplay* vying with *Picture Play* in devoting page after page in praise of the 'sensational new British discovery'. And, a few months later, when *The White Rose* was first shown, Ivor received some really wonderful reviews. The *Los Angeles Examiner* declared that he was 'superb', while several New York papers agreed that the young man was certainly the most remarkable new film discovery for several years. Paul Gallico, in the *New York*

* Benita Hume is now, of course, Mrs. Ronald Colman.

Daily News, wrote: 'Novello has established himself as a fine screen actor in his first American movie.' The *New York Herald* declared, 'After this picture Novello will be one of the most widely sought-after heroes in the movie business', and the *New York Morning Telegraph* published a lengthy eulogy in which its critic maintained that Novello had reached great emotional heights in the film. *The White Rose* was certainly an auspicious American début for the young Welshman, but by the time the picture was commencing a lengthy run at the Lyric Theatre in New York he was on the boat to England feeling quite homesick for Piccadilly, Shaftesbury Avenue—and Aldwych.

Back in London he was interviewed by several newspapers, for he had become by now the kind of internationally-known theatrical personality whose every move made news. A typical article-interview appeared in the *Daily Herald* of June 27th, 1923. It ran as follows:—

'Mr. Ivor Novello is a young man whose dreams have come true. He wanted, above all things, to make a picture under D. W. Griffith. His chances looked remote. But the great director saw him, signed him up, and after many months' delay Novello went off to America to play opposite Mae Marsh. Now he is home again for a holiday, and in a high state of enthusiam.

'"I thought when I went out that I would have to do all sorts of stunts in the movie," he told me, "like jumping off the Woolworth Building to save Mae Marsh from being ground in the propellers of the *Mauretania*! Nothing of the sort. The climax of the picture, for example, is purely emotional".

'"How did you find Griffith as a director?"

'Mr. Novello was enthusiastic: "He's wonderful. He never raises his voice in the studio, but he gets everything he wants. His methods are peculiarly his own. The artists do not read the script, but on the first day he tells you the whole story. Then for three weeks, before we ever see a camera, we rehearse the whole picture right through.

'"It is a great help later when the continuity has to be broken because of the scenery necessities. It is also wonderful experience, because, if any actor happens to be absent from rehearsal, his place must be filled by anyone else who is on the spot. So in those weeks I played my own part and several other people's, which helped a great deal in the understanding of the characters' motivations."

' "How long were you working?"

' "The picture took us several months to make, during which time we travelled all over the place. Griffith is too careful a worker to hustle. After the first three weeks' work he was not satisfied with the photography, so it was all taken again. Each scene is taken six or seven times with three cameras, so that he has a big choice of shots. He shows them the 'rushes' of the picture and listens to their suggestions as to which are the best scenes to keep."

' "That is very unusual."

' "Yes, but extraordinarily helpful. He is so frank, too, and always ready to tell you when you are good—or bad. Some directors let one work on blindly in the dark."

' "How do the studios compare with English ones?"

' "For equipment, about the same, but, of course, the Americans are prepared to spend more money. Griffith admires everything English, however, and half his staff are Englishmen."

' "What do you think are the chances of English pictures in the States?"

' "I have my own solution of that problem. What we must do is to establish our stars in the States. It is to see certain actors that the people in America go to the pictures. They must get used to seeing English stars. Miss Fay Compton, for example, is already very popular there. Others could be international stars, too, if we bothered to build them up."

' "Will you make a picture before going back?"

' "Yes, for Adrian Brunel. I hope to make a picture called *The Rat,* from a story by myself and Constance Collier."

' "How's your fan mail since you've been over there?"

' "Don't talk of it," said Mr. Novello, despairingly, "I have to send off six or seven hundred photos a week!"

'But the fans have the right instinct. Ivor is young, handsome, talented, but, most important, quite unaffected and charming.'

Ivor actually returned to London for a holiday, but he later learned that Griffith would not be making further pictures for a period, and that he was therefore free to do films—or plays—in England. While in New York Ivor and Gladys Cooper had seen a play called *Kiki,* and nothing would content Gladys but that she should play Kiki (with Ivor opposite her) in a London production of the play. On his return from America he found that Gladys, true to her word, had gone ahead with her plans, and was herself going to present the play, in conjunction with Frank Curzon and Gilbert Miller, at the Playhouse. Ivor was delighted, though it was with some misgivings that he accepted a starring part on the stage.

As he explained: 'I had only played three parts in my life —that small scene with Madge Titheradge in *Debureau,* the Chinese hero in *Yellow Jacket,* and the Spanish boy in *Spanish Lovers.* Those three parts had simply nothing whatever to do with playing a modern young man on the West End stage, and I had certain doubts about my ability to do so. *Enter Kiki,* as the play was named for London, was, unfortunately, rushed on, and as the rehearsals flew past I began to suspect that I was miscast. After the first night at the Playhouse I knew I was! The papers gave me hell. My performance was described as "amateurish". I was called "self-conscious"— in fact, I completely got it in the neck. All this completely spoiled the good impression I had made in the other three smaller parts, and for a time the *Enter Kiki* incident not only dashed my hopes of a stage career, but succeeded in giving me an inferiority complex which it took years to overcome. Curiously enough, in spite of the bad notices and the fact that the play ran only for a few months, I quite enjoyed myself acting in it. Playing opposite Gladys Cooper is, of course, always a great pleasure. We had shared something of a success together in the film of *The Bohemian Girl,* and a certain proportion of our audiences each evening were people who had come to see what we looked like in real life.

'Those who saw the play liked it quite well—but it did not run. I played a French theatrical manager of forty-five (the play was adapted from the French original of André Picard by Sydney Blow and Douglas Hoare), with Gladys as a chorus girl who falls in love with me and resorts to various wild devices to win my affections. Looking back, I realize that I was not well cast and it was not a good play. At the time the whole thing seemed like a tragedy, and when it closed I went through a terrible fit of depression. Luckily, several things happened to cheer me up. While rehearsing for the play I had been signed by film producer E. E. Calvert to play the title role in *Bonnie Prince Charlie,* under his direction, for the Gaumont Company, with Gladys Cooper opposite me as Flora MacDonald. My salary was to be the fabulous one—to me at least—of £350 a week. I became quite jubilant. Immediately the play opened we started on the film, and after the run had ended we completed the exterior scenes on the Isle of Aran, finishing up in the Gainsborough Studios in Islington. I enjoyed making this picture very much indeed, and my spirits began to rise once more. The principal thing, however, which helped to combat the failure of *Enter Kiki* was the fact that news of the success of *The White Rose* in New York, and the excellent Press notices for me personally, had boosted me as a film "name"—still somewhat to my astonishment.

'I began to receive offers from British and American companies to star in various films, and my fan mail from filmgoers became enormous,* and meant that "Lloydie" worked day and night answering letters and sending out photographs. It was quite exciting. Nevertheless, I still tended to feel quite depressed and self-pitying over my stage failure. Apparently I had tried to run before I could walk, and had, so to speak, sprained my acting ankles. Would I ever act on the stage again? Constance Collier, my dear friend, came to my rescue with explanations and advice. One evening she asked me to supper, and out of the wisdom of her long experience she

* *Picture Show* reported that his fan-mail was at that period in excess of 2,000 letters a week.

took me to task—firstly for my mistakes, and secondly for not rising above them. I remember her words clearly: "Ivor you've got far too much personality to be anybody's leading man. Unless you strike out on your own you will never be able to meet any leading lady on equal terms—much less Gladys. My advice is—find a play, take it out into the provinces with yourself as the star, become an actor-manager, and see if your film public won't come to see you in the provinces. Then try London again." '

He remembered Constance's advice, and a few months later acted upon it. In the meantime *The White Rose* had broken all records at the Strand Theatre in San Francisco, and had led the dramatic critic of the *San Francisco Chronicle* to write, 'Novello is one of the greatest new screen personalities of the year'. He had finished his role in *Bonnie Prince Charlie,* in the cast of which were Hugh Miller, Adeline Hayden Coffin, Nancy Price, and Arthur Wontner; when the film was first shown in London in November 1923, it was highly praised by the Press and adored by the public. As *The Cinema* stated: 'In the role of the prince, Ivor Novello has the invaluable assistance of an engaging personality and the attractively romantic appearance so typical of a figure who is one of the most fascinating in our history. Novello's acting is effortless and sincere; he is a perfect Young Pretender.'

In the same month *The White Rose* arrived in London, commencing a successful run at the Scala Theatre. The *Morning Post* reported (November 27th, 1923): 'The film was enthusiastically received, and a great ovation was given to the star, Mr. Ivor Novello, who was present on the opening night.' Shortly afterwards *The Man Without Desire,* billed as 'The Amazing Story of a Man Who Lived for Two Hundred Years', also opened in London (having been delayed for nearly a year, due to distribution difficulties). *The White Rose* and *Bonnie Prince Charlie* had rocketed Novello's popularity to fever-pitch, and began an era described by the film trade papers as the 'Novello Boom'. *The Times* (December 15th, 1923) considered that 'Novello's acting set the seal on a great achievement by Brunel', and Brunel's unusual and intelligent direction was highly praised by the *Daily Telegraph* the *Daily Sketch,* and the *Daily Graphic,* the *Daily News* going so far as to say: 'It is one of the most artistic British films ever made, and Adrian Brunel, with this film, has at once leaped into the front rank of British directors.' Even the film trade Press, notably cynical, was impressed by the picture. *Kinematograph Weekly* was certain that 'every exhibitor will welcome this production', and the *Bioscope* pointed out: 'this unusual film will appeal to better-class film audiences, and is certain to be a great success everywhere because of Novello's name'.

In the *Manchester Guardian* C. A. Lejeune wrote: 'This Brunel-Novello picture is a testimonial to native production, and is worth all the British Film Weeks put together.'

Playing opposite Ivor was the lovely Nina Vanna, in a cast which included Sergio Mari, Christopher Walker, and Adrian Brunel himself. (Nina Vanna, a Russian actress of striking beauty, never lived up to the promise shown in *The Man Without Desire,* and disappeared from the screen a year or two later after appearing opposite Novello in Gainsborough's *The Triumph of the Rat.*) Fowell's screenplay, from Hoffe's original story was particularly praised; likewise the photography of Henry Harris. In all, this interesting and beautifully-made film was not only a credit to British studios, but a feather in Novello's cap and a distinct step forward in his career as an actor. By the beginning of 1924 he was certainly riding high, and the *Enter Kiki* incident had been forgotten by everyone—except himself.

Novello continued to compose songs, and did not neglect this aspect of his creative talent.

One of the several songs composed by Ivor in *Our Nell,* which starred José Collins at the Gaiety, had a lyric by Sir Edward Marsh, although his name appeared in the programme as 'Edward Moore'.

Eddie Marsh tells the story of how the song called 'Land of Might Have Been' came to be written. 'One Sunday', he told José Collins, who recounted the incident in *The*

Maid of the Mountains, 'I was spending the afternoon with several others in Ivor's flat, and after tea he began improvising on the piano while the rest of us lolled about on comfortable chairs. After a time the music began to take a definite form, and one by one we pricked up our ears. When he stopped there was a general outburst, "Oh, Ivor, what a delightful tune!" He said he had liked it himself, but had been wanting to see if it took our fancies, and he then asked me if I would like to try my hand at writing the necessary words.

' "But what do you want it to be about?" I queried.

' "Oh, I don't know—Land of Might Have Been."

'So then I sat up all that night with a wet towel round my head. Next day I took him the result. The song was a great success in our circle, and either Olga Lynn or Fay Compton or somebody would sing it at every party.'

Shortly after his three newest films had been successfully, and almost simultaneously, shown in London, Ivor was engaged by André Charlot to write the complete score of *Puppets,** a revue at the Vaudeville, with book and lyrics by Dion Titheradge (Madge's brother), and the stars of which were Stanley Lupino, Binnie Hale, Connie Emerald, and Arthur Chesney (with twenty-year-old Frank Lawton playing one or two tiny parts in the sketches). It was an instantaneous success. The *Daily Chronicle* called it 'the wittiest revue ever seen in London', and went on particularly to praise the score. Other newspaper critics remarked on the tuneful qualities of such of Novello's songs as 'What Do You Mean?', 'Raggedy Doll', and 'Italian Love', but by the time *Puppets* had opened, Ivor's thoughts were already elsewhere. He was feverishly working on plans for the production of his first play.

* When Charlot produced this revue in New York, the *New York Herald* declared: 'The most glorious song in this revue is "March With Me", composed by Ivor Novello, the wistful hero of *The White Rose.*'

6

'The Rat': His First Play

'Mr. Novello, as the Rat, is as big a surprise as Miss Margaret Bannerman was in *Our Betters*. His performance must surely delight even his staunchest admirers. Both in his lighter, more devil-may-care moods, and in his scenes of passion and despair, he is wonderfully effective and affecting. Indeed, the play is not only a success for him as part-author, but especially as chief actor.'—*'The Tatler,' July 7th, 1924.*

I HAVE mentioned previously that Ivor had been experimenting with screen stories for Adrian Brunel, and that *The Rat*, his film story of a young Parisian apache, had never actually reached the filming stage. During his stay in the U.S.A. Novello had polished up this particular scenario, and when he returned to London to appear in *Enter Kiki* he brought out the story from his desk drawer from time to time and revised it, hoping that one day he might play the part of The Rat in a film made from his script.

Back in England, Ivor discussed his screenplay with Constance Collier, and told her of the difficulties he had experienced in getting it accepted as a film. Always ready to advise him, she immediately suggested that he turn his film idea into a play. At first he would not agree, for he just did not think he could do it. Admittedly he had made a success as a composer and as a lyricist, but he had never tried to write a play. That was something Ivor had always considered one of the most difficult of all creative techniques.

As he pointed out to Constance, it was not as if he had had a great deal of theatrical experience which would help him to fashion a play in three acts. He was technically unsuited to be a dramatist. No, no, he decided, he would never attempt such a task. Nonetheless, Constance was quite sure that *The Rat* would make an excellent romantic melodrama for the theatre, and, to show that she had faith in her belief, she offered to help Ivor turn this story into a three-act play. Greatly encouraged, he then agreed to her proposition, and for weeks on end every spare moment—he was acting in *Bonnie Prince Charlie* during the day at the film studios, and in *Enter Kiki* each evening—was spent working on a dramatic adaptation of *The Rat*. At last the first draft was finished, and, rough though it was, both Constance and Ivor were jubilant. They had written a play—and it seemed quite good, too. They had it read by friends in the theatre, not all of whom were enthusiastic, but at length Ivor polished up the first act and, greatly daring, booked a nine weeks' tour of the provinces. Such was his youthful optimism that he began to cast the play while the second act was being polished up, and by the time the third act was completed, he and Constance had made all arrangements for Ivor himself to star in the tour of *The Rat,* with Constance as producer.

The collaborators worked incessantly until four and five in the morning. They sat up, drinking innumerable cups of tea—twenty-three during one night was their record—and the play took shape hour by hour. It was hard work, but they both loved it. With the manuscript finished, however, there came the inevitable question of finance. Although he had earned a great deal for such a young man, Ivor had saved very little. He had invested some of his own money into the film distribution company, Novello-Atlas Renters, the firm which distributed *The Man Without Desire,* but this would not be returned for a year or two. *The White Rose* had paid well, but Ivor had spent literally all his salary from this picture on entertaining his mother and friends in New York. Suddenly, when he most needed it, he found himself without any ready cash. *Bonnie Prince Charlie* had only sufficed to pay his outstanding debts in England from the period before he made the Griffith film, and *Enter Kiki* had just covered his many and varied expenses while he was playing in it. At length, however, he managed to scrape two hundred pounds together, with Constance's aid, and on this meagre capital Ivor Novello launched himself as an actor-manager. (It was not, however, his first venture into actor-management. After the West End run of *Spanish Lovers* in 1922 he had taken out a tour of the play, under his own management and with himself in a leading role. He returned to London, after a short but successful tour, with £300 profit. That had merely whetted his appetite: now he was to try again—but on a more ambitious scale.)

The Press and theatre world were all agog. Novello to become an actor-manager after only four appearances on the stage? How dare he! The tenor of most of the comments was highly critical. Ivor admitted that he did not get a kind word, except from two of his best friends—Mrs. Teddie Thompson, who read the play, loved it, and was most encouraging, and Sir Edward Marsh, who was most amused by it, and believed in it from the very outset. Ivor was grateful to both of them.

With the exception of Madeline Seymour and Isabel Jeans, the cast he engaged for the tour were quite unknown, and included Jean Webster Brough, Dorothy Batley, and Victor Boggetti. They were going to have their first opportunities and were extremely grateful. *The Rat* was to open at Brighton on January 15th, which happened to be Ivor's birthday, but he imagined that no play could have opened in more inauspicious circumstances, birthday or not. The dress rehearsal on the Sunday before the opening lasted from ten o'clock in the morning until four o'clock the following Monday morning, and the cast was literally reeling with fatigue. The musical director got disgustingly drunk and staggered round to Ivor's dressing-room shouting 'Of all the so-and-so awful plays I have ever seen this is the so-and-so worst'. The manager of the theatre, Lawson Lambert, privately confessed to poor, worried Constance that he regretted having booked the play and wished he could substitute another touring show even at that late date. The whole thing promised to be a wonderful 'present' for Novello. After a few hours' sleep the cast assembled again and rehearsed all Monday afternoon, but an atmosphere of gloom hung over the company. Constance was playing in *Our Betters* at the Globe, and had to go back to London after the rehearsal —so she could not even be there on her own first night. Gladys Cooper, Teddie Thompson, and Arthur De Lissa (another dear friend of Ivor's) came down for the opening performance, but Constance went back to Victoria by the six o'clock train, leaving behind her a distraught and unhappy young actor-manager quite convinced that the whole affair was going to be a disaster. Apparently, however, the theatre was packed full. Ivor's films had aroused keen interest in him, and an atmosphere of tensity and expectancy prevailed. Gladys and the others sat in a box, and there was quite a hum of interest when some of the people in the stalls noticed the famous West End star who had come down to Brighton to watch her beloved Ivor's first play.

At last the curtain rose. Ivor sat at the side of the stage listening, and to his astonishment, after a few moments, he began to realize that the play was apparently holding the audience. He made his first entrance to tremendous applause, which made him say to himself, 'Well, they *want* me to be all right'. The curtain fell on the first act to a riotous reception. The character of The Rat, as played by Novello, was definitely maintaining the audience's interest, and Gladys sent round a note, 'I am so proud of you, Ivor. Keep on like this and you've got a winner.'

His spirits soared. Gladys was the one person he had wanted to please and impress, especially as he had always considered that he was partially to blame for the near-failure of *Enter Kiki*. He became more confident, and as the play proceeded the enthusiasm in the theatre grew. The audience loved it, and at the final curtain there was a storm of applause which lasted for twenty minutes. Ivor and his cast took thirty-nine curtain calls. The reception was exciting, the atmosphere was electric, and, although *The Rat* was not an artistic masterpiece, it certainly seemed to be a play which possessed that magic 'something' which assures success wherever it is shown. Ivor scored a personal triumph, while Dorothy Batley was quite exquisite as the little waif who loved The Rat. She was a real 'discovery', subsequently played opposite Ivor in his revival of *Old Heidelberg,* and has had a distinguished career ever since.

Constance was coming down from London on the midnight train after her performance. As she relates in *Harlequinade,* 'Ivor's chauffeur, the famous Arthur Morgan, met me at the station. I stepped from the train and rushed at him, "Well, Morgan, how did it go?"

' "I am afraid, Miss Constance . . ."

' "Oh, don't Morgan," I almost sobbed.

' "I am afraid, Miss Constance, we have a hit on our hands!" he finished.'

And they had. By lunch-time on Tuesday they had sold out for the week, and before the end of that week Ivor had increased his tour from nine weeks to fourteen. That tour had a remarkable success. Wherever *The Rat* was produced it was the same story—packed houses every night. Novello's film reputation obviously meant something, and the public's liking for the play, coupled with its fine first-night reception and the good provincial notices did the rest.

Next came the question of a London run. Ivor and Constance (who, by the way, had written the play under the combined pseudonym of 'David Lestrange') were all for bringing it into the West End, although nearly all their friends and advisors were against it. But at length they made up their minds, and, with the tour over, Ivor returned to London having decided to risk his luck as an actor-manager in the West End. He had lunch at the Ivy with Noël Coward, by now his dear friend of several years' standing. After lunch Noël drove him four times round the park, imploring him not to put the play on in town. He gave three reasons. Firstly, it was not a good play, and suitable only for provincial audiences. Secondly, Ivor was certainly not ready to star on the London stage. Thirdly, another bad press after *Enter Kiki* would surely put an end to his career as an actor. Ivor listened carefully, and, having agreed with Noël on all three points, decided to go ahead with the production.

His confidence was justified, *The Rat,* under his own management, opened brilliantly at the Prince of Wales' Theatre in June 1924, took ten more curtain calls than at Brighton, and ran to packed houses until the following year. It was a solid, undoubted hit. Coward took Ivor out, after he had completed his six-hundredth performance in the title role, especially to say 'I take it all back', an incident typical of the Novello-Coward relationship during the past thirty-five years. It continually amused both these talented men when people suggested that they were rivals, and that each must have felt great jealousy and resentment if the other had a success. Some people even went so far as to belittle Noël's talents in front of Ivor, and run down Ivor in front of Noël, but they were above this kind of petty gossip. They were always the greatest of friends, and their careers ran successfully parallel for many years. Since they both composed music, wrote plays, and acted in them, comparisons were, of course, inevitable, but Ivor himself explained what he thought was the fundamental difference between them*: —

'Noël is a far better workman than I am. He sweats blood. He deeply cares, and I believe I am right in saying that even his lightest comedies have been written with the most meticulous care and attention. Sitting, as it were, at the opposite end of the see-saw, I work the other way. If a thing does not come out at once, quite spontaneously, I scrap it immediately and wait for another idea to come along. Possibly my work is, compared with Noël's, a little slipshod. He cares for the work he is doing more for its own sake, and yet the things that he himself has cared about most, and considered to be his best work, have been those which have pleased the public least. There are certain things which Noël has written that I would have given the eyes out of my head to write—chiefly, I think, the incomparable *Bitter Sweet,* most of the first act

* *Sunday Graphic,* September 5th, 1937.

of *Private Lives,* and two of his one-act plays, *Hands Across the Sea* and *Still Life*. All these I consider to be near-masterpieces, while *Calvalcade* moved me as no other new play has moved me for years. I admire him intensely, and we enjoy a most genial friendship. Noël has—at least as far as I am concerned—developed the missionary spirit to an extraordinary extent. I call it his "finger-wagging". He has "finger-wagged" at me on things of mine that he did not like very much until my head was dizzy. In the end, however, he has always admitted that, in my case, he has invariably turned out to be misguided. He advised me against going on the stage; he advised me not to star in *Enter Kiki*; he was against putting on *The Rat* in London; and so on. If I had followed his advice it would have proved to be fatal. He said to me not so long ago, "What a beastly boy I must have been!" I fervently agreed. In his early days Noël had all the things I liked least—enormous push, great intolerance, unbounded ambition, but a lovely wit, high appreciation of the first-rate, and, without doubt, the best sense of humour in the world. With the years, and with his enormous and deserved success, the bad qualities have disappeared, leaving him one of the wisest, kindest people I have ever known.'

'None of our friends believed we were seriously writing and going to produce a play. They thought we were mad, and met our earnest intention with laughter. Nothing is so hard to combat in life as ridicule.' So wrote Constance Collier of *The Rat* incident. She went on: 'As our friends took us separately aside and warned us of our folly we grew more and more determined to succeed. The only bit of real sympathy we received during the whole undertaking was from Noël Coward. We were tired out and needed help and encouragement, and Noël supplied it at exactly the right moment. Ivor, despite the huge fortune he had made out of music and songs, was going through the usual crisis in an artist's life, and after he had paid all the production expenses and salaries of *The Rat* he was eighty pounds overdrawn at the bank. All the money I had earned had been spent on my husband's illness, so I only had the salary I earned at that time in

Our Betters. However, we were undaunted in spite of opposition, and we produced the play at Brighton. As everyone now knows, it was an overwhelming surprise success. The play ran for nearly a year in London, and Ivor made a world-wide reputation with the play and the film of it which followed. After the London run there followed a triumphant tour, breaking records everywhere.

'Ivor has the best capacity for work of almost anybody I know in the theatre. His energy is untiring, and all this success did not turn his head in the very least. The only effect it had was to make him work harder than ever. He tried to improve his acting, slogged away at his plays, appeared in films during the day, composed music every spare second he had, and never grumbled or complained. Most people rest on their laurels. Not so Ivor. After *The Rat* we acted together in *The Firebrand,* but that did not succeed very well. After this we wrote another play together, *Downhill,* which made a great deal of money. But I always had an affection for *The Rat*. I suppose it was because we suffered so much over it.'

*

To return to *The Rat*. With Isabel Jeans (who really established herself with her performance as Zelie de Chaumat), Maurice Braddell and Jean Webster Brough—as well as Ivor and the brilliant newcomer Dorothy Batley—it was a sensational success at the Prince of Wales' Theatre, not only as a piece of theatrical entertainment, but as a personal triumph for the star and co-author. By now it had become generally known that 'David Lestrange' was actually Novello and Constance, and the public was intrigued by the fact that this talented and handsome young composer and film star had marked his début as both playwright and stage star with one of the biggest hits in the West End. The play, as Ivor would have told you, was simply a thriller, with some good dialogue and situations—a story of the Paris underworld, in which a good-looking apache falls in love with Isabel Jeans, a beautiful Parisian aristocrat, but finally returns to his faithful sweetheart of the Quartier Latin. However, it really 'caught on'.

'Novello Has A Hit' ran headlines in the London newspapers. Even the late great James Agate, in the *Sunday Times,* always a stern critic, adjudged it excellent entertainment, going on to declare, 'Ivor Novello played in the tradition of Sir John Martin Harvey'—praise indeed from Agate. All the other critics were equally enthusiastic.* On September 15th the play was transferred to the Garrick Theatre, but this did not alter its run of success. Novello was the man of the hour. He was photographed at home, in his country cottage at Marlow, in his dressing room, in Hyde Park—and even in the bath. Everything he did made news. He was interviewed by London newspapers every week, and the London correspondents of New York papers 'wrote him up' continually, for Novello, 'the handsomest actor in Europe', was always 'good copy'. In the U.S.A. his films, *The Call of the Blood, The Bohemian Girl, The White Rose, The Man Without Desire* and *Bonnie Prince Charlie,* had made him a famous name, and Hollywood offers continued to reach him. Ivor, however, did not want to leave London and the fabulous success he was enjoying with *The Rat*. He was intrigued with the theatre. He wanted to go on writing plays and acting in them himself. Temporarily, at least, he decided to stay as an actor-manager on the West End stage.

Marian Ryan interviewed Novello for the *New York Telegraph* (August 31st, 1924), and quoted him as follows: 'I have always said that you can be as melodramatic as you like when you write a play, if only you make your people talk and act as people would in such circumstances, and don't make them rant and tear their hair just because the situations seem to call for that. Of course, *The Rat* is good old-fashioned melodrama, but the characters in it talk and act as you or I would if suddenly confronted with such situations. That is why, I think, it is fortunately having a success. People love melodrama. They always will. I have been to any number

* e.g. 'Has all the characteristics of a good thriller' (*Observer*); 'It has established itself as a favourite with the public' (*Daily Telegraph*); 'A well-deserved success' (*The Star*); 'A first-class drama' (*Illustrated London News*); 'A great success' (*Evening News*).

of Sunday night performances of extremely highbrow and intellectual plays, and have watched the audience come out stifling yawns and saying, "What a divine evening! What an experience!" Actually many of them are bored and tired from trying to be too intellectual. I don't claim to be an intellectual and I don't write for these kind of people. And, honestly, I don't think I ever could.'

Ivor continued to make no claims for his plays, but the fact remains that he did write a number of witty comedies, while his plays with music (or, as some call them, his operettas) will stand for many years among the finest works of their kind in the English theatre. But we must return to 1924, the year of Novello's triumph with his very first play. At that time, as regards films, he confessed, 'I was very much in the doldrums'. With some amusement he remembered that when a daily newspaper organized a competition to find the Most Popular Star in British Films, he came out at the bottom of the list.* Yet, two years afterwards, when Ivor had starred in the phenomenally successful film version of *The Rat,* the same paper organized a similar competition—and there was Ivor sitting right on top of the list. Ivor smiled: 'This only goes to show something or other.'

When the run of *The Rat* finally ended, Ivor put on a revival of *Old Heidelberg* at the Garrick Theatre. He adored himself—as he would tell you frankly—as Prince Karl (the part, incidentally, which Ramon Novarro made famous in *The Student Prince,* M.G.M.'s screen version of the play), but he readily added, 'The public did not agree with me'. It came off rather hurriedly, and soon afterwards Ivor was invited to join the cast of Pinero's *Iris* at the Adelphi, taking over the role of Laurence Trenwith. Gladys Cooper was starring in the title role, opposite Henry Ainley, and was delighted to play with Ivor once more. She was even more delighted—and surprised—when the first week Novello joined

* The newspaper was the *Daily News,* April 4th, 1924. Novello was at the bottom of a list which consisted of Betty Balfour, Alma Taylor, Gladys Cooper, Violet Hopson, Fay Compton, Chrissie White, Stewart Rome, Matheson Lang, Owen Nares and Ivor.

the company the receipts went up from £900 to £2,400, demonstrating the enormous popularity which Ivor's films (and *The Rat*) had brought him.

Adrian Brunel, the clever young man who had produced and directed *The Man Without Desire,* an unusual film years ahead of its time, told me recently that when during the 1920's a film was shown in any of the towns which Ivor Novello was visiting on one of his stage tours, it invariably broke all that cinema's box office records of the year. Brunel was only sorry that Ivor could not spare more time to go on personal appearance tours with his picture, because in this way Brunel's company might have got its money back quicker and thus have been able to go ahead with other independent films starring Novello. As it was, Brunel told me, Novello finally signed a contract to make films for Gainsborough, one of the leading British companies of the period. The first of these 'big' pictures was *The Rat,* the film which Brunel had been obliged to turn down two years before owing to lack of finance. By 1926 Ivor Novello had become such a tremendously popular film name that when Astra-National reissued *The Bohemian Girl,* after two years it was still the top British box-office draw, breaking records all over the country. Novello was continually being compared with Valentino, and his name was almost as big an attraction outside a cinema as the fabulous Rudolph himself.

In 1923 Michael Balcon, who had come from Birmingham to London to become one of the most significant names in British films, had started Gainsborough Pictures at Islington Studios, with Graham Cutts as his co-director and Reginald Baker as financial advisor. Here he produced such films as *The Passionate Adventure, The Pleasure Garden* and *The Rat* (all directed by Cutts), *The Lodger* and *Easy Virtue* (directed by Alfred Hitchcock), *The Vortex* and *The Constant Nymph* (directed by Adrian Brunel), and a series of other famous British silent films. Balcon was a very shrewd young producer, and a great admirer of Novello. He had seen and liked all Ivor's early films for other companies, and after he had seen *The Rat* at the Prince of Wales' he decided that he would be prepared to make a film version, starring Novello, of course, with other films to follow. Ivor was delighted to sign a contract, and eventually, under the direction of Graham Cutts, the film was produced at Islington in the summer of 1924, while the play was still running in London.

If *The Bohemian Girl* and *The Man Without Desire* had been highly successful, *The Rat* was enormously so. It had a wonderful reception on its London opening, subsequently becoming one of the most popular British pictures ever made. Balcon was delighted, and privately confessed to Novello that the picture had made an important change in the fortune of Gainsborough Pictures. Indeed, he went so far as to say that this film not only completely ensured the continuance of Gainsborough as a producing company, but had brought about a heartening revival generally in the British film industry, then going through a depressing period after its war-time collapse.

By the mid-twenties Ivor was indeed a famous youngster. He had followed *The Rat* by writing another play, *Downhill* (in collaboration once more with Constance Collier). With Phyllis Monkman, who made a great personal success in this play, Frances Doble and Novello himself, it ran at the Queen's for six months (from June to December 1926), and was afterwards made into a successful film by Michael Balcon. Ivor had also found time to start a club.

As Constance Collier writes: 'Ivor founded a club in Soho in the 1920's, with his friend Henry Kendall, called the "Fifty-Fifty". They had thought of this idea to help the younger actors, who earned small salaries and had nowhere to go after the play at night, to have supper and entertainment at a moderate price. Novello's popularity was such that the club became the rendezvous for all the smartest people in London, and the members for whom it was orginally started were almost crowded out. Nightly the club was so full that one could hardly get a table. It was charming and gay and had a very good orchestra. Sometimes Ivor would conduct or play, or any of the famous stars who happened to be there would get up and give an impromptu entertainment. Ivor liked his friends to go there often, and we were all so fond of him that we went night after night. It was at the "Fifty-Fifty" that Noël Coward and Ivor would sit and ask me to tell them stories of the theatre, and it was Noël himself who persuaded me to write down the little things I remember. And that is how my book of reminiscences, *Harlequinade,* came to be written.'

Film star, stage star, successful playwright, and composer, Ivor Novello was continually exciting Press comment; dozens of articles were published about him in various newspapers and magazines. Some called him a genius, but in an article in *Woman's Pictorial* (October 23rd, 1926) Beverley Nichols declared that Novello was the 'eternal child'. 'He has all the wonderful simplicity of a little boy', wrote Nichols, and went on: 'He is a brilliant child, playing at theatres, music, films. But always a child. He sneezes when he drinks a cocktail. He shouts when he dives into a swimming-pool. He gurgles when he puts on his greasepaint. His mantelpieces are covered with stuffed animals, woolly babies, and birds that squeak. And I should imagine, after seeing that full-blooded, naïve, but essentially entertaining play *The Rat,* that a good deal of it was written with fierce joy when he ought to have been doing homework. His acting is, therefore, always interesting. His whole attitude with regard to the theatre is that of a child crooning ecstatically at its first première. And he adores circuses more than anything else in the world. Its romance is as no other romance. Genius unparalleled belonged to the trapeze artists. Heroes all were the lion-tamers. It seemed that the very flapping of a circus tent was sweet music to him. Novello had the boyish fever for that superb tradition which most of us lose so quickly. He is, and always will be, a child.' Nichols remained one of Ivor's greatest admirers and friends until his death.

Apart from starring in *The Rat* and *Downhill,* making films during the day, running the 'Fifty-Fifty', and composing the scores of West End shows, Ivor still managed to find the time to see all his friends and to give wonderful theatrical parties at his top-floor flat in the Aldwych. The 1920's are famous for their parties. Of them a character in Evelyn Waugh's *Vile Bodies* succinctly observes: 'What a lot of parties—masked parties, savage parties, Wild West parties, Russian parties, circus parties, parties where one had to dress as somebody else, almost naked parties in St. John's Wood, parties in flats and studios and houses and shops and hotels and night-clubs, in windmills and swimming baths.'

Noël Coward remembers Ivor's parties with great affection. As he writes in *Present Indicative*: 'In those days they were great fun. In later years they seem to have become a trifle staid and less spontaneous, but perhaps the fault lies with me; perhaps I have grown blasé, and the thrill of star-gazing has turned sour and curdled. At any rate, at that time a party at "The Flat" was a signal for general rejoicing. "The Flat" sat, and still sits, on the very top of the Strand Theatre, and in order to reach it a perilous ascent was made in a small, self-worked lift. Ivor's guests crushed themselves timorously together in this frightening little box, someone pulled a rope, there was a sharp grinding noise, a scream from some less hardy member of the party; then, swaying and rattling, the box ascended. Upon reaching the top it would hit the roof with a crash, and, more often than not, creak all the way down again.

'Many people preferred to toil up seven long flights of stairs rather than face the lift, but I was one of the braver spirits, on one occasion actually making six complete journeys before I could induce it to stop. The big room in the flat had a raised dais running across one end. Upon this there were sometimes two, at other times no grand pianos, sometimes a gramophone, and nearly always Viola Tree. The high spots of the parties were reached in this room. Charades were performed, people did stunts, Olga Lynn sang, and Fay Compton immediately did an imitation of Olga Lynn singing. Visiting musicians were subtly lured to the piano. Native musicians rushed to it. Rival leading ladies had verbal scuffles. Divorced couples hobnobbed with each other, and with each other's co-respondents. Bitter enemies met face to face, and either swept majestically from the room or stayed to ruffle Ivor's hair.'

★

Novello had his setbacks, of course. He once said to me of this period of his life: 'I have a suspicion that Fate has a sense of humour, and a rather malicious one. Fate says 'Ah! That boy's had a success. He is getting a bit above himself. Now for a few slips!" And I had them. The success of *The Rat* and *Downhill* had given me such confidence that I really felt that I was up there on the top, and that up there I was going to stay. Not on your life! I went "highbrow" for two plays and flopped badly. I played Benvenuto Cellini in *The Firebrand,* under Gilbert Miller's management, and we ran ten weeks to very bad business. (That lovely actress Ursula Jeans made a big personal success in this, by the way, and the cast also featured Constance Collier, Hugh Wakefield and George Howe.) And, after I had been happily starring as Roddy in my second play *Downhill* for some months, I rashly decided to attempt the wonderful title role in Ferenc Molnar's great play *Liliom,* put on by my own management and produced by Theodore Komisarjevsky. This, with Fay Compton and Charles Laughton both giving magnificent performances, ran at the Duke of York's for three rather miserable weeks.* So subdued was I at this setback—and the serious inroads made upon my capital—that I afterwards revived *The Rat* at the Prince of Wales', and for a time breathed with relief at the continued success of this "certainty". But, sure enough, hardly had I settled back to enjoy another successful run than I had been persuaded to play the leading part in *Sirocco,* which everyone knows was one of the most celebrated theatrical failures of the past twenty years. A rather curious fact about my stage career is that although I make no claims that my plays are in any way better than anyone else's, they

* Ivor has written of the first-night of this play: 'Something happened to the producer's novel smoke-effect; the smoke drifted into the auditorium and nearly drove the gasping and coughing audience into the streets!' (*News of the World,* October 8th, 1933.)

are apparently right for *me*. Whenever I have been in a play written by anyone else it had failed. *Deburau,* by Sacha Guitry, ran for three weeks; the revival of *The Yellow Jacket,* by Benrimo, lasted for eight weeks; and *Spanish Lovers* for only three weeks. *The Firebrand,* by Justin McCarthy, *Liliom,* by Molnar, and *Sirocco,* by Coward, all lasted for a few weeks only.'

★

And so we come to *Sirocco*. This new Coward play was produced at Daly's in November 1927, by which time Novello (in spite of *The Firebrand* and *Liliom*) was continuing to enjoy extraordinary popularity with filmgoers. Coward, in his witty autobiography *Present Indicative,* has given an amusing description of the *Sirocco* incident, and Ivor assures me that his version agrees with Coward's, with the exception of one or two small points. In any case, the facts are these.

About two years before *Sirocco* was produced Noël had given Ivor the play to read, with a view to his putting it on under his own management at the Garrick, to follow *Old Heidelberg*. Novello was not much impressed with it, however, and eventually told Noël that he did not think *Sirocco* was up to 'Coward standard'. And there the matter rested. In the summer of 1927 Ivor had closed his revival of *The Rat* and was filming in Bavaria, in Margaret Kennedy's *The Constant Nymph,* directed by Adrian Brunel, with Basil Dean (the producer of the stage version) in charge of production. Dean, in order to persuade the busy and popular Novello to star as Lewis Dodd in the film of *The Constant Nymph,* had promised to put on a play especially for him in the autumn. Ivor was delighted with the arrangement, as he regarded Basil Dean as one of our finest producers, and had previously been most disappointed when he was turned down by Dean for the part of the stage Lewis Dodd in favour of Noël Coward (and afterwards John Gielgud), when the play was first produced at the New Theatre in September 1926.

The picture completed, Dean and Novello returned to London, and the producer told Ivor a week or so later that he had arranged a luncheon at the Ivy with Noël Coward, to discuss a Coward play for Novello to star in. At this meeting it transpired that the play was *Sirocco.* Noël assured the astonished and slightly embarrassed Ivor that he had re-written it and completely transformed it, and that with Basil as producer and Novello as Sirio Marson it simply could not go wrong. Ivor's heart sang, for although Noël had made an enviable reputation by then (with such plays as *I'll Leave It To You, The Vortex, The Rat Trap, Fallen Angels, Hay Fever* and *Easy Virtue*), in Novello's opinion no doctoring could make right a play that was essentially wrong. He was not at all happy about *Sirocco.* At length, however, Coward and Dean literally talked him into it. 'After all,' Ivor thought to himself, 'a new Coward play and a Basil Dean production—it cannot possibly fail.' So he reluctantly agreed to do it, and that was how matters stayed for two days. Then Noël rang up, with a note of uncertain triumph in his voice. 'Ivor,' he said, 'you can forget all your doubts about *Sirocco.* I am going to play it myself.'

Ivor tried to hide the relief he felt. 'Oh, well,' he said jauntily, 'if that's the way you feel about it, that's all right with me.'

Two hours later Noel rang up again, simply falling into the telephone with laughter. 'Oh, Ivor, you really have got to be offended for me. I told Basil I had decided to play the part and he laughed in my face. "You play that part?" he cried. "You simply haven't one qualification for it. Sirio has got to have looks, temperament, a distinctive Italian appearance—in fact, everything Novello has and you haven't. Ivor *must* play it, of course!" '

Ivor received this second phone call with mixed feelings. His first impulse was to say, 'Oh, no, Noël. You took it away from me. Now you can keep the part.' But the die was cast. He found himself saying 'yes' all over again—and rehearsals commenced.

Rehearsals went comparatively smoothly. In fact, as Novello remembers, everybody concerned was quite pleased with themselves. Even Ivor thought the play had improved in production. After the dress rehearsal, a few friends who were in front came round to the dressing-room delirious with excitement. 'Noël's got another *Vortex!*' they cried. And, curiously enough, they had all by this time begun to believe that they were going to have a hit. On the day of production Noël and Ivor went to Golder's Green Hippodrome to see a matinée of *Clowns in Clover,* which starred Cicely Courtneidge, Jack Hulbert, and Ivor's friend June (with whom he had appeared in *The Lodger*). They were both gay and full of fun and highly enjoyed the show. On the way back to London in the car they sang silly songs, and both could hardly wait for the opening night.

At Daly's that evening—that momentous, tragic, unforgettable November evening—the house was packed and excited. It was a Coward First Night, and it was also a Novello First Night—not to mention a Dean First Night. There was an electric atmosphere in the theatre; the audience was keyed up to a pitch of expectancy. When Ivor made his first appearance he was greeted with furious clapping and positive hysteria from the gallery—which seemed somehow to annoy the rest of the house. The atmosphere suddenly became tense. The play, an excellent idea with some quite beautiful writing, seemed pitifully thin as the first act proceeded, and Novello, with some experience of audiences both in the provinces and in London, thought he could sense a kind of hostility in the air. He soon began to realize that they might be in for a bad time. And they were.

During the second act certain sections of the gallery began to make vulgar noises while he was making love to Frances Doble. That hardly helped the play, but things went from bad to worse. Ivor learned later that in the second interval a number of free fights broke out between pro-and-con audiences in the gallery, and this reminded him wryly of the story of a dear but antiquated singer of serio-comic songs on the music-halls. The gallery were giving her the 'bird' when a clear voice above the rest of the crowd cried, 'Give the old cow a chance!' To this she gratefully replied, 'Thank you, sir. You are the only gentleman here!'

As Ivor declared, 'Not even a cow at Daly's got a chance on the night *Sirocco* opened!' He himself had an unforunate last line to speak as he made his exit in the last act. Having thrown Frances Doble all around the stage, broken crockery, and generally behaved like a most frightful cad and perpetual bully, the line he had to say was 'I go to my mother'. This got the big laugh of the evening, and, following the roar of derisive laughter, the curtain fell on combined cheers and boos—mostly boos. Failure, real devastating failure, was there at Daly's Theatre that night. And everyone knew it—except the producer. It was unfortunate that the curtain was allowed to go up and down the way it did, but Basil Dean, who had avoided the first night and had sat in the Ivy in splendid isolation, smoking endlessly and riddled with nerves, had returned backstage just before curtain-fall, and had mistaken the great roaring and screaming out front for applause. Blandly he kept the curtain ascending and descending, to the supreme discomfort of the cast. Everyone was crestfallen and confused, but Coward took the whole disaster extremely well. Ivor told me: 'I must say Noël behaved superbly. He was not going to let us face it alone. He knew they had hated his play, but he came on to the stage to face them. By that time the noise and hubbub had become so awful that I couldn't help seeing the funny side of it all. I wanted to step forward and say to the audience: "Listen, dears, this is not the French Revolution. Nobody has been shot. This is only one small play which we have done. You don't like it—all right, let's call it a day." And I believe if one had been allowed to get one word out, and had treated the situation with humour, the evening might have ended quite differently. But when Basil came on to take a bow he was received with renewed booing. Frances Doble, poor thing, was playing her first leading part, and the audience had liked her very much. Knowing this was her big chance, Noël, therefore, ignoring the roars and boos, led her to the front of the stage. Poor Frances, with tears rolling down her face, blurted out in near-hysteria her carefully-rehearsed first night speech. "This is the happiest night of my life," she sobbed. The audience stopped booing and fell out of their seats with laughing—and the whole evening ended in confusion. Incidentally, "This is the happiest night of my life" became a catch-phrase in the theatre, and was used whenever there was a real stage fiasco for several years to come.'

George Coulouris, the well-known Hollywood actor, who recently returned to the London stage, was in the cast of *Sirocco* and declares that in all his years on the London and Broadway stage he had never experienced such an opening night. 'The audience were really terrifying', he told me.

For Ivor this disaster had come on top of other recent theatre failures, for even *Downhill* had not been as big a success as *The Rat,* while *Old Heidelberg, The Firebrand* and *Liliom* had lasted only a few weeks between them. *Sirocco,* thought Ivor, was his death-blow in the theatre, and he began to believe quite seriously that his double success as author and star of *The Rat* had merely been a flash-in-the-pan, a fluke. 'After all,' he said to himself, 'I have only been on the stage for six years. I've got a lot to learn. Or (frightening thought) perhaps I'm just not cut out for the theatre?'

And, since no West End management came forward with offers of fat parts in new plays, Ivor made up his mind to make films exclusively his career. All his screen appearances had been well-received, and he decided to entrust his future to his old friend Michael Balcon, the producer of *The Rat, Downhill, The Lodger, The Vortex* and the other Novello screen hits which had made him the most popular actor in British films. Thus it was that in the late autumn of 1927 Ivor abandoned the stage and forthwith signed a contract with Balcon to become the leading star of Gainsborough Pictures.

7

Novello and the Silent Cinema

'I have always had an immense respect for Novello's talents, and an intense personal admiration for him. He was a professional actor in the very best meaning of that phrase—sensible, conscientious, patient, and a really brilliant artist. Friendly and unassuming, he made filming with him a pleasure. I shall never forget those tremendously exciting days at Islington when we were producing Ivor Novello films which were to make British cinema history.'
—*Sir Michael Balcon.*

THE arrangement made by Ivor and Michael Balcon for the young man to star in a series of productions at Islington Studios was a happy one for both of them. It revived Ivor's drooping spirits after his comparative failures as a star in the theatre, while to Balcon it meant the continued production of films at his studio starring the most popular 'name' in British pictures—one who, in spite of his tremendous movie reputation, had never really thrown himself wholeheartedly into film-making. What had been the extent of Novello's career in British films following his return from the U.S.A.? After the enormous success of the film of *The Rat* in 1926, starring Ivor, Mae Marsh and Isabel Jeans (repeating her stage role as Zelie), Balcon and the director, Graham Cutts, were very anxious to make a sequel.

Balcon wanted to get Mae Marsh over from Hollywood, but she was involved with bringing up her two children, and her husband did not want her to leave home again for a lengthy period. Actually she almost didn't appear in *The Rat*. When Balcon had suggested making a film version of Novello's stage success, Ivor immediately said that he wanted Mae Marsh to play opposite him as the faithful Odile. He had, of course, co-starred with Mae in Griffith's *The White Rose,* and they had become the greatest of friends. Indeed, her husband, journalist Louis Lee Arms, threatened to leave her at one time because he believed that she and Novello were having an affair. One of the members of the Griffith company had confided her suspicions to Louis, for Ivor, Lloyd Williams, Mae, and her little daughter were inseparable during the making of the picture, and the gossip writers in the fan magazines had begun to smell out a love story where none existed. But that had all been cleared up, and Ivor and Louis, his jealousy quietened, had become the best of friends.

Balcon agreed to co-star Mae in *The Rat,* so Ivor at once cabled her and received an immediate acceptance. Several weeks elapsed before the picture finally went on the floor at Islington, and when Mae finally arrived in London she told Ivor and Balcon that she was going to have her second child—which she hadn't known when she accepted the offer—and she didn't think she could play in the film after all! It was much too late to effect a change of plans, however, and Novello and Balcon went ahead with the picture, after employing a trained nurse to be constantly in attendance upon Miss Marsh, and also erecting a special dressing-room on the set, where she could lie down between shots.

Poor Mae was ill throughout the making of the entire film, but Sir Michael Balcon told me recently that Ivor was the soul of kindness and consideration. He was gentle, patient, and helpful, and made Mae feel a great deal better than she might have done had she been working opposite another star. Whenever she suddenly came over ill in the middle of a shot—as was invariably the case—Ivor would pick her up straight away, carry her to the dressing-room, and fuss over her until she had quite recovered. He was genuinely fond of Mae, and he worked doubly hard to see that she made the film under the most comfortable conditions; she has never forgotten his kindness to this day. *The Rat* was thus shot under difficult circumstances, but it turned out to be an excellent and entertaining film. It certainly enjoyed the biggest box-office success of any British picture in the year 1926. So a second film was made some months later, with the same locale and characters. Titled *The Triumph of The Rat,* it was made and released in March 1927, a year after the release of *The Rat,* and duplicated the latter's success. Again Graham Cutts directed, with Hal Young as the cameraman; co-starring were Ivor and Isabel Jeans, repeating their former roles, and Nina Vanna, Ivor's old friend from *The Man Without Desire,* playing Odile (instead of Mae Marsh). This sequel found Pierre, The Rat, living in society, being kept by Zelie, who, in turn, is being kept by a rich Parisian industrialist. The story was quite daring and *risqué* for that period, and aroused quite a little controversy in the Press. However, the *Kinematograph Weekly* of September 9th, 1926, summed up popular sentiment about the film when it commented: 'This is a really excellent follow-up to Novello's previous success, *The Rat.*' The picture went on to become a box-office hit all over Britain and the U.S.A.

Ivor's third film for Michael Balcon was the now-historic *The Lodger,* adapted from the novel by Mrs. Belloc Lowndes, which was, of course, freely based on the story of the notorious Jack the Ripper. Opposite Novello was stage star June, with Malcolm Keen as Joe, the detective who suspects that Jonathan Drew, played by Novello, is really a mysterious killer. Drew arrives at the small Bloomsbury lodging-house of Mr. and Mrs. Bunting at a time when London is in a state of excitement over a notorious and unknown murderer known as 'The Avenger'. Each of his victims has been a pretty, fair-haired girl, and since the Buntings' daughter, Daisy, is both fair and pretty, Joe, the young detective who is in love with her, views with growing suspicion the mysterious activities of the strange lodger. Drew and Daisy fall in love, but events throw suspicion on the lodger, and eventually he is almost torn to pieces by an enraged mob before it is revealed that he is not the murderer.

The *Bioscope* (September 16th, 1926) stated: '*The Lodger* is possibly the finest British production ever made', and there was no doubt that this brilliantly written piece of fiction had been brought to the screen by Hitchcock with tremendous skill. It was only Hitchcock's third film, but he handled it like a veteran. The tension was admirably sustained, the tempo was fast, the photography was excellent, and Novello's sensitive performance marked him out as one of the truly important screen personalities in our studios. It brought forth unanimous critical praise, and *The Lodger* made many reputations—Balcon's, Hitchcocks' and undeniably Novello's. It was a colossal success, and has since been shown time and time again as an example of the finest British silent films. Indeed, as I write, the British Film Institute are including *The Lodger* in its 1950 Season of Great Films, being presented at the Institut Français (along with such classics as Griffith's *Hearts of the World,* Bramble and Asquith's *Shooting Stars,* Dovzhenko's *Earth* and Ruttman's *Berlin*).

For Novello particularly it established a reputation as a great film actor. Since *The Call of the Blood* he had progressed—from *Miarka* to *Carnival,* from *The Bohemian Girl* to *The Man Without Desire,* and from *The White Rose* to *Bonnie Prince Charlie*—in each film developing more and more into a very gifted and resourceful young player. The critics had been kind to him from the outset, particularly for his performances in Griffith's *The White Rose* and Brunel's *The Man Without Desire,* but Ivor was a perfectionist. He was never satisfied. He knew he had a lot to learn, and the glowing Press notices he received both in England and America only served to convince him that he had a long way to go before he could really be called a perfect film actor. In *The Rat* and its sequel he had merely played a 'devil-may-care', handsome young scoundrel, the kind of part which made him thousands of admirers wherever the films were shown, but in *The Lodger* he undertook something of a more serious nature. Jonathan Drew*—pale, strange of manner, distraught, mysterious—was not the kind of character to excite sympathy. For most of the picture the audience was led to believe that this lodger with his odd behaviour was, in fact, a vicious sexual maniac. Drew was a most difficult and arduous role to sustain, but, nevertheless, Novello's bulging Press books bear witness to his remarkable success in the part. Even those critics who had previously dismissed him as just a handsome young screen hero realized that with *The Lodger* British films now possessed a young and versatile star of international standing who could rival Hollywood's best. When Ivor looked back on all the movies he had appeared in—in Italy, France, Hungary, Africa, London, Hollywood and Florida—he unhesitatingly picked out the first film he made with Alfred Hitchcock as the most significant step forward—indeed the turning-point—in his career as an actor.

Balcon and Hitchcock were anxious to collaborate with Novello on another film, and finally it was decided to make a screen version of *Downhill,* the second play written by Ivor and Constance. Production was commenced in April 1927, at a time when *The Lodger* was earning 'rave' reviews wherever it was being shown, both in England and the U.S.A. (where, by the way, it 'established' Hitchcock). Unfortunately *Downhill* was not a particularly filmic story, and did not by any means emulate the success of the first Hitchcock-Novello effort, even though Ivor, Isabel Jeans, Annette Benson, Lilian Braithwaite and Ian Hunter all gave good performances.

Ivor played Roddy Berwick, a young man who, during his last term at the public school, has an accusation brought against him by a girl at the local tuckshop, which he does not deny out of loyalty to his friend. For this Roddy is expelled, and his father casts him out. In an endeavour to earn his own living the boy drifts on to the stage, runs through a legacy, marries a scheming actress and is deserted by her, gambles, drinks, becomes a gigolo, wins the Calcutta Sweep, goes to Paris, and finally sinks down in the social scale until

* Henry Ainley played Drew in a stage version of *The Lodger.*

he ends up on the Marseilles Docks as a penniless wharf-hand. Ivor comments: * 'As you will see, the film was not without incident!'

In *Michael Balcon's Twenty-five Years in Films* (World Film Publications, 1947) the following amusing note on *Downhill* appears:—

'A young woman in the local village, finding herself in a state of health not proper to a spinster, called on the headmaster of the school. The Head, being somewhat narrow-minded, dealt with our hero, the school captain, who was obviously sheltering his best friend. On being told he was to be expelled, Novello (as Roddy) exclaimed—or rather the written sub-title put these words into his mouth: "Does that mean, sir, that I shall not be able to play for the Old Boys?" ' (Ivor told me that this became a catch phrase at Islington Studios for years afterwards.)

Downhill was released in the U.S.A. under the title *When Boys Leave Home,* and although it was not a particularly good film, it continued to maintain Novello's extreme popularity in America. He received two more offers to go to Hollywood—from M.G.M. and Paramount—but he had already signed to appear in further pictures for Michael Balcon. The first of these was *The Vortex,* a version of Noël Coward's sensational play, to be directed by Adrian Brunel. Novello's contract with D. W. Griffith, by the way, still held good, but the young man was never called upon to fulfil his side of the bargain, for after *The White Rose* Griffith's fortunes had begun to wane. He was abandoned by his backers, and in the mid-twenties the great director of the *Birth of a Nation, Intolerance, Way Down East, Hearts of the World, Broken Blossoms* and *Orphans of the Storm* was forced to cease independent production, after making *America* and *Isn't Life Wonderful.* Following an absence of a year or two he returned to films, but this time not as his own master, as he had been for a dozen years. He never regained his former reputation. Thus Ivor was never required to follow up his

* In *Index to the Work of Alfred Hitchcock,* by Peter Noble (British Film Institute, 1949).

success of *The White Rose,* much to his regret, as he always considered that Griffith was the first real genius of the cinema.

Even if Griffith had resumed independent production, however, it is doubtful whether Ivor could have found the time to make an American film, for after the success of *The Rat* he had become the biggest money-making star in British pictures. He was certainly the busiest young man in the English theatre, for while he was starring nightly in *The Rat* on the stage, he was making the film version of this at Islington Studios during the day, and collaborating with Constance Collier on his second play at every available spare moment at week-ends. *The Triumph of The Rat* soon followed; and afterwards came *The Lodger, Downhill,* and *The Vortex* in quick succession. All were big hits; all added to Ivor's by now immense popularity and reputation.

*

In his autobiography *Nice Work,* Adrian Brunel discusses the making of *The Vortex,* a production he welcomed since it reunited him with Ivor, an actor and person he admired tremendously. Three years previously Brunel had given the young man what still remains one of his finest screen roles, in *The Man Without Desire,* and it was to his eternal regret that he never succeeded in obtaining the backing for the Brunel–Novello projected film version of *The Rat.* Adrian subsequently joined Michael Balcon at Islington, there to alternate with Graham Cutts and young Alfred Hitchcock on the direction of a series of Gainsborough productions. His first film there was *Blighty,* a war story written by Brunel himself in collaboration with Ivor Montagu and Eliot Stannard, with a cast including Jameson Thomas, Lilian Hall Davis, Ellaline Terriss and Godfrey Winn, then a young actor making his film début. *Blighty* was an excellent film, and Brunel quickly followed it with Noël Coward's *The Vortex.* In his argument with the Lord Chamberlain before the play was produced, Coward claimed that it was a moral tract, but even so it only just scraped past the censor. As is well known, the play concerns a mother who has a lover, and her son who takes drugs. Balcon had obtained the film-rights of this play, as well as a number of other West End stage hits by Novello, Coward, Margaret Kennedy and others, but before going ahead with the production he sent Jeffrey Bernard, of the distributors' office, to see the British Board of Film Censors, and get their reaction to the play's theme. Neither Balcon, Brunel, nor Novello were impressed when Bernard returned, exclaiming triumphantly: "It's okay, except that the mother must not have a lover, and, of course, the son must not take drugs!'

The script of *The Vortex* was therefore rewritten, and when Coward read it he almost had a fit, for the screenplay bore little relation to his powerful drama. Finally, however, a 'doctored' version, which he reluctantly passed, went into production, with Ivor playing the part of the son, Nicky, and Willette Kershaw, the American stage actress, as Florence Lancaster—the part made famous on the London stage by Lilian Braithwaite. Frances Doble played Bunty, with Alan Hollis as Tom, Florence's young lover. Brunel was disappointed with the finished picture, for he knew what a good film it might have been before the censors got hold of it. To his intense surprise, however, it was exceptionally well received, and Ivor, as he remembers, 'was simply praised to the skies' for his acting as the sensitive, hysterical Nicky.

Brunel also recalls that in an attempt to help 'put over' what he knew to be an emasculated version of *The Vortex* he decided to embellish the production with a display of technical devices which might divert the attention of critics who expected to see Coward's play on the screen in its original and somewhat sensational form. Thus, every day he would think out some little twist, some intriguing camera angle, some unexpected shots—an extra coating of sugar for the doughnut as it were—to make up for the lack of jam in the centre. These desperate measures were welcomed by his cast and unit, and especially by Ivor, who composed a joyous slogan which he sang to musical accompaniment:—

A cute shot a day
Keeps the critics at bay!

Brunel's next picture with Ivor was a version of Margaret Kennedy's *The Constant Nymph,* also produced by Michael Balcon. The play had been adapted from her own novel by Miss Kennedy, in collaboration with Basil Dean, who also produced it. Dean then joined the film production unit as 'supervisor' of the picture, and the company left for the Austrian Tyrol, where, on the shores of Achensee, the location work was completed.

Novello played the famous role of Lewis in a cast which included Mabel Poulton as Tessa (the film part which established her), Frances Doble as Florence, Benita Hume, Dorothy Boyd, Mary Clare, J. H. Roberts, Tony de Lungo, Keneth Kent, Harold Scott and Elsa Lanchester.

Robert Andrews and 'Lloydie' travelled to Austria with Ivor, and the making of this film was a continual delight for all three. By Ivor it was regarded as a most pleasant holiday; he had just completed three years of really strenuous work on plays, films, and compositions, and was beginning to feel the strain. With *The Constant Nymph* over, he returned from the Tyrol much healthier and happier, and particularly pleased with himself because Basil Dean had promised to star him in a new play on the London stage immediately the film was completed. We have already seen what happened to this production—the ill-fated *Sirocco*—and thus we arrive at November 1927, when Ivor, dispirited by his stage failures, decided to sign a contract with Michael Balcon to make films exclusively for a year at least—and probably longer.

★

'I had a dreadful pang', Novello confessed, 'when I signed on the dotted line, but it seemed to me that I had been shown almost too clearly that the stage was not for me. I could only remember my failures, and I went through what I think was the hardest and most bitter period in my long experience. So afterwards I threw myself into the joys of filming. I had never been able—for any length of time—to do continual pictures because of my stage engagements, and since Michael Balcon made a number of films abroad under arrangement with foreign companies, this meant that I could now avail myself of the delights of travelling combined with film-acting. The first movie I starred in under my new contract was one called *The Gallant Hussar,* made—by arrangement with Josef Somlo—entirely in that lovely country Hungary, where I had a wonderful stay.'

G. M. Bolvary, the well-known Hungarian director, made *The Gallant Hussar,* with Evelyn Holt playing opposite Ivor. As the *Kinematograph Weekly* (September 20th, 1928) remarked of it, 'This is a romance which will please all Ivor Novello's admirers'. Its release, however, had been held up for some months, and it was finally shown at a time when talking films had begun to be popular. Consequently neither *The Gallant Hussar,* nor *The Return of The Rat,* nor *A South Sea Bubble,* which followed it, repeated the success of *The Vortex* and *The Constant Nymph,* for they were silent films competing with talkies; as a result, *The Gallant Hussar,* in particular, tends to be overlooked when one recollects Novello's film appearances. *The Return of The Rat,* the third in the series, starred Ivor, Isabel Jeans, Mabel Poulton, and Gordon Harker. It was by no means as good as the first two 'Rat' pictures, and Ivor was keenly disappointed. Curiously enough, although it was not released until 1930, when sound films like *Rio Rita, On With the Show,* and *Gold Diggers of Broadway* were being shown, this picture was quite successful—a great tribute to Novello's name.

A South Sea Bubble was made in Algiers and Biskra, and Ivor and company enjoyed what turned out to be a prolonged African holiday. Adapted from the novel by Roland Pertwee, it told the story of Vernon Winslowe, descendant of a pirate, who is ruined by his friends, and then, in revenge, persuades them to go with him on a wild-goose chase after some fake buried treasure. The director was T. Hayes Hunter, an American who had made England his home; playing opposite Ivor was his dear friend Benita Hume, with Annette Benson, Harold Huth, Ben Field and S. J. Warmington completing the cast. Although released in early 1929, when *The Broadway Melody* and others had made British filmgoers feverishly 'talkie-conscious', *A South Sea Bubble* was fairly popular,* and as the *Cinema* noted (July 26th, 1928), 'Novello seems to be an invaluable draw'. It was to be, at any rate, Ivor's last silent film.

He was still the top male star in British films, as he had been for half a dozen years. As an indication of this, one may note that in 1928 the *Picturegoer Magazine* ran a Popularity Competition among its readers, the result of which showed that Novello was definitely the most popular male actor—British or Hollywood—whose films were shown in our cinemas. He headed the list of six, followed by Ronald Colman, Ramon Novarro, Matheson Lang, Harold Lloyd and Milton Sills.

On his return from Africa Novello had found his thoughts turning continually towards the theatre. The excellent reviews he had obtained for his fine performance in *The Constant Nymph* cheered him; yet he found himself thinking over and over again: 'I have sold my birth-right. Where is my beautiful theatre? I must make up for the stage failures somehow.' He began to think to himself: 'What had been the best things in his two plays so far? Comedy.' He realized that he should concentrate on comedy. 'Why not try to write a comedy? Ridiculous! Why not?' So write one he did. He worked on an idea night and day—and at last he had finished it. Called *The Truth Game,* it had a wonderful part for himself. He was simply bursting to play the role on the stage. 'But could he do it? What about his film contract?' Ivor had completed only seven months of the year for which he had signed up, and he racked his brains for an excuse to get out of the remaining months. 'There must be *some* way out of the contract.' At length, deciding to brave it out and tell the truth, he went to Michael Balcon and asked him point-blank if he had any objection to his doing a stage comedy in the autumn. Balcon's face fell. 'My dear boy, of course I do not mind, if you can fit it in with your filming. But do you think

* Sir Michael Balcon recently stated that this was a highly underrated film, and that, although it somehow got lost in the talkie rush, it featured one of Ivor's most satisfying performances.

it is wise?' What Balcon meant was that, in his opinion, Ivor was far better away from the stage—so why not leave it alone? Ivor, however, was convinced that he could 'get away' with a light comedy in the theatre, and finally Balcon agreed.

'That was typical of "Mickey" Balcon', Ivor pointed out to me when he recounted the incidents leading up to his return to the stage in his own play. 'He was—and still is—one of the kindest, most generous, most lovable men I think I have ever known, and I am proud to number him among my oldest friends. And not only is he such a darling person, but he is the shrewdest and most talented film producer this country has ever had. When you think back to *The Rat, The Lodger, The Vortex, Easy Virtue* and all the others at Islington, and then remember that he produced all the wonderful Jessie Matthews and Hulbert-Courtneidge films at Shepherd's Bush, as well as all those memorable Hitchcock thrillers in the 1930's—and then look at the exciting, brilliant, and completely individual series of films he had been producing at Ealing Studios in the 1940's—you realize what a great contribution his particular genius has made to the British film industry. I shall, in any case, always be grateful to him for those exciting and successful films I made for him at Islington, the only really happy period I have spent in pictures.'

8

Back to the Stage

IVOR wrote *The Truth Game* (which he first entitled *Taken By Storm*) with Constance Collier in mind as Mrs. Brandon, Viola Tree as the gawky Lady Joan, and Lily Elsie, if he could get her, as the heroine, and with himself as Max, the persistent hero. This was a most ambitious idea, and all the more ambitious because Ivor privately considered that he had no justification at all for appearing on the stage again so soon. However, optimistically, he went ahead. Constance was the first to read the play after he had polished it up, and was immensely amused by it, though, oddly enough, she did not like some of the lines in which she herself—as Mrs. Brandon—was made fun of. Ivor was most amenable, and promised to take out any lines which offended her. The next person he approached was Lily Elsie, but she was very shy and quite unable to make up her own mind about returning to the stage in his play. Viola Tree had given up the theatre—for 'good' she assured him—and was beginning a very successful career in journalism. She, too, turned down the part, but advised Ivor to take the play to her friend Sir Gerald du Maurier, with the object of asking him to read it, and, if he liked it, to advise Lily Elsie to play in it—and also to produce it.

Viola Tree had told du Maurier all about the play, and Ivor read him one scene, which pleased him sufficiently to make him write to Lily Elsie saying that he thought it would be a good idea if she returned to the London stage in this new Novello comedy, which he would be delighted to produce. That was a lucky stroke for Ivor.

Excitedly he read the play to Lily Elsie, and, to his delight and surprise, she immediately said 'Yes'. He could hardly believe his good fortune. Not only was he going to act with the great Lily Elsie, but she was going to be under his own management. She was perfect for the part. Time had definitely stood still for this wonderful woman, and Ivor considered that she looked as young, if not younger, than in the days of *The Merry Widow,* when she was twenty.

Having done very well from his films, Novello had the sum of £4,000 to spend on the production. It looked promising. He certainly had gathered together a wonderful cast—Lily Elsie, Constance Collier, and Viola Tree (who eventually could not resist playing such a good part as Lady Joan obviously was). They were to open 'cold' at the Globe Theatre, and without a provincial try-out, since Ivor had decided to dispense with that theatrical custom. He found, however, that he had to pay a month's rent in advance for the theatre, and another for the last month of the run. That brought him back to earth with a bang, but he was determined to do the whole thing in style. The designs for the sets were exquisite—and exceedingly expensive. Elsie was to wear at least seven new creations, and the production was to be just about as *chic* as it could be. He had a feeling of optimism such as he had never had since *The Rat* was about to open in London, but, as he confessed, 'I think perhaps that was the one time I forgot to touch wood.'

His first jolt came at the very first rehearsal on that first exciting Monday morning, on the stage of the Globe Theatre. There he was, excited and nervous, and there was his illustrious company all assembled. But where was the producer? Where was Sir Gerald? Ivor had always supposed that producers came to the first rehearsal, but Sir Gerald had sent his stage manager to start the whole thing off. It seemed a little peculiar, to say the least, and Ivor felt uneasy. However, the first rehearsal commenced, and he pinned all his hopes on Constance. Surely *she* would be devastating? So she was—but in the wrong sense. Where, he asked himself, after an hour's rehearsal, was that inimitable drawl of hers which he had heard in his mind in every line as he wrote it? There was not a trace of it; Constance was playing the part absolutely 'straight', without a tinge of comedy. Viola, on the other hand, hit the note of her character exactly. As the days went on the reason was not far to seek. Viola loved her part, but Constance hated hers. The rehearsals continued, but the clouds were gathering. After ten days Sir Gerald had still not made an appearance. The cast were in a state of nerves and the author was almost distraught. Ivor admitted that he should have 'bearded Gerald in his den and hauled him by sheer force to the Globe', but at the time he was, he said, 'paralysed by du Maurier's enormous reputation'. The young man simply did not know what to do next. Then the storm burst.

From his cottage in the country Noël Coward rang up. 'Constance is here, Ivor', he jerked out, obviously not liking his task at all. 'And I think you ought to know what's up. She does not want to play the part, and if you hold her to it she will let you down at the last moment.'

'Right,' Novello responded. 'Let me speak to her.'

Constance came on the line: 'I am sorry, Ivor dear . . .'

'You don't like the part, do you, dear?' said Ivor.

'Well . . .' she began.

'It's all right, Constance; I'll get on to Ellis Jeffreys. Don't worry about it at all. Good-bye.'

Of this incident Novello told me: 'I am quite ready to believe now, looking back on this, that Constance was acting from the best of motives. In fact, she says now that she gave up the part because she was terrified that the play was going to be a failure and that I was going to lose a lot of money, and she thought that if she gave up the role I would cancel the whole production. At that time I did not believe a word of this, and her defection on top of all we had gone through together nearly cost me a friendship which I valued more highly than I can say.'

Accordingly, however, Ivor rang up Ellis Jeffreys, who had not acted in the West End for some time. On hearing that

Lily Elsie was playing opposite him, and that Sir Gerald was producing, Ellis enthusiastically agreed to come up to London the next morning and have the part read to her. Next day at the Globe, while the others were waiting in suspense on the stage, Ivor read her the part of Mrs. Brandon in the dressing-room. She appeared to be delighted with both the role and the play, and accepted the part with pleasure. Rehearsals again commenced, but there was still no sign of du Maurier. In spite of frantic telephoning and pleadings he did not show up to one rehearsal, and because they were having no direction of any kind, except from Novello himself, a noticeable lack of confidence began to creep over the entire company. Two weeks of rehearsals without the producer being present! It was almost unbelievable. Ivor went down to 'Red Roofs' (his country house near Maidenhead) for the week-end, full of grave premonitions. Two weeks of precious rehearsal time had been virtually wasted. What should he do next? Unknown to Ivor, Fate was preparing to deal him another blow.

On Monday morning, just before he was starting the journey back to London, Ellis Jeffreys rang him up.

'Ivor,' she said, 'I am sorry, but I cannot possibly play the part. I don't understand the role.'

'But, Ellis,' he implored, 'you *did* understand it! You loved it! You said how delighted you were to come back to the West End in such a splendid part. For God's sake don't let me down now!'

'I am sorry, Ivor,' Ellis replied, with a note of finality in her voice, 'I shall came to rehearsal this morning, but only to explain why I cannot play.'

Rehearsals were by now proceeding at the St. James's Theatre, where Sir Gerald at last condescended to make an appearance—since he had an office in the theatre. When Ivor arrived he found such an atmosphere of gloom, despondency, and mutual suspicion as he had never before—or after—encountered in a theatre. That was Black Monday with a vengeance! There were only two exceptions—Lily Elsie and Viola Tree. Both looked at Ivor sadly, but they were distinctly friendly. Sir Gerald had left a message that he wanted to see

Ivor in his dressing-room. When the young man got there he found Ellis and du Maurier waiting for him, looking very serious and depressed. Ivor turned to du Maurier: —

'Gerald,' he implored, 'please tell Ellis it's all right. You know it's all right. It's a wonderful part, isn't it?'

Du Maurier turned to Novello. 'Ivor, I can hardly say that,' he replied, 'you see, I haven't read it!'

The boy, barely able to believe his ears, was stupefied into silence.

At this moment Lily Elsie swept into the dressing-room and informed Ivor and du Maurier that she was going home unless something was settled quickly.

'Elsie,' cried Novello, clutching at a straw, 'Gerald hasn't read the play!'

At that she rounded on Gerald in a fury.

'But, Gerald, you told me—in fact, you *advised* me—to do it!'

Gerald ignored this, but turned to Ivor, crying out: 'Please, Ivor, I beg of you not to do this play.'

'But,' the boy stammered, 'if you haven't read it, how can you know anything about it? There's a wonderful curtain in the second act . . .'

By this time he was desperate, and tears were not very far away.

'My dear boy,' responded Gerald, 'you won't even get to the end of the second act—mark my words!'

Lily Elsie, by now thoroughly sorry for Ivor, drew herself up to her full height and spoke to Gerald coldly: 'I just want you to know', she said, firmly and deliberately, 'that your advice about doing this play meant nothing to me at all. I said I would do it because I believed in it. And I still do. Please inform me when rehearsals commence again.' With that she was out of the dressing-room in a flash. Her outburst gave Ivor back all his confidence. He thought of all the money he had already spent, of the hours he had worked on the play, the rent he was paying week by week for the theatre, the dresses ordered, the cast waiting about, the first night arranged. That all this should be thrown away was unthinkable.

Du Maurier was looking at him. 'Well,' he said, 'you are not going on with it, are you?'

'Going on with it? Of course I'm going on with it, and as you haven't bothered to read the play, I am going to get some one who will. What's more'—this to poor Ellis—'I shall get Mrs. Brandon played by the finest actress in London!' And with that Novello also swept out of the dressing-room.

'I have never forgotten or really forgiven du Maurier for his behaviour over that play', said Ivor, continuing the story. 'He put me into a really tight corner, and I had to do some quick thinking. I went through the names of all the West End stars who could play Mrs. Brandon, finally deciding on Lilian Braithwaite. She was perfect for the role. But would she do it? She was, at that time, acting at the Garrick in an indifferent drama called *The Moving Finger,* which I knew was not due to last very long. I had never known Lilian very intimately, but I knew her as an extremely intelligent actress, who had proved in Noël's *The Vortex* and Sidney Howard's *The Silver Cord* that she possessed magnificent emotional powers. But how could I get her to consider my play when all the West End was ringing with my troubles, and the bills outside the Globe announcing *The Truth Game* had changed so often that it had become a pastime to go down Shaftesbury Avenue to see which names had been altered each day?

'Anyway, I got in touch with Lilian. She immediately invited me round to her dressing-room at the Garrick, and she was all sympathy and kindness. "You poor darling, what are they doing to you?" she exclaimed. This note of sympathy after all I had gone through was too much for me, and tears came to my eyes. Lilian, ever practical, immediately opened a cupboard and gave me a large glass of port. "Now tell me," she said, "tell me the whole story—and don't leave anything out."

'I told her. I poured forth the whole sad tale. Her reaction was instantaneous. "Darling," she exclaimed, "I will play that part if it is the worst in the world."

' "But it isn't!" I sobbed—having had two more glasses of port, I was now drunk as well as unhappy. "It's a gorgeous part. They have all turned it down, and they are all wrong."

' "Well, anyway, I am going to play it," Lilian finished.

'Her decision was made, you must remember, in the knowledge that two famous actresses had relinquished the part, that the most famous producer in London had jibbed at the play, and that in my case I had appeared in a series of spectacular stage failures, culminating in *Sirocco*. That is what I call friendship. Fortified by both the port and her decision, I next went to see Marie Tempest, with the idea of asking her husband, W. Grahame Browne, to produce my play for me.

'Marie was wonderful, and showed me the same sympathy as Lilian. She and Willie Browne read the play on the spot, and at once promised to help. Indeed, Marie went so far as to cry, "Ivor, we will make a success of this play if I have to scrub the theatre!" All I can say is if she *had* scrubbed the theatre, she would have done it superbly—and worn her best hat to do it!

'Next morning we all met for rehearsal. "Elsie" and I, very tentatively, played the first scene as we had rehearsed it. Willie Browne came on the stage. "But Ivor, this is perfectly charming! What are they all talking about?"

'You can imagine the gradual reconstruction of our confidence and my deep gratitude to Lilian, to Willie Browne, to Viola Tree (who had never wavered in her faith in me), and to my beautiful, adorable "Elsie".

'And now comes the sequel: *The Truth Game** opened in London at the Globe in October 1928, enjoyed a sensational first night, and played for six riotous months in London, followed by a triumphant tour round the provinces, and another London season at Daly's. It was a tremendous personal success for Lilian, and for "Elsie" and Viola. I also played in the same despised comedy for six months in New York. It was made into an excellent film by Metro-Goldwyn-Mayer in 1932, and remade by this company some years afterwards. It is constantly being performed by repertory companies and by

* In the first-night programme the author was given as 'H. E. S. Davidson', a thinly-disguised pseudonym (He's David's Son)—but all London knew that Ivor had written it.

13. In the title role of Ferenc Molnar's *Liliom,* the original London production of this play (directed by Komisarjevsky in 1926-27), with Charles Laughton as Ficsur.

14. As Roddy in the film version of his second play, *Downhill,* produced by Michael Balcon and directed by Alfred Hitchcock in 1927—with Annette Benson and Robin Irvine.

15. As Max Clement in his own play *The Truth Game,* Globe, 1928, with Lily Elsie, making her return to the stage, as Rosina. In the New York production in 1930 Billie Burke played Rosina opposite Novello.

amateurs. It was a colossal, resounding, unquestioned success. But, what is most important, it restored my confidence in myself. After all those terrible rehearsals, those unhappy weeks, the agony I suffered, the self-torment and self-pity—after all that, my play was a hit. After the curtain had fallen on the opening night, with the echo of applause still ringing in my ears, I sat in my dressing-room, surrounded by friends, and reading a sheaf of telegrams and good-luck messages. A knock came on the door. It was Gerald du Maurier.

' "This makes me look rather an ass, doesn't it?" he smiled. I was still bitter and resentful, but at that time there was no point in rubbing it in, and we shook hands heartily. So ended an incident which I shall never forget, but which, fortunately for me, ended happily. And *what* a celebration party I gave at The Flat after that memorable first night!'

The Truth Game occupied Ivor for most of the year 1929. He followed the West End run with a profitable tour, and at the same time busied himself with his next play, which he titled *Symphony in Two Flats*. He had made a great impression as the light-hearted Max in the comedy, *The Truth Game,* so now he wrote a tragic role for himself—that of David, a young composer who loses his sight and almost loses his wife, too. Novello had done so well with his first solo play that he again decided to present the new one under his own management, and to continue his career as an actor-manager in both London and the provinces. With the same company—with the exception of Lily Elsie, who wanted a rest after a year's run of *The Truth Game,* and was replaced by lovely Benita Hume—Ivor appeared in *Symphony In Two Flats,* which opened at the New Theatre in October 1929, a year after the wonderful vindicating first night of his previous play at the Globe. The new production repeated the success of *The Truth Game*; both Novello and his play were acclaimed once more, and all his past failures seemed to have been forgotten. He was described as the 'Wonder Boy of the English Theatre', 'the Man with the Golden Touch', 'Our Most Promising New Playwright', and so on. 'Novello Scores His Fourth Big Hit as Actor-Manager-Playwright', ran newspaper headlines. The critics almost fell over themselves to praise his new play. Michael Balcon, who was present on the opening night, immediately went round to the dressing-room to congratulate Ivor and to make an offer for the film rights—provided Novello would make his return to films in the star part. Ivor gladly agreed, as he could arrange to make the picture during the day while playing at the New in the evenings. *Symphony In Two Flats* was a real success, not only for Ivor, but for Benita Hume (who repeated her role in the film version). It was the play which really established her.

The period in which Novello was first 'accepted' as a youthful giant of the English stage was 1928–29. He was acclaimed as one of the most promising of new playwrights in a year which featured new plays by Somerset Maugham, Noël Coward, Reginald Berkeley, Frederick Lonsdale, H. M. Harwood, Edgar Wallace and J. B. Fagan among others. *The Truth Game* and *Symphony in Two Flats* were as successful as those other contemporary hits of the West End stage which included *The Desert Song, Thark, Dracula, Canaries Sometimes Sing, Hit the Deck, The Girl Friend, The Sacred Flame, The Vagabond King, Interference, On Approval, The Terror* and *The Beloved Vagabond.*

For his performance in these two widely differing plays, not forgetting his work in *The Rat,* Novello was at last considered to be among the leading West End stage stars, thus enjoying the distinction of being in the company of such 'names' as Sir John Martin Harvey, Gladys Cooper, Fay Compton, Jack Buchanan, Tallulah Bankhead, Sir Gerald du Maurier, Marie Tempest, Ivy Tresmand, Sydney Howard, Cedric Hardwicke, Brian Aherne, Sonnie Hale, Clara Eames, Phyllis Monkman, Derek Oldham, Winnie Melville, Edith Evans, Jack Hulbert, Isabel Jeans, Cicely Courtneidge, Lilian Braithwaite, June, Ronald Squire, Ellis Jeffreys, Herbert Marshall, Edna Best, Jeanne de Casalis, Binnie Hale, Bobby Howes, Mary Jerrold, Harry Welchman, Edith Day, Ralph Lynn, Tom Walls and many others.

But not only was he a successful stage actor, but the young man was in continual demand to appear in films.

His fan mail was still the highest of all British film stars. He remained Britain's Number One Star. The film papers were full of articles and interviews with the versatile young man who had been at the top since *Call of the Blood* in 1919; the following quaint effusion, which appeared in the *Picturegoer,* was contributed by one of his many fans: —

POEM TO IVOR

I take my pen to write a line
To Ivor, that dear star of mine
Of all his roles that I have seen,
Each in its way has perfect been;
I went to see him in 'The Rat',
I felt that naught could equal that;
But when 'The Triumph' had been shown,
His masterpiece I had to own!
Alas! I know I have no skill,
Pages and pages of verse to fill;
But this I must with ardour say
To Ivor: 'Luck' in every way!

The film of *Symphony In Two Flats* was subsequently made at Islington Studios, under the supervision of Michael Balcon, and directed by Gareth Gundrey (the co-director of such British silent successes as *Hindle Wakes, Mademoiselle from Armentieres* and *Roses of Picardy.* An interesting fact concerning it was that an American film actress, Jacqueline Logan, was brought over, at the insistence of the U.S. distributors, to play the heroine in the 'American version' of this film, with Benita Hume remaining in the original version.

Cyril Ritchard played Leo Chevasse, the rich philanderer who almost succeeds in breaking up David's marriage after he has become blind. Others in the cast included Clifford Heatherley, Maidie Andrews and Minnie Rayner, all of whom, of course, had been in the original play. *Symphony In Two Flats* was Ivor's first talking film, and it revealed that his delightful speaking voice was eminently suited to the new medium. Sound had smashed the careers of dozens of American and British film-stars; for various reasons their voices had just not been suitable for talking films. Ivor's was perfect.

While he was appearing at the New Theatre, his last silent pictures, *The Constant Nymph, The Gallant Hussar, The Return of The Rat* and *A South Sea Bubble,* were still being shown at a time when half the cinemas in England were exhibiting talking films only. But Ivor's silent pictures continued to be popular, and many magazine articles were devoted to him and his great cinematic popularity. Even so, some writers had asked: 'Can Novello keep his position in talking films?'

The answer was on the screen in *Symphony In Two Flats.* Trained as a singer, studying under one of the greatest elocution teachers in the world—Madame Clara Novello Davies—and with several years' experience on the stage, Ivor had developed a fine speaking voice. He was ideal for the new medium. Talking films only served to enhance his popularity. As the *Bioscope* (July 23rd, 1930) put it: 'Novello, in his first talkie, plays with easy and natural charm, revealing a delightful sense of humour in the lighter moments.'

★

Towards the end of the play's run, in the summer of 1930, Ivor, having finished the film, received an offer from the Shuberts, the well-known New York impresarios, to take *Symphony In Two Flats* to America after its West End season. He was highly excited. He had never acted on the Broadway stage—and now he was to do so in his own play, featuring his own music! Quickly Ivor cabled back his acceptance, and in August, when they closed in London, the whole company sailed for Montreal, Canada, where the play was 'tried out' before its New York season. The 'try out' was most promising and augured well for Broadway.

At the Shubert Theatre, New York, in September 1930, they finally opened, with Benita Hume, Lilian Braithwaite, Minnie Rayner, Maidie Andrews and Ann Trevor, with Raymond Massey as producer, but, alas! without Viola Tree, whose journalistic and domestic ties had kept her in London.

Ivor regarded Viola as something of a mascot to him. She had always encouraged him; she had introduced him to Sir Edward Marsh, for years one of his greatest friends and advisors; and she had stuck by him during all the troubles which marked the rehearsals of *The Truth Game*. Viola had repeated her success in that comedy in *Symphony In Two Flats,* and Ivor began to believe that her presence brought good luck to his endeavours.

'I think if Viola had come to New York with us it would have been a different tale', he once reminisced, and continued: 'We opened in New York on the hottest day of the entire year, and ten minutes before the curtain was to rise a thunderstorm broke over the city. This was followed by the most torrential rain I have ever seen, so that not only were wet late-comers arriving at the theatre all through the first act, but when they got there they could not hear a word for the insistent crashes of thunder. Somehow we got through that first night, and we got a fairly pleasant Press. But partly because we opened so early in the season, and partly because of the heat, and because most of the cast were unknown in New York anyway, *Symphony In Two Flats* failed to run, and finally came off after only seven weeks.* I could not bear the idea of going back to England without making a Broadway success. I had tasted blood. I loved New York, and during the final weeks of the stay I had made plans to follow it with *The Truth Game,* since the Shuberts had kindly offered to take a chance with a second play. I cabled Viola to come over to play Lady Joan, and made her realize the urgency. Then, luckily for me, I got Billie Burke to play Mrs. Brandon. And, with myself as Max, we opened at the Ethel Barrymore Theatre in December 1930, to a wonderful house, a glittering first-night, and a huge success. The New York critics were ecstatic about this new English comedy, and particularly by the performances of Billie and Viola. I was delighted. To have achieved a dual success in that toughest of all towns was

* As Novello wrote in *The News of the World,* October 15th, 1933: We opened in a heat wave and closed in a heat wave. Unfortunately it was the *same* heat wave!'

just about as much as I ever expected out of life. I shall always be grateful to the Shuberts for giving me a second chance. Lesser managements would have sent us back to London by the next boat after the failure of *Symphony*. Not so the Shuberts. God bless them!'

The American Press and public remembered Novello with affection from his visit in 1923 to make *The White Rose*. Since that time most of his British films had been shown with success all over the U.S.A., and Ivor arrived in New York in 1930 with the reputation of being one of the cleverest and busiest young men in the English theatre and cinema. *The Truth Game,* one of the season's hits, was soon snapped up as a film by M.G.M., who also offered Ivor a dual contract as actor and writer. Ironically enough, during the run of *Symphony In Two Flats,* not one film company had approached Ivor, but with the success of *The Truth Game* they all came a-running. Indeed, he could have signed with half a dozen Hollywood companies, but finally he chose M.G.M. (As it turned out, he made the wrong choice.) When *The Truth Game* ended its Broadway run most of the cast returned to London. Ivor, however, after a brief holiday, travelled out to California to begin his Hollywood contract. A new era in his life had commenced.

9

Hollywood

WHEN Novello arrived in Hollywood in the summer of 1931 the Celluloid City had just gone through a major revolution. Three years previously the firm of Warner Brothers had startled Hollywood with the introduction of sound films, and by 1930 every other company was engaged in the making of 'talkies'. Great silent stars, whose voices were for various reasons unsuitable to the new medium, found themselves discarded in favour of British and Broadway actors and actresses who could talk as well as act. By 1931 a whole new group of sound-film stars had begun to establish themselves in Hollywood; most of them are still active at the present time.

It was with mixed feelings that Ivor set off from New York to California. Everyone had told him that Hollywood would break his heart in six months, but that, anyhow, he would have 'one hell of a time'. The nearer he got to Los Angeles the more miserable and friendless he felt, but a surprise was in store for him. In New York Ivor had given a party, to which had come, among others, Joan Crawford and her husband, Douglas Fairbanks Junr. He had told them that he would shortly be going to California, and they had asked him to let them know when he was due to arrive. Ivor had done so, and to his delight, when he arrived in Hollywood, there on the platform to met him was Joan Crawford. This was such an unexpected and friendly gesture that Novello's spirits rose at once. That night he dined with Joan and Doug, and the next morning she called for him and took him to the M.G.M. Studios, where she insisted on introducing him to everyone. As Ivor recalled, 'I could not have had my entry into Hollywood made more easy and delightful, and shall always be grateful to Joan for that charming gesture'.

His immediate job at M.G.M. was to prepare a screen version of *The Truth Game*. He was given an office and handed a 'first rough draft' of an already prepared screenplay of his play.

'Take it home and read it', directed Bernie Hyman, one of the studio supervisors.

That night, his second in Hollywood, Ivor sat alone in his apartment and read the draft. It gave him the first taste of what it was like to be an author in Hollywood. The script was simply awful. 'Rough' just wasn't the word for it! He began to feel ill. The adaptor (anonymous, apparently, since there was no credit on the title page) had tried to make the screenplay exactly like the play as it had been produced on the stage. Ivor, with even his limited knowledge of screenwriting, realized at once that this was the wrong approach. He knew that it was filmically hopeless right from the start merely to photograph a stage play, and that theatre productions needed to be translated onto the screen entirely in terms of the cinema if they were not to be static and 'stagey'. This had not been done, and, in addition, some really appalling jokes had been introduced to 'liven up the action'. Their very 'unfunnyness' made Ivor shudder, and he spent an unhappy evening making copious notes in the margin of the script.

Next morning Novello walked into the studio to see Hyman, and his face must have told the whole story.

'I see you have read it', remarked Hyman.

Ivor nodded, too full to speak.

'Terrible, isn't it?' added Hyman.

From that moment Novello knew that Bernie was a man after his own heart, obviously a kindred spirit. Relieved, he sat down and they had a cup of coffee, followed by a conference with other studio heads, at which Ivor made everybody roar with laughter by exclaiming: 'Let's face it. I don't know why you bought my play, though I'm very glad you did. Now let's alter the whole thing and try to make a good film out of it.'

'You're the first author we have ever had at the studios who has voluntarily suggested altering a word of his own play', chuckled Hyman afterwards. 'You've made Hollywood history.'

And so Ivor began to work on the screenplay of his comedy, and during the next few months he wrote no less than eight different versions of *The Truth Game*. As he told me somewhat ruefully, 'After nine months' work, about all that remained of my play when I had finished with it were the names of the characters and the title—and both these were altered on the first day of production!'

He said of his Hollywood stay: 'There was a sunlit patio where I used to sit, with creepers growing over the trellis-work, and the big Pacific rollers booming along the shore in front of me. I was staying in the house of Edmund Goulding, the English film director, who has been in Hollywood for twenty years. I lived in nothing but a beach-suit. Between work and meals I used to roll off the patio into the sea and go for a swim. Then a sunbathe, then work again. It was a very pleasant existence, but I still longed, strange as it may seem, to get back to London.'

The film of *The Truth Game* was eventually directed by Jack Conway, under the title of *But the Flesh is Weak,* as a vehicle for Robert Montgomery, then one of M.G.M.'s biggest stars.* Novello secretly hoped that he himself would be asked to star in the part of Max, which he had created on the London stage as well as on Broadway, but things did not work that way in Hollywood in those days. M.G.M., who had gaily put him under contract both as an actor and writer, just did not seem to know what to do with him. They already had Robert Montgomery, Clark Gable, Ramon Novarro, John Gilbert, Robert Young and half a dozen other male stars, all

* M.G.M. made a second version ten years afterwards. Titled *Free and Easy,* it was directed by George Sydney and starred Robert Cummings (in the Novello role), Ruth Hussey, Judith Anderson, C. Aubrey Smith, Nigel Bruce and Tom Conway. It was re-issued in 1949.

of whom had to be supplied with starring roles. Novello's appearance on the M.G.M. lot, therefore, caused little or no sensation. If any new plays or film stories were bought, such stars as Gable or Novarro were immediately thought of to play the leading parts. M.G.M. could not seem to see Ivor as a star, and in any case they had their hands full with their other very expensive contract artists. Thus, as far as his acting was concerned, Hollywood represented to Ivor the most frustrating period of his life. Nonetheless he managed to enjoy himself as much as possible, and made many new friends, though he still missed London and his old friends very much. He never stopped working, however. In addition to writing the various screenplays of *The Truth Game,* and collaborating on the screenplay of the Robert Montgomery–Madge Evans picture *Lovers Courageous,* he was asked by M.G.M. to go to work on rather an amusing assignment. This company had bought the rights of the novel *Tarzan, the Ape Man* by Edgar Rice Burroughs, to star Johnny Weismuller and Maureen O'Sullivan, and Novello, that master of slick, polished, drawing-room conversation, was detailed to write the dialogue of this jungle epic. Could anything have been more ludicrous? However, Ivor had quite a good time on the Tarzan picture, deciding that if Hollywood wanted to do mad things he would enter into the spirit of it all. Naturally he chafed a good deal—firstly, at not appearing in the film version of *The Truth Game,* and, secondly, at not being used by M.G.M. as an actor at all. However, he made up for all his disappointment by throwing himself eagerly into a protracted period of work, and, in addition to his film writing, he also found time to write two new plays. So his Hollywood stay was not entirely a wasted period in his career, and was, on the whole, quite enjoyable.

One day a dog wandered on to the patio of Ivor's beach house, settled down, and refused to leave. Ivor thought he must belong to somebody in the film colony, so he tried him with various names. At 'Garbo', 'Janet Gaynor' and 'Ramon Novarro' he gave no sign, though he wagged his tail furiously at 'George Arliss' and 'Zazu Pitts'. Nevertheless he remained unclaimed, and advertisements failed to find his owner. So Jim, as he became known, a lovable 'cross' between an Airedale and an Alsatian, stayed with Ivor and went back with him to England some months later. Strangely enough, Jim strolled into Novello's life on a Wednesday. The following week a letter came from England from Ivor's father, telling him that his own pet dog, Jim, a fox-terrier, had suddenly died on that very same Wednesday. That was the last letter Ivor ever received from David, for he died a week or two later.

The home-sickness increased, further accentuated by the shock of the death of his father, and at the end of six months Ivor approached Irving Thalberg, then in charge of production at M.G.M. Studios, put the whole case before him, and asked for his release from his contract. Thalberg was quite distressed. He simply could not understand at all how this young Englishman could possibly be dissatisfied with Hollywood, especially since he was receiving a fat cheque every Friday for doing practically nothing. Eventually, however, Ivor made Thalberg see that he really was unhappy in the film city, and the producer suggested that he should be fair to M.G.M., who had brought him out to California at great expense, by giving Hollywood a further three months' trial.

'If at the end of that time you are still determined to go back to London and to give up your contract, then I shall not stand in your way', he informed Ivor. So there the matter stood for the next three months.

Of course, Hollywood did not entirely consist of work and home-sickness. Ivor's greatest friends in Hollywood were Joan Crawford and Douglas Fairbanks Junr., Ruth Chatterton, Edmund Lowe, Paul Lukas, Lilyan Tashman, Laura Hope Crews, Kay Francis, Richard Cromwell and a small contingent of the English colony in California. Ivor met many world-famous stars, and on the whole enjoyed the parties at which he encountered many of the most interesting personalities in the film city. He became brown and healthy, spent a great deal of time on the beach, and learned to become a skilled exponent of surf-boarding. Apart from the more cheerful social aspects of his stay, however, he learned something about himself. He began to see himself in perspective. In England the name of Ivor Novello was practically a household word. In London he knew everybody, everybody knew him, he went everywhere, was always treated as an important young man, and had—as he thought—achieved quite a lot one way or another. In Hollywood, he discovered, he just did not mean a thing. There they hardly knew the names of the great stage stars of New York, let alone the names of the famous theatrical personalities in London. Of course, Hollywood is a much more cosmopolitan place to-day, but twenty years ago it was extraordinarily insular, a 'hang-over' from the bad old days of silent films, when the movie industry was a thing apart from the American theatre. Thus, in perspective, Ivor realized that the experience was a good one for him. Those who knew him well will affirm that there had never been a chance of Novello ever becoming too conscious of his own importance, but his stay in Hollywood made him realize just how much he still had to attain if he really wanted world recognition and acclaim. But it was not only Ivor Novello about whom Hollywood showed its ignorance. Once he happened to show a particularly beautiful photograph of Gladys Cooper to a well-known Hollywood executive.

'What a lovely girl,' exclaimed the producer. 'Who is she? She ought to come out to the Coast.'

'Why should she?' replied Ivor. 'She is at the top of her profession—virtually the queen of the London stage.'

'Is that so,' was the uninterested reply. The incident was typical.

Looking back, Ivor decided that he grew in stature as a person, possibly because he was so very much alone, and also because he had been taken down a peg or two and found himself mattering very little to anyone else in that extraordinary community.

He spent a great deal of time with Joan Crawford, whom he admired, and became good friends with Marie Dressler, Norma Shearer, and her husband, Irving Thalberg. One morning Ivor's telephone bell tinkled. At the other end of the wire was his very old friend Lilyan Tashman. She told him that she was just setting out for her bungalow at Malibu, and was going to call by on her way. Half an hour later they were hugging each other and talking as hard as they could go. Then Lilyan suddenly remembered: outside, she told Ivor, were her friends Paul Lukas, Kay Francis—and Greta Garbo.

Ivor had never met Garbo, although he had worked—with, he believed, seventeen other writers—on the screenplay of her film, *Mata Hari,* and here she was actually waiting outside his house! He couldn't wait to meet her, and rushed to welcome her. In she came, dressed in trousers, a striped sweater, a sailor's reefer coat, and a beret pulled tight over her lovely hair. She wore dark blue glasses and walked with a mannish stride. She seemed shy, but after a while she began to talk with Novello, and gradually her reserve melted. They must have chatted for nearly two hours, with Ivor telling Garbo about London, Berlin, Sweden, all the theatre and film people he knew in Europe, and the theatres of London, Paris and Stockholm. Garbo was delighted when she discovered that he knew a few words of Swedish and was a friend of Ernst Rolf, the cabaret artist. She prattled away, gay, relaxed, and very happy. There was nothing of the great star about her. She was simple, unassuming, unaffected. Her face fascinated Ivor. Even the old clothes, the glasses, the tight beret, could not hide her beauty. As he told me: —

'Let me say, once and for all, that she is infinitely more beautiful off the screen than she is on. In the cinema you miss that divine honey-coloured skin, those wonderful blue-grey eyes, with real gold lashes that seem to hang half-way down her face like ostrich feathers. And there is a real warmth about Greta in person that never really begins to appear on the screen.'

Suddenly Garbo stopped talking, as if she had realized that she had broken down her reserve for far too long. She rose to go.

'Auf wiedersehen', she smiled.

'Really 'auf wiedersehen"?' Ivor queried. He wanted so much to see her again.

'Really "auf wiedersehen"!' She seemed quite definite

City at that time, sharing with Norma Shearer and Joan Crawford all the plum roles in M.G.M. films. Following *Mata Hari* (which Ivor had a hand in writing), she began discussions with Erich von Stroheim, the great silent star and ex-film director of *Greed* and other famous films, on a screen version of Pirandello's *As You Desire Me*. There was some talk of Novello callaborating with Stroheim on the screenplay, but by the time it was planned to go into production Ivor had obtained his release from his contract and had made all arrangements for his return home.

Hollywood in 1931 was quite an exciting place. The introduction of dialogue in 1929 had thrown all the studios (except Warners, who introduced it in the Al Jolson picture *The Jazz Singer*) into confusion and fear. By the time all studios were finally equipped with sound dozens of great silent film stars found that their careers had virtually come to a stop. For various reasons their voices were not suitable to the new medium, and stage stars from New York and London were quickly brought in to take their places. During 1930 Hollywood 'played it safe' by concentrating on making film versions of stage successes, using well-known stage names. By 1931, however, some of the more courageous studios began to experiment a little with the new medium of sound, and by 1932 some brilliant and 'un-stagey' talking films had been produced, many of which are still remembered to-day.

At M.G.M., while Ivor was working there, such pictures as *The Champ* (Wallace Beery and Jackie Cooper), *Emma* (Marie Dressler and Richard Cromwell), *A Free Soul* (Norma Shearer, Leslie Howard, and a sensational newcomer called Clark Gable), and *Lovers Courageous* (Robert Montgomery and Madge Evans) were being produced. On the latter, written by Frederick Lonsdale, Ivor collaborated with that clever playwright on the dialogue, and became great friends with the star, Montgomery, whose next film was Ivor's *The Truth Game*. In this he played opposite Nora Gregor in a distinguished cast which included Heather Thatcher, Nils Asther, C. Aubrey Smith, Eva Moore and Edward Everett Horton.

16. As Felix in his own play *I Lived With You,* with Ursula Jeans and Thea Holme, Prince of Wales's, 1932, which marked Novello's return to the London stage after two years on Broadway and in Hollywood.

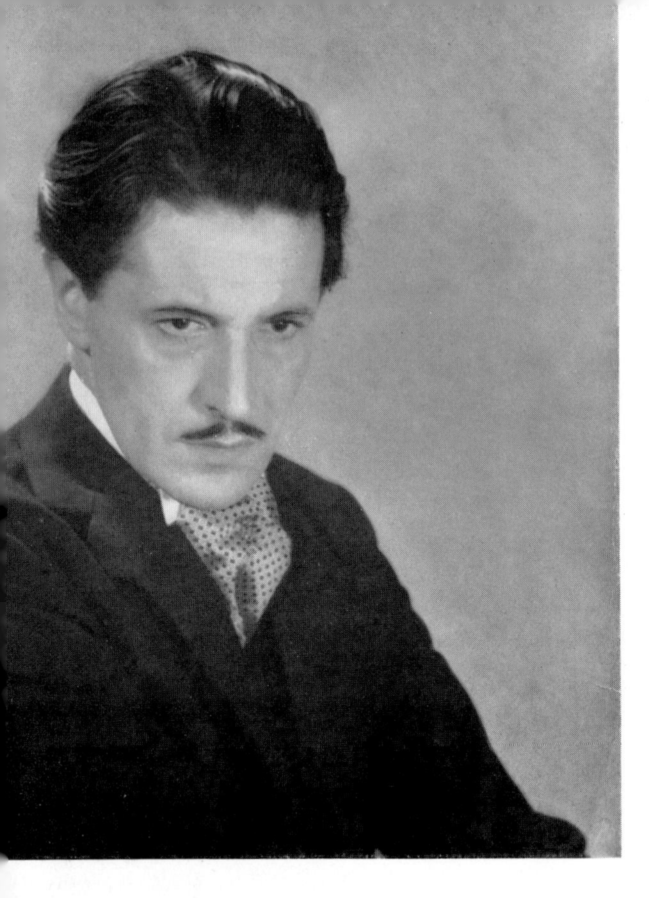

17. As Jacques Clavel in
own play *Murder in Mayf*
Globe, 1934, the cast of wh
included Fay Compton, Ed
Best, Zena Dare, and Rob
Andrews.

18 (below left). With Ma
leine Carroll in the fi
Sleeping Car, directed
Anatole Litvak in 1933.

19 (below right). With F
Compton in the screen v
sion of *Autumn Crocus,* dir
ted by Basil Dean, 1935.

Other pictures which Ivor remembered were being made in Hollywood during his stay there included *Arrowsmith, Dishonoured* (Marlene Dietrich's second American movie), *Dr. Jekyll and Mr. Hyde, Forbidden, Lost Squadron, Frankenstein, The Man I Killed, Scarface, The Silent Voice, Friends and Lovers, Waterloo Bridge,* and *What Price Hollywood?* Lowell Sherman was the director and star of the latter; Ivor asserted that he was one of the greatest wits in Hollywood, the 'Clifton Webb of his day'.

The biggest stars at that time were the importations from the stage—stars whose voices were their greatest assets, and whose stage technique was admirably suited to the talking film. They included Ruth Chatterton, Fredric March, Ann Harding, George Arliss, Maurice Chevalier, Jeanette Macdonald, Basil Rathbone, Joe E. Brown, Kay Francis, John Boles, Robert Young, Laurence Tibbett, Vivienne Segal, Constance Bennett, Sylvia Sydney, Walter Huston, Elissa Landi, Chester Morris, Robert Montgomery, Irene Dunne, Pat O'Brien, Grace Moore, James Cagney, Edward G. Robinson, Paul Muni, Joan Bennett, Kent Douglas (who later changed back to his own name, 'Douglass Montgomery'), Claudette Colbert and Eddie Cantor. Most of them are still appearing in Hollywood films.

In the early 1930's players like the above were constantly being signed up by Hollywood. The rush to put stage stars under contract involved Novello, for his New York production of *The Truth Game* had made him into a big Broadway name overnight. Unfortunately, like certain other stage 'names', Ivor was contracted to a studio chock-full of stars, with not enough films to go round. Had he signed to star for one of Hollywood's smaller companies, it is likely that he would have stayed in California. In that event, therefore, we should probably never have had those delightful Novello musicals. So we must be grateful to the powers-that-be who allowed Ivor to break his contract and come home to his beloved London theatre in the spring of 1932.

On his return to his home studio from his unhappy experience in *Once A Lady,* Novello was more certain than ever that there was no point in his staying in Hollywood, and so, after the further three months was up, he went once more to Irving Thalberg and begged to be released from his contract. Thalberg was most charming about it, and gave his consent with only one stipulation. This was that if ever Novello returned to Hollywood he should at once take up his M.G.M. contract where he left off. Ivor was relieved, and at once assented. A great weight seemed to be lifted from his brain. He bade good-bye to all his American friends, took one last look at the glorious Californian sunshine, and headed back as fast as he could to the London he loved so well.

On the journey back to New York Ivor had a rather macabre experience. Three days before he left Santa Monica, where he had a beach house, he gave a party to all the people who had been so charming to him in Hollywood. Edgar Wallace was coming, with Ramon Novarro, Ruth Chatterton and Billie Burke, but on the morning of the party Wallace rang up to say he had a slight cold and was afraid he would not be able to come along to say good-bye. Three days later Ivor left California for good. With him he took the dog Jim. Jim's quarters were in the guard's van, and three times a day, on that long, tiring journey, Ivor took him his meals. At Chicago they changed trains. As soon as they were off again he took along Jim's mid-day food. In the guard's van was a Negro porter sitting on an enormous packing case, making out his list of passengers. Ivor asked him if he would be nice to Jim during the journey, and added: —

'What an enormous case. I hope there is no one inside.'

'Sure there is', the porter replied casually. 'It's a film writer who died in Hollywood.'

At that he turned the label over and showed it to Ivor. He glanced at the name and received a terrible shock. In the case was the dead body of Edgar Wallace!

10

Home Again

'Ivor Novello is a much better actor than anybody with his looks has ever been.'—*'Country Life', April 2nd, 1932.*

APART from the scripts of *But The Flesh Is Weak* and *Tarzan the Ape Man,* Novello had worked intermittently on four other M.G.M. films at Culver City, but in his spare time, on the beach at Malibu, or in a deck-chair by the side of one of his friends' swimming-pools, he had mainly worked on two new plays. The first, *I Lived With You,* had a magnificent part for himself. The other, *Party,* had an excellent part for the leading lady and a good one for the leading man. He worked on *I Lived With You* for months, polishing it up, adding a few lines here, taking away redundant passages there, and finally he had completed what he thought was a satisfactory comedy. On the way back to England he polished up the second play, *Party,* thus arriving at Southampton with two new completed plays under his arm. He had never felt so happy at being back in his own home town. His Aldwych flat seemed even more cosy, more inviting, more friendly than ever it had been before. The faithful Bobbie Andrews was there to meet him, and so was his mother—still as youthful and as full of life and enthusiasm as ever. London seemed a magical city, and Hollywood—that crazy town—was far away. Ivor had returned home, and nobody who has been out of England for nearly two years, as he had, will ever know quite what it feels like to be back home once more. It was a wonderful feeling.

Plans and questions were jostling each other in his head. Had he been forgotten after all this time? Ivor need have had no fears. For his next venture in actor-management (in association with Richard Rose) he chose *I Lived With You,* and for the theatre to stage it he decided on the Prince of Wales', the lucky playhouse on the stage of which he had conquered London in *The Rat* six years before. As Prince Felix in *I Lived With You* he had a tremendous triumph, and on the opening night he received a tumultuous reception. When he came forward to make his curtain speech the audience clapped for a full two minutes before they would allow him to speak. London, that wonderful city, had certainly not forgotten its own Ivor. The London audience, ever faithful and like no other audiences in the world, had welcomed him back with open arms. He was home!

I Lived With You tells a story of a homeless and starving young man, with an interesting profile and a charming accent, who meets a young girl from Fulham in the Maze at Hampton Court, and so impresses her with his personality that she takes pity on him and asks him to her home. There he is adopted as one of the family. It subsequently transpires that the young man is a Russian prince, with a naïve disregard for conventions, no particular morals, and a pliable disposition. Under his influence the Wallace family of Fulham changes considerably—Mr. Wallace takes a mistress. Mrs. Wallace takes to vodka, young Miss Ada Wallace accepts the protection of her employer, and Gladys—the girl who 'discovered' him—becomes quite distracted over his profile. Finally he is persuaded to leave, and the family settles back into its comfortable and conventional rut. It was a charming idea. Auriol Lee produced the play, which saw some fine acting from Ursula Jeans as Glad, Thea Holme, Minnie Rayner, Eliot Makeham, Jean Webster Brough and Robert Newton, with Novello himself scoring a great personal success as the prince.

Novello had always considered Ursula Jeans (who played

opposite him in *The Firebrand*) as one of the outstanding young actresses on the London stage, and he was glad that she received acclaim for her work in his play. Minnie Rayner gave a grand, genial, rollicking performance of the kind which she repeated in several Novello shows. In fact, Minnie became something of a mascot to Ivor, appeared in all his plays, and remained until her death a faithful friend and an actress as clever as she was reliable.

London loved *I Lived With You,* and its critical reception was extremely favourable. The *Evening News* critic declared that he liked the play, and predicted a 'huge success'. The *Daily Telegraph* pointed out, 'Novello's comedy was liberally besprinkled with quips which provoked that immediate ripple of laughter in the audience which indicates that they are without doubt enjoying themselves'. And there were other excellent notices. 'I enjoyed Novello's new play', wrote Alan Parsons, the *Daily Mail* dramatic critic. 'It is pleasant to have Mr. Novello home again; he is far too good to be exiled in the wastes of Beverley Hills' (*The Observer*). 'Ivor Novello gives a sparkling performance in his own very amusing play. The situations are novel, the lines are funny, and the casting is brilliant' (*Sunday Chronicle*) 'Vastly diverting, with a splendid performance by Novello' (*Daily Sketch*). 'A lively entertainment, with lines that shake the house with merriment, in the midst of which Mr. Novello continuously glitters' (*The Times*). These were only a few of the reviews. James Agate, in the *Sunday Times,* declared that it was Mr. Novello's best play to date, and made for an exceedingly jolly evening. He went on to remark jocularly, 'The piece was obviously written by Mr. Novello for that good actor Mr. Novello, and it should succeed, since I can imagine nothing more likely to be popular than a theme of Dostoievsky treated in the manner of Ian Hay!'

In all, *I Lived With You* received an excellent Press, and proved to be an auspicious return to the London stage of one of its young idols. J. K. Prothero summed up the general concensus of opinion in a lengthy critical piece which he wrote for *G.K.'s Weekly* on April 2nd, 1932, when he declared:

'Ivor Novello, with *I Lived With You,* has grown considerably as a dramatist since his previous efforts. He has drawn the character of Felix, a Russian prince picked up in Hampton Court Maze by a Fulham typist, with real cleverness. He has exactly gauged the speculative capacity, the unlimited range of ideas, with the complete inoperativeness in regard to action which makes this type of play so baffling to the ordinary Western European. Nothing is too subversive, nothing too fantastic for discussion. The mentality of this engaging person entertains every kind of revolutionary morality, changes every possible social postulate. Altogether full marks to Mr. Novello for his insight and for the really brilliant manner in which he exploits all the facets of the hero. The whole thing is excellent entertainment.'

The prodigal son had been welcomed back.

★

While *I Lived With You* was running in London, Ivor met Bernard Shaw for the first time. One Sunday night he went with Sir Edward Marsh to see Yvette Guilbert at the Arts Theatre, and Shaw was sitting just behind. Eddie introduced them. For some time Novello had been toying with the idea of a stage version of Bunyan's *Pilgrim's Progress,* and had rather fancied himself in the role of Christian. And was not Mr. Shaw always writing about the dramatic quality of Bunyan's dialogue? Here was Ivor's opportunity—and he quickly put the suggestion to Shaw. Why not a Shaw dramatization of *The Pilgrim's Progress,* with Novello as Christian? Shaw beamed on the young man.

'That is an excellent idea', he declared. 'Really excellent. But you are a dramatist. Why not do it yourself?'

So that was that. One day, Ivor assured me, he would get down to writing a play of the great Bunyan book, but the opportunity to star in a new Shaw play was missed, and will never occur again. Ivor's Bunyan play remained unwritten.

After the West End run of *I Lived With You* Ivor should have had a break before the provincial tour which was booked for the autumn. But he had become a glutton for work, considering that his Californian stay had been a complete waste of time. Already his next play, *Party,* had been produced at the Strand Theatre, with Lilian Braithwaite quite superlative as an ageing, kind-hearted, but acid-tongued actress and Benita Hume as the temperamental Miranda Clayfoote, Joan Swinstead, Margaret Vines and Victor Boggetti. This was a play about the theatre, and, in defiance of all theatrical conventions and superstitions that a play about the theatre never succeeds, *Party* proved to be a very big success indeed. Sebastian Shaw was playing the part of Lord Bay Clender, but he wanted leave of absence for one month, so Ivor took over the role. He recalled that he had a lot of fun playing a perfectly ordinary young man after a series of more temperamental characters, and in any case, as he explained: —

'I was much happier playing all through the terrific heat of that particularly hot August than I should have been dangling my legs in a swimming pool day after day for a month.' Like all actors, he would rather have been acting than doing anything else, and his entire career was a reflection of his tremendous industry and enthusiasm.

There was an interesting story behind the production of *Party*. Ivor told me that he wrote it mainly to please himself. He never really intended it for a commercial run, visualizing it as a Sunday night show to be played to a special theatrical audience who would laugh, he hoped, good humouredly at the jokes against themselves. On the other hand, *I Lived With You* was, he considered, a good commercial play. Having got that off his chest and started on its successful run, he approached Bronson Albery, the West End theatrical manager, who had at that time a lease on the Arts Theatre, and discussed with him the possibilities of the play being produced at this intimate playhouse. Albery agreed, but there was no thought at that time of the play ever being transferred to another West End theatre. With Lilian Braithwaite, Benita Hume and Sebastian Shaw rehearsing under the direction of Athole Stewart, *Party* began to leap into pulsating life, and Ivor and the others began to realize during rehearsals that the comedy was much better than they had all thought.

One morning Ivor's friend Gladys Henson strolled into the theatre to watch a rehearsal. After about half an hour she bounded out of her seat and rushed to a telephone. Ten minutes later her husband, Leslie, and his partner, Firth Shephard, were sitting in the stalls. Before lunch Leslie and Firth had made a proposition to Ivor for an immediate production of *Party* at the Strand Theatre. And that was how one of Ivor's most successful plays was put on in the West End almost by accident.

Party was more highly praised by the critics than any of Novello's plays. For six months it became a real vogue.* Not only was it a success with theatrical people, but the general public loved it. Ivor had never admitted that he had based the role of the ageing actress on that wonderful creature, Mrs. Patrick Campbell, but all theatrical London guessed the identity of the character as Lilian Braithwaite played it—and how superb she was. One night Mrs. Campbell came to *Party* and went back-stage to see Lilian.

'Oh, Lilian,' she exclaimed in that wonderful voice of hers. 'You make me so much nicer than I really am!'

After Ivor had played in *Party* for a month he spent the autumn of that year touring the provinces in *I Lived With You*. While on tour he wrote his seventh play, *Fresh Fields,* which took him ten days to write (and subsequently played to capacity for fifteen months). He began the play on a Friday morning in Manchester, and he had it completely finished by the Saturday morning of the following week while playing in Birmingham.

'I did not have to rewrite one word,' Ivor remembered. 'Heaven knows, I do not hold this up as an example, or even as an encouragement to write quickly. It was just good luck. I had got hold of an idea, and, having well in mind the actresses for whom I was writing the play, I just could not get my thoughts on paper fast enough. To write a play in ten days will probably never happen to me again.'

Fresh Fields opened at the Criterion in January 1933, and

* M.G.M. outbid all other studios for the film rights and bought it as a vehicle for Joan Crawford, but it was never subsequently made.

ran until the March of the following year, with Lilian Braithwaite as Lady Lilian Bedworthy and Ellis Jeffreys, both of whom had wonderful opportunities for comedy acting. The cast included Minnie Rayner once more, 'without whom', Ivor affirmed, 'I could never feel that a play of mine was complete'. Robert Andrews (that fine young actor, and one of the wittiest men in London, who was one of Ivor's most intimate friends for thirty years, and has appeared in several other Novello plays), Eileen Peel, Fred Groves and Martita Hunt completed the cast. Athole Stewart, who had produced *Party,* also produced *Fresh Fields,* which really focused attention once more on Novello as one of the most brilliant and industrious young actor-playwrights on the London stage. His abortive trip to Hollywood had been forgotten. His absence had made not one jot of difference to his loyal public, and *I Lived With You, Party* and *Fresh Fields,* as successful a triumvirate of new plays as one could ever wish to have produced within a period of a year, put him back right on the top of the tree. He achieved the unusual twin triumph of popularity with the public as well as critical esteem.

Fresh Fields was yet another big Novello success. The *Morning Post* wrote of the 'gusts of uproarious laughter'. W. A. Darlington, in the *Daily Telegraph,* found it very funny, going on to write, 'How well this dramatist knows the theatre'. The *News Chronicle* declared that it was certain to be a success, especially because of the acting of Lilian Braithwaite and Ellis Jeffreys; while Alan Parsons in the *Daily Mail,* pointed out: 'Ivor Novello, who is rapidly becoming one of our most prolific playwrights, fortunately retains through all his various dramas the pleasant knack of turning out bright, smart comedy lines which keep up a general ripple of laughter and at the same time reduce the more impressionable members of the audience to a state of hysteria. I greatly prefer his new comedy to his other plays.' Even the staid *Observer* commented, 'So spontaneous is Novello's flair for the theatre, and so brilliant is the support of his chief interpreters, that the entertainment has scarcely a dull moment, and many that lace their interest with the choicest ingredients'.

The first night of the play saw Ivor and his mother in the stage box, from which he took a bow before the curtain rose to a packed and enthusiastic audience, many of whom had come for miles to see the clever young man's latest creation. The fact that *Fresh Fields* was obviously a riotous success was of particular pleasure to Ivor, for his mother had just recovered from a ten-months' illness, and this marked her first evening out for nearly a year. After the show she sat on the stage at the first-night party receiving congratulations from cast and friends on her recovery and on her beloved son's new play. It was indeed a happy celebration for Madame Clara, to whom each new Novello triumph was a further addition to her happiness and pride. She had seen her son grow up from a gentle, sensitive boy into an accomplished composer in his teens, and subsequently reach an honoured position as a great film and stage star and one of England's most promising young playwrights. How proud she must have felt, and how proud Ivor was of the brilliant woman who had been mainly responsible for all his successes—the great lady without whom he might never have achieved so much in so short a time.

Ivor himself did not play in *Fresh Fields,* for when it began its run at the Criterion he had opened at the Playhouse in the same month in his next new play, *Flies in the Sun.* In this he played the part of Seraphine, one of a group of idle decadents basking in the sun on the edge of the Mediterranean somewhere between Marseilles and Capri. The play, utterly unlike all his others, was produced under the management of Gladys Cooper, who had been running the Playhouse for six years.* Gladys also played in *Flies in the Sun,* but, unfortunately, it ran for only a few weeks. Theatregoers did not seem to like 'Novello's attempt to be wicked', as some of the critics put it, and although Gladys Cooper gave a magnificent performance of a character entirely different from

* The cast included Denys Blakelock, Thea Holme, Dorothy Hyson, Joan Swinstead, Anthony Bushell, Jevan Brandon Thomas and Tom Macauley, with designs by Hamilton Gay, who was responsible for the décor of several Novello plays in the 1930's.

her own sympathetic, fresh-air personality, the play somehow went wrong.

Ivor afterwards confessed: 'All the wrong people liked the play—and all the right people loathed it. That is why I think it failed.'

From *Flies in the Sun,* a play about people he did not know much about, Ivor turned to *Proscenium,* a play about people he knew very well—theatre-folk. He was again warned before he wrote it that no play about stage people had really succeeded in London since Pinero's *Trelawney of the Wells,* although his own previous play, *Party,* had somewhat given the lie to this. He was also told that the time had not yet arrived for sentiment, and that true love and devotion were still pre-war jokes. Ivor trusted his own judgment, and *Proscenium,* a sentimental story about the theatre and its people, was successfully produced at the Globe Theatre on June 14th, 1933, with Fay Compton, Joan Barry, Zena Dare, Dorothy Boyd, Keneth Kent, and Ivor himself playing two parts—that of a hard-bitten major-general of fifty in the Prologue, and his son for the rest of the play. Strangely enough, he received more praise for his seven-minute character-study than he did for all the rest of the parts he had played in his entire stage career. The experiment gave him great courage and great hope, for it made him feel that 'when he got past playing heroes and such-like the big field of character-acting would still be open to him'. Ivor considered that the reason he scored such a pronounced success as the middle-aged general was mainly that he based the character, in appearance and personality, on his dear father, with the result that the character really grew into an authentic person since it was allied so closely to real life. Ivor also played Romeo to Joan Barry's Juliet in an interpolated scene from Shakespeare's play, and he was magnificent. It roused his ambitions to play more Shakespearean roles.

Proscenium proved yet again that the old bogey about plays on the theatre being failures could be disproved time and time again. If a story of the theatre is human enough to be set in any other walk of life it can always be a success. A good play is always a good play, no matter what the subject may be. In the casting, however, he experienced some difficulty. For the part of the mother he had approached several attractive youngish actresses, most of whom turned up their noses at the idea of playing Ivor's parent. One of them indignantly pointed out that if Ivor was to play her son he would have to have been born when she was only five! Finally, on a suggestion of 'Lloydie's', Ivor approached Zena Dare. Very tentatively he suggested that she might like to play his stage mother, quickly adding, 'Please don't be offended!'

All Zena replied was: 'Darling, if it's a good part, I'll play your grandmother. Of course I'll play it.'

And play it she did—so beautifully and with such splendid technique that it landed her right up at the top of the small group of stars playing the smart society-matron type of role, adding a new and wonderful West End comedienne to the rapidly diminishing list. Miss Dare has been associated with Novello in several plays since that time, and has certainly never regretted playing Ivor's mother in *Proscenium*.

'Zena is absolutely wonderful at rehearsals', he said to me. 'She goes about with a starry eye and a glittering smile, knowing for a fact that she has not got one funny line, and, however funny it is, she personally could not get a laugh from it. She suffers from nerves and fits of depression during the entire rehearsals, and the nerves persist during performances. But, in spite of this, she is surer than any rock in the world—surer than anyone I have ever acted with. I believe that the girls of Zena's age were given an added warmth which their predecessors did not possess, and in which their successors are lacking, because when Zena appears on the stage the whole audience falls in love with her. You can give her a line which, if said by anybody else, would be definitely catty, but, as Zena says it, the line loses all bitterness—and is still riotously funny. She had in *Proscenium*—and still has—that wonderful, indefinable quality which, for want of a better word, I call "magic".'

Proscenium was well received by the Press. A typical

comment was made by W. A. Darlington, dramatic critic of the *Daily Telegraph*: 'Ivor Novello is a wonderfully handy man in a theatre. He knows it inside out, and there is not a lever in all its complicated machinery that he cannot handle with effect.' It played in London for more than seven months, during which time Fay Compton left the cast for six weeks to have an operation on her throat, and Madge Titheradge, the actress who had given Ivor his first chance in *Deburau* at the Ambassador's twelve years before, took over her part and played it superbly. After she had ben playing it for a few weeks she, too, was suddenly taken ill one night, and Fay, straight from the nursing home, took over the role for that one performance.

'I shall never forget the stir in the audience that night,' Ivor wrote, 'when the stage manager came on the stage to make his speech. "Ladies and gentlemen," he began, "I am sorry to have to tell you that Miss Madge Titheradge has been taken ill." "Oh! ! !" cried the audience. The stage manager went on, "But her part to-night will be played by Miss Fay Compton!" There was a great "Ah! ! !" from the auditorium, followed by tumultuous clapping. It really was wonderful of Fay to do this for me, and I think also that she enjoyed the dramatic twist.'

In 1932 Methuen published three of Novello's plays in one volume,* and his good friend Sir Edward Marsh contributed a Foreword which, for its sincerity and excellent critical adjudgment, deserves complete reproduction here: —

'Ivor Novello is first and foremost a man of the theatre, predestinate from his cradle. Never was there a more stage-struck little boy. All his pennies were saved up for the Pit, and if there were not enough he wormed his way into the leading lady's dressing-room and wangled a ticket for the Upper Circle. His first disillusionment was when the Fairy Queen came to tea with his mother in mufti; and he wrote his own plays for his toy playhouse when he was seven. Yet his stage gift was not the first to develop. When I made his acquaintance he was a popular composer of twenty-two, and

* *I Lived With You, Party,* and *Symphony In Two Flats.*

it seemed that this must be his career. But all through his musical successes ideas for plays were continually coming into his head; he longed to be an actor. And although when at last his wish had come true, he was soon, to use a cant phrase literally, "claimed by the films", his heart was always with the boards and the footlights—he wanted to act with his own body and voice, to be in touch with an audience with no machinery between.

'I say all this to bring out the fundamental strength of his play-writing: that it is an ingrained impulse and a labour of love. He writes to please himself and (like the Elizabethan dramatists) as many other people as possible. Because he is a man of brains and character, his mature plays have a significance beyond their outward show; but what he starts from is the fun of imagining characters and situations and action, not the desire to embody an idea. As I said, he is a man of the theatre.

'Since my qualification for writing this note is that, apart from being nearly as stage-struck as he is, I am (in a good phrase of Maurice Hewlett's) "always benevolent to his invention", I will make no bones about giving a list of what I believe to be the merits of his work. The first is that he can conceive and draw characters which "get across". Some of them are real people, acutely observed and completely credible; some of them could have no existence outside the theatre; but they have this in common, that they give glorious opportunities to the players. His very first piece, *The Rat,* made reputations for himself and his heroine, and went a long way towards establishing Miss Isabel Jeans in her present position as our most irresistible siren. But these parts were of the stagey kind, and it was not till *The Truth Game* that he began to draw from the life. This play, for all the triviality of its charming little plot, contains two personages which enriched the stage and should have a permanent value. Mrs. Brandon, the Society tout, who makes her living by commissions on the sale of every conceivable article from cocktail-glasses to country houses, is a closely-studied and only slightly-heightened sketch of an actual contemporary type, and quite as much of a document for the social historian as any humour of Ben Jonson's; and what a chance she gave Miss Lilian Braithwaite! Lady Joan Culver is a creation of another order. This plain, gawky, penniless, hourly-less-marriageable duke's daughter, never in any discomfiture parting with either her native aristocracy or her suicidal sense of humour, is a fantasy, if you like, but a fantasy which keeps in touch with lovable human nature. Miss Viola Tree made her adorable; but she only brought out what was already there.

'Of the characters in the plays here printed, the reader will judge. In the hero of *I Lived With You,* Prince Felix, the playwright, by almost uncanny divination, has embodied what a cosmopolitan friend of mine recognized as the quintessence of all the Russians he had known in twenty years; and the minor personages have given each player material for a vivid portrait. In Auntie Flossie, the household drudge, unconsidered by the genial but dunder-headed family she serves except as a purveyor of meals and "charing", who yet has an inward pride and clearness of vision which makes the exotic noble recognize her instinctively as his equal, I seem to find a touch of poetic quality which is perhaps not quite brought out in an otherwise effective and finished performance.

'Mrs. MacDonald, in *Party,* has been generally acclaimed as a triumph for both author and actress. Her biting wit does not shake our belief in her loyal and golden heart; and in the perennial naughtiness of an *enfant terrible* who can rise on occasion to the *terribilita* of a Michelangelo, we can find nothing incongruous with a commanding intelligence and a burning fire of devotion to the art of acting. Miranda, in the same play, is alive to her finger-tips, various as the wind, but always the same person. Completely as she lives up to her oddly *Pilgrim's-Progress*-like surname of Clayfoote, we yet accept the qualities which win her Mrs. MacDonald's admiration and affection, and the emergence of a better self under that lady's influence, no less than her final relapse into callousness towards poor Lord Ellerton.

'Dialogue shall come next. Novello has a faultless ear for the spoken word, and I doubt if there is a speech in these plays which rings stiff or stilted. This naturalness is a valuable quality when it goes with point and spirit; and he has a pen which bubbles unceasingly with "quips and cranks and wanton wiles" that keep his audiences shaking with laughter. Readers will find them on every page, some subtle and some frankly and deliciously silly; so I will only quote one of each kind from the amusing *Truth Game*. "You never even seem to remember that you're a duke's daughter", says Mrs. Brandon to Lady Joan in the course of a lecture on her misuse of such assets as she has; and the reply is so unexpected: "I believe there's some doubt even about that." And for sheer absurdity there is the footman's explanation that he was christened Mafeking "because it was such a Relief when I was born". Both these lines used to cause explosions which must have been heard in the street.

'Most important of all is the constructive art which makes a play a harmony and a whole. Here the two latest plays mark a great advance. I always thought the first act of *The Rat* a little masterpiece of swift movement combined with the firm "planting" and rich illustration of atmosphere, character, and situation; but the rest was not on the same level. *Downhill* was picturesque-picaresque. *The Truth Game* was an agreeable but superficial anecdote, kept alive by a series of episodes which only just hung together. *Symphony In Two Flats* is composed of two distinct plays, a melodrama and a farce, audaciously sandwiched in alternate layers, like Trollope's *Can You Forgive Her?* where the adventures of a comic widow play Box and Cox with the moving tale of Lady Glencora. This procedure might be justified on æsthetic grounds by the doctrine of Simultaniety devised by the Dead Poet in Miss G. B. Stern's *Little Red Horses,* who wrote his poems in parallel columns to light up "the profound discovery that while something is going on in one place, something else, either startlingly different or startlingly the same, is going on at exactly the same time in another place". But the real justification, it must be admitted, was the more practical one that neither of the plays was long enough by itself to fill the evening bill. Together they did this to admiration; and to me, for one, the scene in which the blind musician learns that it is not his symphony which has won the prize—though of the theatre theatrical—never lost its shattering poignancy.

'In *I Lived With You* Novello has for the first time found a substantial theme and sustained it without divagation from beginning to end. It is a clash between two violently-contrasted views of life. The Tartar aristocratic and autocratic *authadeia,* or doing-as-you-please (why have we no word for this?), impinges on the English lower-middle-class respectability (we have plenty of words for that): the attractive poison (for such it is to them) works through the veins of the Wallis family and brings them near to dissolution; then the one and only brain they have takes charge and expels it from their system while there is still something to save. This story is developed with grace and ease of appropriate invention, and what the old painters called "keeping"; it is seen consistently through spectacles of just the right shade of pink to hold what might be painful within the region of comedy. To illustrate the playwright's resourcefulness in giving a "twist" to a situation, I will relate that once the tale was carried to its most austere conclusion: the adorable and intolerable Felix disappeared into the night for ever. This was too much for either audience or author to bear, and I was afraid he was going to sacrifice the logic of his play to a happy ending; but he found a solution which gives nothing away, and yet leaves Felix and Gladys in each other's arms.

'In *Party* construction is less to the fore, but it is there. Good judges who read the play, and were satisfied with the scenes devoted to giving the "party-atmosphere", made two criticisms: the story of Bay, Rosie, and Miranda, which was supposed to hold it together, was too slight for its purpose; and, when it was finished, there was nothing left to go on with. Both these doubts were silenced by the performance. The lurid, tender, comic little plot turned out to be both moving and exciting, and, when it was disposed of, a motive which had underlain the play from the outset came to the surface and proved to be its real subject: the passion which good players have for their art, and the difference in the forms it may take—a difference of type; perhaps, alas! of generation —in the old actresss an almost disinterested love of beauty for its own sake; in the young one a clinging to the only means by which she can satisfy her personal ambition. The author had kept his good wine to the last. Mrs. MacDonald's allocutions over the eggs and bacon she has cooked herself and Miranda's reception of Sir Gerald du Maurier's fantastically improbable offer of an engagement by telephone at three o'clock in the morning were found to be the best part of the play.

'There are many comparisons that I might, and will not, make between Ivor Novello and Noël Coward; but it will be interesting to contrast them as moralists. Both have a contempt for any rigid code, yet both are on the side of the angels; but Noël (I can't keep up calling them by their surnames)—Noël as a satirist—has a bitterness which is foreign to Ivor. The difference between them may be put thus: that Noël makes us ashamed of ourselves, and Ivor tolerant of one another. There is a set-to in *Party* between two former chorus-girls, one of whom has married a peer and the other a comedian. If Noël had written the scene, I expect the peeress would have been dragged through the mud and gone off in eternal dudgeon. In Ivor's version, after a short slanging-match she gets the giggles and falls on her old friend's neck. This is an excellent instance of the sunny good-humour which shines through all his plays. He cannot bear to be on bad terms with any of his characters, and in the most worthless of them he discovers some redeeming trait before the curtain falls.

'I am glad that *Symphony In Two Flats* has been included in this volume, because, with all its own considerable charms and merits, it is chiefly interesting as a measure of the progress its author has made in the two or three years since it was written. If he will give himself his due, and put his main reliance on those among his many gifts which distinguish the dramatist from the entertainer, he will surely win a high place in the theatre of his time, and perhaps write a play which will survive it.'

*

While *Proscenium* was running, *Fresh Fields* was still playing to packed houses at the Criterion, making the third time in a year that Novello had had two plays running simultaneously in the West End. A month or so previously there had been *Fresh Fields* and *Flies in the Sun,* while almost a year before he had *I Lived With You* and *Party* running at the same time. He was certainly both a prolific and brilliant man of the theatre. When *Fresh Fields* had passed its 200th performance at the Criterion in early 1933, Novello was interviewed in the *Observer* (January 2nd, 1933). Discussing the technique of playwriting, he stated: 'In spite of the success of *The Rat, The Truth Game, Fresh Fields, Proscenium,* and others, I have suffered to a certain extent from the imputation of amateurishness. It probably came about because I first happened to get known through writing a popular song, and then because I did a lot of film acting before I ever went on the stage. This was about ten years ago, when film acting and stage acting were far more apart than they are now. Hence I started to some extent by playing leading parts in the theatre, and had to make all my mistakes, as it were, in public, instead of having learned my job through years of work in the provinces. But I do not think that this is to say that I had done much less hard work than most other people in the theatre. As regards the job of writing plays that the public wish to see, I do not think I have any particular formula for success, except possibly two rules: avoid gloom, and try to get a good cast. By "gloom" I do not mean necessarily tragedy, which can be thrilling or exciting. I mean, hammering on at the same theme, on the same note, through many scenes. I think it enormously important for a dramatist to possess a sensitivity to this—to be able to hear at a rehearsal when a scene is running too long and getting nowhere, and then to cut ruthlessly and at once. My experience as an actor has helped me greatly to write plays which have proved to be "good theatre", and I think that this very specialized technique requires a writer with a good knowledge of the theatre, or a love of the theatre, and preferably both.

'As for casting, I know I have been immensely lucky in the casts of all my plays. Neverthless, I write them always with certain actors and actresses in mind, and I move heaven and earth to get them when I am ready to start production. It is not only luck, but great determination. What I owe to comediennes like Lilian Braithwaite, Ellis Jeffreys and Viola Tree! I cannot express my gratitude to these three great ladies for the help they have given me in making my plays leap to life.'

In an article headed 'The Busiest Young Man in England' which appeared in the *Daily Dispatch* on October 20th, 1933, Novello's contribution to the theatre was appraised:—

'Ivor Novello', wrote the critic, 'manages to perform the work of half a dozen men without turning a hair. He is actor, manager, author, and composer, and yet achieves to turn out play after play with astonishing facility. On Monday his new play, *Sunshine Sisters,* is opening at the Palace Theatre, Manchester, and when it comes to London on November 8th he will then have three plays running simultaneously in the West End. The busiest young man in England is acting eight times a week in his own play *Proscenium,* which is still running with great success, and nearly all his spare time is taken up with rehearsals of *Sunshine Sisters. Fresh Fields,* at the Criterion, of course, is a well-established hit. In addition to all this, Novello starts work on the film of *Autumn Crocus* in the same week that *Sunshine Sisters* opens in Manchester.'

Sunshine Sisters, with Dorothy Dickson, Phyllis Monkman, and Joan Clarkson as the daughters of a decaying music-hall star, played by Veronica Brady, opened at the Queen's on November 8th, 1933, but received only a fair press. On its opening, theatregoers beheld the extraordinary sight of two Novello plays running simultaneously in two adjoining theatres, for *Proscenium* was nearing its 200th performance at the Globe.

Sunshine Sisters, produced by Athole Stewart, who had also produced *Party* and *Proscenium,* was the story of Ma Sunshine and her three theatrical daughters, who are introduced by the younger son of an aristocratic family into the home of his mother, the Duchess of Frynne. The quartet are quite happy in the baronial halls until they realize that the eccentric Duchess imagines them to be painted creatures from another planet. The comedy of errors ends happily when two of the Duke's sons marry two of the Sunshine sisters, while the third returns to the stage and stardom. An amusing play, though not by any means Novello's best, it ran at the Queen's for a few months, and gave wonderful parts to Phyllis Monkman, Dorothy Dickson, Irene Browne, Joan Clarkson, Maidie Andrew, Jack Hawkins, Veronica Brady, Sebastian Shaw and Joan Swinstead. Phyllis Monkman, in particular, established herself as one of the most brilliant comediennes on the English stage with a really delicious performance which recalled her scintillating work in *The Co-optimists.* (In 1926 Phyllis had deserted the musical comedy stage to make a hit in a dramatic role with Ivor in his *Downhill.* Two years later she co-starred with him again—under very different circumstances—in a one-act play of his called *The Gate Crasher,* which was featured in George Black's first programme of Non-Stop Variety at the Palladium. Ivor and Phyllis were very good, but the playlet, as he admitted, was not.)

To celebrate his 'hat trick' in the theatre, Ivor was honoured by the Gallery First Nighters' Club, who held a dinner to which were invited a glittering galaxy of theatrical celebrities, including, of course, Madame Clara Novello Davies and the many stage stars who had appeared in various Novello plays since *The Rat* in 1924. Ivor made a charming speech in reply to the toast, pointing out that this was the first dinner he had ever been given in recognition of his work in the theatre.

'I have been going to the theatre ever since the age of five,' he said, 'and although music was my first love, I have no cause to regret having made the theatre the main object and purpose of my life. I have experienced reverses and made a lot of mistakes, and I have many wonderful people to thank for the help and advice along the road to success. I have often looked up at the gallery audiences on first nights—for all the enthusiasm was always up at the top of the theatre, the stalls merely echoing it. But I could scarcely have hoped that one day I would be their guest of honour at one of their famous dinners. I am very grateful to them for their encouragement and for this heart-warming gesture.'

After the West End run of *Proscenium* Ivor took it on a long tour, in which the theatre was invariably sold out the week before the play opened. It was successful and, as Ivor remembered, 'hilarious', but much as he enjoyed himself on the tour, however, he did not cease working on a new play idea, which he called *Murder in Mayfair.* Before planning a London production of this, Ivor decided that he had not seen enough of the world, and set off with Robert Andrews, Lloyd Williams and Richard Rose, his partner in theatre management whom he had met in America while playing on Broadway in *The Truth Game*. The quartet went on a cruise in the Mediterranean, taking in everything from Algiers to the Holy City. Cyprus, Jerusalem, Cairo, Athens, Rome—they visited all these cities and many more—and so enjoyable was this holiday cruise that Ivor almost forgot that the theatre existed. He was thoroughly and completely rested and ready to return to work once more.

In the late summer of 1934 rehearsals for *Murder in Mayfair,* commenced, with a cast almost the same as *Proscenium,* including Fay Compton, Zena Dare, Robert Andrews and Ivor. He had written the part of Auriol in this play as an unhappy and disillusioned post-war product. Ivor did not want to play her as a sensuous, dark-eyed vamp type with a pale skin and dark shadows under her eyes. He was all for more subtle casting, so he chose Edna Best, the general public's idea of a lovely fresh English beauty. Edna, instead of seeing her part as a villainous one, realized the awful tragedy of this girl's life, and she played Auriol with such skill and passion —and so completely against her own looks—that she scored the greatest success of her career since her remarkable performance in *The Constant Nymph* in 1926. Fay Compton, in a much less showy role, Zena Dare as the murderer's mother, and Robert Andrews as the neurotic young murderer —a part entirely outside his usual range, but one in which he acquitted himself magnificently—all made personal successes in *Murder in Mayfair,* which filled the Globe Theatre for six months. As the French pianist, Jacques Clavel, Novello gave a mature and moving portrayal. It still remains among his best performances.

Typical of the many articles praising Ivor Novello which appeared in the mid-1930's is one by the famous dramatic critic, Sydney W. Carroll,* which ran as follows: 'Are good looks in an actor an asset or a handicap? Can they be rescued by, or are they aggravated by, intelligence? Ivor Novello is probably the handsomest player on the English stage. What precise part does his appearance play in his success?

'With a recollection of the theatre that goes back for many years, I cannot remember anyone with more striking distinction in externals, allied with sensibilities, intelligence, and imagination of such an unusual and versatile order. Kyrle Bellew, the juvenile who was associated with Sir Henry Irving in several of his productions, was a graceful and picturesque figure. Forbes-Robertson had always a melancholic and ascetic beauty. Lewis Waller had good looks of the brazenly heroic brand. William Terris was every inch a man. Hugh Conway was a mysteriously arresting youth who flashed across the horizon, and there are many others one can think of.

'But no one can claim such a fusion of physical gifts with mental alertness and variety as this young Welshman who has been placed by his own abilities and sheer force of character and determination in the forefront of his profession.

'Observe that magnificent head, with its coal-black hair swung from a forehead shaped as a sculptor might have loved to form it. That profile approximating to nobility, denoting command in every part; that determined chin; those large and luminous eyes, such as Dante might have had—these

* *Daily Telegraph,* November 8th, 1934.

surely cannot belong to a mere mummer? Surely some Greek statue of a young, athletic poet has been brought to life?

'It is the fashion with certain folk to laugh at Ivor Novello. By several of his critics he is definitely placed in a second-class group. Often he is compared with Noël Coward and others of his contemporaries, much to his detriment.

'I, myself, have always been one of Novello's staunchest admirers. I believe in him both as an actor and a playwright. No one I know shows more promise. My knowledge of music, or, rather, my ignorance of it, does not permit me to give any authoritative view of his possibilities in that quarter. But at a time when, like Coward, he was being laughed at for his earliest efforts on the stage, I used my position as a dramatic critic to "give the little boy a hand" and encourage him to continue. He has done so to good purpose.

'The truth is that Ivor Novello has made himself first of all a commercial success because he has realized that without finance in these days the man of the theatre can accomplish very little. He writes plays of a deliberately profit-making character; not because he cannot write pieces of a higher standard, but to keep his theatrical pot boiling. He acts parts which are far below his real standard of talent because he knows that there is a big public for that class of work. He likes to be the head of a theatre, to give employment to a number of brilliant fellow-workers, and he aims at a target which he can hit every time.

'But to say that this man is not a first-class actor is just nonsense. See him in his present thriller, *Murder in Mayfair*. Note the consistency of the portraiture, his nervous sincerity and concentration, how he acts with every one of his fingers, how every mood of the temperamental foreign pianist works itself out to perfection, and how subordinate he can be when the situation calls for deference to the other player.

'Despite the danger of prophecy, I declare that one of these days Novello will come into a higher field than he has yet attempted; that he will be hailed in England even as John Barrymore was hailed in his country. He can if he will, I am certain, write better plays than he has yet done, but is it nothing to have entertained thousands of playgoers?

'Whatever Novello attempts will be tried with a thoroughness, an earnestness, and a joyousness of that rare type only found in the real artist of the theatre, the man who loves it for its own sake, and who cannot be separated from it even in its lighter and less serious moments.'

11

The Sound Film

IVOR was beginning to think that his days of anxiety about his career were over. The Hollywood period had dealt a strong blow to his confidence, of course, and the nine months of wasted effort in California would always remind him of the vagaries of a career in the movies. However, the undoubted success of *I Lived With You, Party, Fresh Fields, Proscenium* and *Murder in Mayfair* was gratifying and exciting; it revived his self-confidence, and in the case of his performance in *Proscenium* it made the critics realize that the brilliant boy of the 1920's had become an extremely fine young actor of the 1930's. Life was very pleasant for Novello by this time. Not only was he a leading stage star and playwright, but he had returned to films in a talking version of his great silent success, *The Lodger,* followed by several other movies.

Before Novello went to Hollywood in the summer of 1931 he had been our most popular film star, even though he had made only one talking picture, *Symphony In Two Flats.* His initial American sound film, *Once A Lady,* is perhaps, best forgotten, even though Ivor, a polished veteran of screen acting, gave a performance of charm and skill. While he was in California Ivor received various offers from British film companies asking him to return to London to star in several early British talking pictures. His M.G.M. contract at that time, naturally, prevented this, but after his reappearance on the London stage in *I Lived With You,* he was immediately besieged with film offers once again. He finally accepted two of them—from Twickenham and Gaumont-British.

Twickenham Films signed him to star in a sound version of his great silent success, *The Lodger,* made eight years previously, and at the same time this company bought the film-rights of *I Lived With You* on condition that Ivor would himself star in the film as his own delightful creation, Prince Felix. The other big British company of that period was Gaumont-British-Gainsborough, with Michael Balcon in charge of production. Ivor had made *Symphony In Two Flats* at Islington for Balcon, and, of course, he had starred in a dozen British silent hits for him at Gainsborough, so he felt a kind of allegiance to 'Mickey', as everyone affectionately called him. Thus it was that Ivor signed to co-star with Madeleine Carroll in *Sleeping Car,* a light comedy, for Gaumont-British at Shepherd's Bush at the same time as he had contracted to star in *The Lodger* and *I Lived With You* at Twickenham. He then became involved in one of the busiest periods of his career.

He managed to sandwich *Sleeping Car* at Islington in between the two pictures which he made at Twickenham; at the same time continuing to act on the stage in his plays, *I Lived With You, Party, Flies in the Sun* and *Proscenium.* It may have seemed inexplicable why, in the mid-thirties, Novello suddenly decided to make no more films, but the above indicates why he eventually reached this decision. The theatre was always his great love. To him film-making was quite a pleasure; it was an amusing adventure and extremely well paid. The theatre, however, was magic. The theatre was his life. The two years immediately following his return from Hollywood were busy ones, and Ivor began to realize that he simply could not write plays, star in them, supervise their production in London, arrange provincial tours, learn new roles, and also make films during the day. Something had to suffer. At first he had thought it was possible to combine the two mediums, but the work involved in making *The Lodger, Sleeping Car* and *I Lived With You* eventually showed him that this was not going to be possible.

Ivor used to arrive at the theatre every evening tired out after a long day's filming, which had meant getting up sometimes as early as five-thirty or six o'clock in order to get to the studio and be made up and on the set soon after eight o'clock. He knew that his work in the theatre was suffering. He did not seem to find time to complete his new plays or work on the ideas that were jostling themselves in his brain. Filming during the day, acting on the stage in the evening, learning his lines for the film at midnight, and getting up the next morning in the early hours were all proving too much of a strain. By the time he had finished making *I Lived With You* Ivor had come to a momentous decision: he would not star in any more films.

When one considers that he took this step at the height of his film fame, that decision seems all the more remarkable. Nevertheless, except for the film version of *Autumn Crocus,* which was shown in 1935, Novello kept to his word, and concentrated on his compositions and his plays and on acting in the live theatre. Understandable though his action might have been, it was, nevertheless, a great blow to those thousands of admirers who had followed his film career since *The Call of the Blood,* and had seen him grow into our greatest film star in British pictures like *Bonnie Prince Charlie, The Lodger, Downhill, The Vortex, The Constant Nymph* and *Symphony In Two Flats.* It was also a great blow to British films, but Novello had made up his mind.

The talking version of *The Lodger* was directed by Maurice Elvey, with Elizabeth Allan playing the part made famous by June, A. W. Baskcomb and Barbara Everest as Mr. and Mrs. Bunting, and Jack Hawkins as Joe. The director used a new adaptation of Mrs. Belloc Lowndes' novel,* and made a very creditable thriller, even though the Hitchcock version had set a high standard. As the tortured young lodger, Novello, looking not one day older than when he had previously played the role, gave a splendid performance. Although physically he had not altered one jot in the eight years, his

* By Paul Rotha and Miles Mander.

range as an actor had considerably improved. Technically he showed a great advance; he had taken the sound medium, with its stress on underplaying, in his stride, Emotionally he was well suited to the sensitive and subtle camera eye—his own beautiful eyes, limpid and expressive, were ideal for the cinema. *The Lodger* was extremely successful, and Julius Hagen, head of Twickenham Films, and director Maurice Elvey immediately began preparations on the screenplay of *I Lived With you.*

However, Ivor had committed himself to star in *Sleeping Car* at Shepherd's Bush, and hardly had *The Lodger* been completed then he was hard at work on a new and entirely different screen role, at the same time playing Prince Felix every night in *I Lived With You* at the Prince of Wales' Theatre. *Sleeping Car* told the story of a handsome, amorous sleeping-car attendant who, like the fabled sailor, has a wife in every port of call. He uses his position as a first-class attendant on the sleeping car from London to Paris and Bucharest to flirt with every lovely unattached—and attached—female who is travelling aboard. It takes the glamorous and sophisticated Madeleine Carroll to tame this fickle lover, and her adventures in so doing made a light-hearted, filmic trifle which was so popular that filmgoers in their thousands wrote and demanded that Ivor and Madeleine should be teamed in further vehicles.

★

Gainsborough became a public company in 1930, and two years later Michael Balcon left Edward Black in charge of production at Islington while he went to Shepherd's Bush Studios to supervise production for the Gaumont-British Picture Corporation, which in the 1930's shared with Associated British Pictures and Alexander Korda's London Films the distinction of being the leading film company in this country. The first picture produced by Balcon at Shepherd's Bush was the celebrated *Rome Express,* followed by *After the Ball, Tell Me To-night, Waltz Time, I Was A Spy, Orders Is Orders, Britannia of Billingsgate, The Ghoul* and several other celebrated films—including *Sleeping Car*. The latter was directed by Anatole Litvak, a Russian, who had come from France a year previously to direct *Tell Me To-night*, a musical comedy starring Jan Kiepura, which proved to be wildly successful. Litvak followed up this excellent musical by directing *Sleeping Car*, another popular romantic comedy which established his reputation in England. (He subsequently went to Hollywood, where he has become known for his direction of such films as *The Sisters, All This And Heaven Too, This Above All* and *The Snake Pit*, among others.)

Sleeping Car was made in an atmosphere of hilarity. Litvak and his two stars thoroughly enjoyed making this jolly picture, and Michael Balcon did everything possible to persuade Novello to stay at Shepherd's Bush and star in a series of movies as successful as those on which they had both collaborated at Islington Studios in the 1920's. As he reminded Novello, *The Rat* had cost only £18,000, but had grossed more than £80,000! But Ivor had determined to stay in the theatre as soon as he finished his next film commitments, and he kept to his decision.

Contemporary with *Sleeping Car* were such films as *Falling For You* with Jack Hulbert, *Waltz Time* with Evelyn Laye, and *It's A Boy* with Leslie Henson, all of which were in various stages of production at Shepherd's Bush while Ivor was appearing there. By the time *Sleeping Car* was completed, the new version of *The Lodger* had been shown, and Novello's popularity rose once more to the heights it had achieved in the late 1920's in such pictures as *The Constant Nymph, The Return of the Rat* and *A South Sea Bubble*.

The early 1930's were a difficult period for British films generally. Hollywood pictures were still predominant, and American stars continued to be extemely popular here. Michael Balcon, Alexander Korda, John Maxwell, Basil Dean, Julius Hagen, Adrian Brunel, Maurice Elvey, Herbert Wilcox, Alfred Hitchcock, Victor Saville and other British producers and directors were, nevertheless, making excellent films, all of which helped to boost British stars like Jessie

Matthews, Robert Donat, Jack Hulbert and Cicely Courtneidge, Brian Aherne, Madeleine Carroll, Conrad Veidt, John Longden, Benita Hume, Gracie Fields, George Formby, Elisabeth Bergner, Laurence Olivier, John Mills, Rene Ray, Anton Walbrook, Anna Neagle, Michael Redgrave and Ivor Novello.

Novello, among the most popular romantic stars on the British screen, chose to make his virtual retirement from the cinema at a time when his popularity was at its highest. Thenceforward he concerned himself exclusively with writing plays, composing, and starring on the stage.

After his first big musical play, *Glamorous Night,* had become a hit at Drury Lane a year or two later, Associated British Pictures outbid all other Hollywood and British film companies for the film rights, and Ivor and Mary Ellis tentatively agreed to co-star in the film version, to be made after the play's run had terminated. Actually, by the time Associated British had scheduled production of the film, Ivor was appearing in *Careless Rapture* at Drury Lane, and planning to follow this with *Crest of the Wave*. He knew from experience how impossible it was to combine filming and stage-acting, so had to reject the film, somewhat reluctantly. Mary Ellis eventually played her original role of Militza, with Barry Mackay as Anthony Ellis, and Otto Kruger and Victor Jory (both from Hollywood) as King Stefan and Baron Lydeff respectively. Brian Desmond Hurst directed *Glamorous Night* at Elstree Studios, and it became a much acclaimed British film—so popular indeed that Associated British subsequently made plans to follow up with film versions of *Careless Rapture* and *Crest of the Wave*. The 1938 British Film Crisis prevented these plans maturing, and the outbreak of war a year later put a stop to all schemes for the producing of large-scale musical films in our studios. But Associated British had always cast a longing eye at Novello's series of plays with music, and several years later they produced a Technicolor version of *The Dancing Years,* his fourth 'hit' musical in a row. It became one of the most popular British films of 1950.

While Novello was playing every evening in *Crest of the Wave,* and working day after day with Lewis Casson on his forthcoming production of *Henry V* at Drury Lane, Herbert Wilcox bought the talking film rights of *The Rat,* with the idea of starring Ivor in the part he had made world famous a dozen years previously. Ivor's great friend Ruth Chatterton, who had come from Hollywood to star in Somerset Maugham's *The Constant Wife* at the Globe Theatre in the summer of 1937, was to play Zelie in the film version, with Rene Ray as Odile. (This was to be Ruth's second film for Wilcox, the first having been *A Royal Divorce,* in which she played Josephine to Pierre Blanchar's Napoleon.) Ivor was delighted at the thought of co-starring in a film again with Ruth, even though he had rather rueful memories of their previous picture together, but again the same story was repeated. Try as he might, he could not fit in his stage commitments with the film at Elstree, and eventually the idea of his starring as Pierre had to be abandoned. The part was subsequently played by Austrian film star Anton Walbrook, who had arrived in England via Hollywood to play Albert to Anna Neagle's Victoria in the celebrated Herbert Wilcox picture, *Victoria the Great.* That film and *The Rat* established Walbrook as one of the biggest stars in British pictures, and, as Ivor wryly admitted: 'He gave a much better performance than I would have done.'

Novello's admirers, with memories of *The Lodger, The Constant Nymph* and *Autumn Crocus* (the last film he starred in) fresh in their minds, would probably disagree. But the fact remains that he kept the promise he made to himself after *Sleeping Car*—not to appear in further films—and with the notable exception of *Autumn Crocus,* in which the opportunity of appearing with his friend Fay Compton was too tempting to miss, he stayed firm in his resolve.

★

For her performance in *Sleeping Car* (and in the previous Gaumont-British production, *I Was A Spy*) Madeleine Carroll received an offer from Fox which she accepted a year later.

The same company also made Novello an offer to star in a series of Hollywood films, but he was obliged to refuse, not only because he did not want to leave London, but because he was committed to make *I Lived With You* at Twickenham, and was also preparing three new play productions, in one of which he was himself to play a leading part. Somewhere inside him an imp of mischief at first urged him to take the offer, made him itch to sign the contract and return in triumph to California, where he had spent so many miserable months in 1931. But reason prevailed. He cabled his refusal, and immediately got down to the immense amount of work which had piled up.

At Twickenham he starred in *I Lived With You,* directed by Maurice Elvey, with Ursula Jeans taking her stage role of Glad, and with a young actress called Ida Lupino playing her very first screen part—as Ada. Minnie Rayner, Eliot Makeham and Cicely Oates played their original roles in the film, while Jack Hawkins played Mort, and Victor Boggetti the part of Thornton. As the Russian prince who turns a Fulham household upside down, Novello made a handsome figure, and his delivery of his own dialogue simply sparkled with wit and good humour. As *Film Weekly* stated: 'Novello gives a clever study in a film which is definitely unusual entertainment.' Ida Lupino made quite a hit in the picture and shortly afterwards she, too, departed for Hollywood, while Ursula Jeans duplicated her stage success, and later made notable appearances in several British and Hollywood films (including *Cavalcade,* for which she went to Hollywood in 1933, immediately following *I Lived With You*).

Julius Hagen was immensely delighted with his two Novello films, and endeavoured to persuade Ivor to make at least one picture a year for a three-year period. But Novello was adamant. He had realized that he had to make up his mind either to concentrate on being a film star (for possibly, as he well realized, a limited period), or to make music and the theatre completely his career. After long deliberation and much advice from his mother, Noël Coward, Robert

Andrews, Edward Marsh and Phyllis Monkman, and other friends, he turned down the offer. It was a momentous decision—but he never regretted it. He assured Hagen that if a 'very special part' in a 'very special film' came along he would consider it, or if a screen version of one of his own plays was to be made then he would probably like to appear in it himself. But he made no promises. Subsequently Hagen offered him a starring role in *Spy of Napoleon,* opposite Dolly Haas, but once again Ivor was too busy, and at length Richard Barthelmess was brought over from Hollywood to play the part. Strangely enough, it had been Ivor's resemblance to Barthelmess in the first place which had prompted D. W. Griffith to sign him to a contract in 1923. To complete the circle of coincidence, Hagen brought out Griffith himself from Hollywood, after the completion of *Spy of Napoleon,* to make a sound version of his great success, *Broken Blossoms,* in which Emlyn Williams (in the original Barthelmess role) played opposite Dolly Haas.

Hagen, knowing that Ivor had made *The White Rose* for Griffith in the U.S.A., then attempted to promote a production involving a collaboration between Griffith and Novello once more, but although many plans were made, all of them fell through. Indeed, in the end Griffith, after several conferences and quarrels, stepped out of the picture and went back to Hollywood; *Broken Blossoms* was eventually directed by John Brahm. So the great D. W. returned home without making his much-publicized 'come-back', and the opportunity of seeing Ivor Novello in another Griffith film had been lost.

Besides Julius Hagen, Korda and Balcon had both tried to interest Ivor in further film appearances. *Sleeping Car* had been a big popular success all over the country, and the latter felt that he would like to team Ivor and Madeleine Carroll in another romantic comedy. Again Ivor had to refuse, for the time being at least. With *I Lived With You, Party, Proscenium* and *Murder in Mayfair* he was riding on a wave of popularity and stage successes during the period 1932–35, and he felt that he did not want to break his run of luck by ceasing his theatre activities to make another film or two. It had become quite obvious to him and to his advisors over the previous year or two that he could not combine both film-making and acting on the stage at the same time. Since it had now resolved itself into a choice of the two mediums, Novello knew which he must choose.

A year or two later, however, he changed his mind, but only for very special reasons. His old friend Basil Dean was preparing to make a screen version of Dodie Smith's play *Autumn Crocus,* with Fay Compton playing her original part of Fanny Gray, the spinster school-teacher on holiday in the Tyrol, who falls in love with Andreas, the handsome innkeeper of the hostelry where she is staying. Her performance in this play will always be remembered as one of Fay Compton's most memorable creations, and Ivor, who had loved the play when he saw it at the Lyric Theatre in 1931, jumped at the idea of playing opposite her in the part which Francis Lederer had created in London (and later acted on Broadway). The opportunity of acting with his beloved Fay in a film to be directed by Basil was too much to resist, and when *Murder in Mayfair* had almost ended its run at the Globe Theatre Ivor immediately went into the film.

At this time Basil Dean was making a series of British pictures at Ealing Studios for Associated Talking Pictures, a British company with affiliations to R.K.O. Radio of Hollywood. Ealing was under the control of Reginald Baker, who had been associated with Michael Balcon at the old Islington Studios from 1923 to 1928, the period when Novello was their biggest star. (Baker invited Balcon to join Ealing in 1938, since which time they have been the most successful combination in British films.) Baker was overjoyed to see Ivor once more working under his ægis, and Basil Dean had long wanted to direct a Novello film since he had worked with Adrian Brunel some years previously on *The Constant Nymph.* (Incidentally, Baker's son, Peter, whom Ivor used to dandle on his knee when the child visited the set at Islington, is now the well-known publisher and M.P.)

Autumn Crocus, released in 1935, and with Fay repeating her stage success, was a production made in an atmosphere of nostalgia and reminiscence. Ivor and Reginald Baker would sit for hours talking of the days at Gainsborough when Novello films like *The Rat, Downhill, The Lodger* and *The Vortex* had helped to establish Gainsborough as the major studio in this country; with Dean Ivor would humorously recall the awful first night of *Sirocco,* that failure in which he and Basil had unhappily shared. The film was quickly completed, and Dean was very happy about Ivor's acting and fine appearance as the Austrian innkeeper. He made plans to star Ivor in a series of A.T.P. productions, but two things prevented this from materializing. One was that Dean eventually relinquished control of Ealing Studios, and the other was that Ivor had embarked on the first of that series of musical plays which was to make his name resound once more throughout the world, and to result in his music being performed and sung more than any other British composer's in his sphere, with the possible exception of Noël Coward. That first play was the fabulous *Glamorous Night,* and after it had been launched on its amazing career all thoughts of further films evaporated from Novello's brain. Music was his first love, the theatre his second. The cinema had always had to take a tertiary position in his affections, and for the next dozen years he was to reject several British and Hollywood film offers, as the pressure of work and the continued popularity of his shows made a combined film and stage career impossible. At one time Novello had found it comparatively easy to combine three, and sometimes four, careers. Now, however, he had at last hit upon the kind of work for which he was ideally suited—the creation of musical plays with excellent roles for himself. His years both as a successful composer and a brilliant playwright had finally yielded their combined artistic dividends. With *Glamorous Night* he created a smash-hit by the brilliant fusion of his many talents, and he decided that this was to be the work of his lifetime. For fifteen years he continued along this channel of creation, with what results the world knows.

12

'Glamorous Night'

'Ivor Novello is now the most considerable personality on the English stage.'—*Paul Holt in the 'Daily Express', April 15th, 1936.*

WITH the exception of a few songs for Jack Hulbert and Cicely Courtneidge in their revue *The House That Jack Built,* which ran at the Adelphi from 1929 to 1930, Novello had not written a note for ten years. Royalties were continually coming in from all his song hits between 1915 and 1926, which included 'The Little Damozel', 'Dreamboat', 'The Valley', 'Megan', 'The Valley of Rainbows', 'And Her Mother Came Too', 'Night May Have Its Sadness', and dozens of other well-known titles. But he had not been entirely happy with his revue experiences, and decided to wait until his music could be performed by a large orchestra. Nevertheless, he was beginning to feel guilty about neglecting the thing he loved most, and to which he owed his start. His partner, Richard Rose, was always saying, 'Why don't you write a big musical show for yourself? You can write wonderful plays and wonderful music; why not combine the two?'

Ivor had always replied that to write a big musical show for himself would mean that he would be obliged to sing—which he most definitely could not do. Hum a little to himself while working at the piano—yes. But sing one of his songs in public—definitely no.

However, the bug had entered into his brain, and with each month had become more insistent. Could he write a big musical? He was not sure. Then, quite suddenly, the opportunity presented itself.

Ever since Noël Coward's *Cavalcade* had run at the Theatre Royal, Drury Lane, for a year in 1932, nothing had quite 'come off' at that great theatre of tradition. *Wild Violets* was succeeded by *Ball At The Savoy,* and this in turn was quickly followed by *The Three Sisters,* which had been a great disappointment, the run lasting only a short time, in spite of the fact that it had a score by Jerome Kern and a libretto by Oscar Hammerstein II. Drury Lane was in trouble again.

H. M. Tennent, formerly with Moss Empires, and then the recently appointed Managing Director of this theatre, was faced with the problem of finding something to follow the 1934-35 pantomime, a show which could hold up to the *Cavalcade* tradition. One day over lunch, Harry Tennent was chatting with Ivor about his problems at Drury Lane, and, more to cheer Harry up than anything else, Novello—then playing in *Murder in Mayfair*—asked him whether the Drury Lane directors would consider a musical play written by himself. Tennent asked him if he had anything concrete in mind, and Ivor, with not a thing in his head, proceeded to tell him a story which he made up as he went along. Gradually he began to get carried away by his own enthusiasm, and the improvised plot got better and better. By the time the lunch was over Ivor had told Tennent almost a complete plot of what was later to become *Glamorous Night,* a Novello production which began a new era of successful spectacle at Drury Lane. 'One thing must be clear, though, Harry,' warned Ivor, amazed at his own intrepidity, 'I want an orchestra of at least forty players, a cast of one hundred and twenty, and I want to devise and supervise the entire production, without interference from anybody!'

Tennent agreed, and thereupon suggested the plan to his directors. To Novello's surprise they immediately commissioned him to write their next show—on his own terms! So there he was, with a commission on his hands—and he simply *had* to do it. Actually, by the time coffee was served at that historic luncheon, Ivor had convinced himself that the plot of *Glamorous Night* had been in his mind for years, and was all ready and waiting to be typed for first rehearsals. The ideas simply poured from his brain, and within a few weeks the play was completed and he had commenced work on the melodies, some of which remain to-day among the most lovely music in the English theatre. Novello was determined to get away from the conventional musical comedy, the kind of production for which he had written music and lyrics twenty-five years before. He wanted to produce something spectacular, combining the thrills of the old Drury Lane melodramas, which were the joys of his childhood, with a romantic operetta framework involving large-scale singing and opportunities for the creation of the most ambitious music he had yet attempted. Before long he had devised, written, and composed *Glamorous Night,* and Leontine Sagan, whom he had long considered one of the most gifted producers in London, was engaged to produce the play—incidentally becoming the first woman producer to work at Drury Lane.

The most important problem, as always, was a leading lady. For Ivor there was no question as to who she should be. He had adored Mary Ellis, the young American singer, in the show *Music in the Air* at His Majesty's in 1933 (and in the original American *Rose Marie* in 1925), and nothing would satisfy him but that she should be his Militza. He knew that she was magnificent, tempestuous, possessing a glorious voice and a wonderful stage presence. He longed to exploit her wealth of talent on a more ambitious scale, and he was confident that *Glamorous Night* was absolutely 'made' for her.

He rang up Mary at her country home.

'How would you like to be in a musical play of mine at Drury Lane?' he enquired, somewhat diffidently.

'Darling, I'd love it, but only if *you* are in it!"

'In it? Of course I'm in it. Try and keep me out! I have written some lovely music for you,' Ivor went on, looking up at his ceiling and expecting it to fall on him. (He had not written one single note.)

'When can I hear it?' Mary asked excitedly.

'To-morrow,' he replied, as he put down the telephone and dashed to the piano. He worked all day and most of the night on five new songs for Militza, including the now-famous 'Shine Through My Dreams' and 'Fold Your Wings', which he completed by four-thirty a.m. The next day Mary arrived at Ivor's flat, her eyes blazing with excitement, but, alas! a contract for Hollywood in her handbag. He outlined the story of *Glamorous Night* to her, and she liked it immensely. Then he played her the music, which she adored.

And then came the snag. She had signed a contract to star in *All the King's Horses,* opposite Carl Brisson, for Paramount in Hollywood, and was due to sail immediately, returning to London only a week or so before rehearsals were due to commence at Drury Lane, in the spring of 1935.

'But never mind,' cried Ivor, 'I will send you the script and the music in Hollywood. You can study it out there, and when you come back you will know something about the play and the music.'

A few days afterwards Mary Ellis sailed for the U.S.A., and from the boat she sent Ivor a cable:

'Your lovely music is ringing in my heart.'

Then followed weeks of extensive work. Ivor completed the play, it was finally approved and accepted by Drury Lane, and Leontine Sagan began planning the staging.

Although she was deservedly famous for her production of such plays as *Children in Uniform,* and had already directed Ivor's *Murder in Mayfair,* for which she received great praise from the critics, Miss Sagan was not well versed in musical productions. As she said to Ivor: —

'You will have to tell me all about it, as I really know nothing about this aspect of the theatre.'

But Novello was not worried. He had worked with her before and knew that she was a brilliant, inventive, and imaginative director who would bring a wealth of talent to the production of his first musical play.

One evening he dropped into Drury Lane to see the pantomime, always a big hit, and by now quite a tradition of the theatre. As he sat in the stalls he gazed all round the magnificent old playhouse. 'I can hardly believe it,' he said to himself as he leaned back in his seat and looked at the stage, 'but the next show here is mine, completely and unquestionably mine.' That was a great moment in Novello's life, but greater moments were to come.

Everything was ready. They planned rehearsals for a certain date, but, unfortunately, Mary Ellis was still in Hollywood, receiving a fantastic salary. Paramount had followed *All the King's Horses* by co-starring her with Tullio Carminati in *Paris in Spring,* and they had further films lined up for her. Although thrilled with her part and the songs of *Glamorous Night,* Mary found it difficult to make up her mind. Should she stay in Hollywood, or star on the London stage? Ivor was becoming desperate. Not only had he written the part with Mary Ellis in mind, but he felt that it was almost impossible to readjust his ideas to the acceptance of someone else in the role. The delay was further aggravated by a London stage strike, but finally Ivor's happiness was made complete when he received a cable from California:—

> 'Darling, of course I am coming to play the part, Sailing on Thursday week—for certain—repeat—for certain.'

Novello went into Drury Lane at that first rehearsal completely and absolutely satisfied. He was quite sure that this was to be a turning point in his career, and he felt supremely happy. Mary arrived from New York in excellent spirits, knowing the whole of the first act already, and in glorious voice. The rehearsals were a joy from beginning to end, and after a period of exciting, strenuous, but highly optimistic rehearsals, *Glamorous Night* was launched on its spectacular career. Noël Coward told Ivor, 'Don't be afraid to ask for anything at the Lane, because you'll get it at once'. Ivor took his advice. To William Abingdon, the famous stage director of Drury Lane for many years, he declared:—

'For this show I want an enormous shipwreck scene, with a luxury liner sinking in full view of the audience!'

Abingdon did not turn a hair. He thought for a moment

and then tersely remarked, 'Okay—it will be done exactly as you want it.' And it was.

Besides Mary Ellis the cast included Lyn Harding, the villain of so many Drury Lane melodramas, Barry Jones, Clifford Heatherley, Olive Gilbert, who has since been in five other Novello musicals, Minnie Rayner, Trefor Jones, the tenor, and Elizabeth Welch, that delightful personality from the New York stage. Ivor played the leading man's role himself.

As W. Macqueen-Pope wrote in his book, *Theatre Royal, Drury Lane*: * 'Novello knew his Drury Lane and knew the formula. What he gave in *Glamorous Night* was a very clever mingling of Drury Lane drama and Drury Lane musical play, with plenty of spectacle. It was a type of show never seen here before, and it was to prove the ideal Drury Lane mixture, for it held all that was best of the old and the new formulas.

'There had been a good deal of debate amongst the "know-alls" of the theatrical profession as to whether Ivor Novello could do a show for the great theatre. "God knows it wants one badly enough," they said, "but is he the right man?"

'And, indeed, the condition of the Lane was parlous.

'The first night was May 2nd, 1935. Memories reverted to another fateful night when the theatre was in straits and a man had arrived to put it right. On a January night in 1814 Edmund Kean had trudged through the snow, friendless, hungry, forlorn, and disregarded, but supremely confident, to save Drury Lane. He had turned into that same stage door with not a friendly voice to greet him.

'On that night in May 1935, the plight of Drury Lane was much the same. But the scene at the stage door was different. Principals and chorus passed in, telegraph boys brought wires of good wishes by the handful, floral offerings arrived in lorry-loads. Then, in the lull which occurs when the company are in and the overture has not begun, a slim, lithe figure, with a hat pulled down over his eyes, darted through the famous portal. The onlookers saw just a glimpse of him, but enough to shout "Good luck!" Inside, unlike Edmund Kean, he

* W. H. Allen, 1945.

received smiles from everyone. But, like Kean, much depended on him. As the orchestra broke into the overture the great battle for the survival and triumph of Drury Lane had begun. How it ended everyone knows.

'It was indeed a glamorous night. The great glittering show hypnotized its smart, hardened first-night audience, for Drury Lane in front was as brilliant as Drury Lane backstage. All the players were acclaimed. Standing in line with his great company, Ivor returned thanks, giving Leontine Sagan, dance-director Ralph Reader, and everyone there their just due, in a modest speech which came straight from, and went straight to, the heart.

'It was a night never to be forgotten. Drury Lane, thanks to Ivor Novello, was itself again.'

One could hardly put it better than that celebrated historian of the theatre, Macqueen-Pope. It was indeed a triumph.

Maurice Willson Disher, dramatic critic of the *Daily Mail*, headed his enthusiastic review 'Great New Ivor Novello Play', going on to declare: 'Cheers, shouts, yells, and a tornado of clapping greeted Mr. Ivor Novello's first entrance at Drury Lane last night. As the one who had "devised, written, and composed" the glamorous piece called *Glamorous Night* for the reopening of the world's most glamorous theatre, he was given this proof in advance of public good will. His welcome was warranted.

'Anthony Allen, the part he plays, is the young inventor of a new television process, who is given £500 by Lord Radio (in a futurist setting) to keep quiet about it.

'The scene shifts to Krasnia, where "backward English" is spoken—as we can tell from the notice, "On Gnikoms", in its opera house.

'King Stefan of Krasnia loves Militza, a gypsy prima-donna, whom we hear and see at a grand gala performance ending in an attempt on her life.

'Here is Anthony's chance. He disarms the would-be assassin and is invited to the gypsy's boudoir. Then he has to return to his ship for the duration of the cruise, plus her cheque for £1,000. She follows.

'Gay scenes aboard ship end in a spectacular wreck. Our hero and his prima donna reach the shore, where they are married gypsy fashion.

'But her country is in danger, and to save it she has to agree to become queen. He returns to England and witnesses her coronation by means of the television he has invented.

'Beyond all doubt, *Glamorous Night* is wildly, inspiringly, intoxicatingly triumphant.

'It is a sheer delight, a feast of colour, music, and drama.

'Besides Mr. Novello, who must take the lion's share of the credit, must stand Miss Mary Ellis, a leading lady splendid enough even for so vast a pageant as this.

'The King of Krasnia was charmingly represented by Mr. Barry Jones, and the Prime Minister most sinisterly by Mr. Lyn Harding.

'There is a whole host of singers, dancers, and actors in the company: Mr. Trefor Jones as the tenor of the Krasman Opera House, Miss Minnie Rayner as the gypsy's faithful attendant, and Miss Elizabeth Welch as a singer aboard ship are among the most notable.

'As Drury Lane's first woman producer, Miss Leontine Sagan has increased her fame. As the artist chiefly responsible for the décor, Mr. Oliver Messel has set the seal upon his.

'It has taken Mr. Ivor Novello—writing and composing his first full-scale musical play and acting the leading male role himself—to provide Drury Lane Theatre Royal with the biggest hit it has had for many years.'

That was not all. 'I lift my hat to Mr. Novello', wrote Ivor Brown in the *Observer,* while James Agate was content to remark, 'The Novello show had a tremendous reception, and one left Drury Lane wondering why one should bother about the National Theatre when one has this.'

Almost before the sounds of the first night cheers had died away, Drury Lane had elicited guarantees of £100,000 at the box office; it was the most splendid and historic success at this theatre since *Cavalcade*. In *Glamorous Night* Novello had made the biggest stage hit of his unique career. He was, as he was the first to admit, lucky in having Mary Ellis and a wonderful cast, Leontine Sagan, designer Oliver Messel, Ralph Reader, and the others, and extremely fortunate in having his musical play staged at Drury Lane. But it all added up to a great personal triumph without any precedent in the English theatre for scores of years. He had written, devised, composed and starred in a splendiferous and entertaining production at one of the world's most renowned theatres. Already celebrated as a stage and screen star, composer of world-famous songs, and a dramatist of wit and skill, Novello established himself with *Glamorous Night* in the unique position which he successfully held since that time. For more than a dozen years he continued to create plays and musical plays which have become a tradition of the English theatre. He always had, however, a sentimental attachment to *Glamorous Night,* since this was the first of the series, the initial triumph in his long list of successes. It has been revived many times, made into a popular film, broadcast and televised, and its music is still sung and played all over the world. It was the foundation-stone of a remarkable new career for a remarkable young man.

Novello wrote to me of his feelings at the time of his first Drury Lane show: 'In a busy and not unexciting life I have had many thrills and many adventures. But no thrill I have ever known and no adventure I have ever undertaken has given me the tremendous thrill which Drury Lane has provided. For I, like every member of my profession, have the greatest veneration and respect for this grand theatre, which is more national than any specially founded "National Theatre" could ever be. Has it not endured for 272 years? Is it not the epitome of the whole of the British Drama? Is it not the greatest and most famous theatre in the world, the most dignified, and at the same time the most human?

'Drury Lane has always obsessed me. I have always loved it, and even as a small child of nine my ambition was to play there, and, if possible, to write a play for its historic boards.

'I have seen every production there since 1902. I have not missed one. I have vivid memories of all the great scenic effects shown there in the famous dramas and the equally famous pantomimes—the great names—the magnificent spectacles—all these are as clear in my memory as on the day I saw them first.

'I know the history of the theatre; I know its traditions; I treasure the knowledge that the actors at "The Lane" were known as "His Majesty's Servants" and wore red coats; that a military guard was mounted; in fact, that Drury Lane is really a piece of English history.

'Up to this year it had never been my luck to appear there. The nearest I ever got to it was when I played the piano "off stage" at a charity matinée. But I believe that everything comes to him who waits—more especially if he helps it along! and I hoped that one day I would have a chance.

'That chance came. Drury Lane wanted a show. I made up my mind that the show should be mine. And here I am!'

After *Glamorous Night* had been running for three months Ivor completed a light comedy which he had written especially for his old friends Lilian Braithwaite and Isabel Jeans. Called *Full House,* it opened at the Haymarket Theatre on August 21st, 1935, and ran for a year, with both Miss Braithwaite and Miss Jeans giving delightful comedy performances in a cast which included the clever and versatile Robert Andrews, Heather Thatcher, Maidie Andrews and Frank Cochrane. By now the London dramatic critics had grown a little blasé on the score of Novello's many-sided talent, but, nonetheless, *Full House* was exceptionally well received, and added to Novello's reputation as the creator of nothing but hit shows.

Since *The Rat* and *Downhill* he had certainly appeared to wield the magic touch—*The Truth Game, Symphony In Two Flats, I Lived With You, Party, Fresh Fields, Proscenium, Murder in Mayfair, Glamorous Night* and *Full House.* It was an imposing list of plays. How they reflected the versatility and brilliance of the ever-youthful Welshman. Each one had been produced and cast with Novello himself supervising; each one had given acting opportunities to a well-known group of players who appeared time and time again in his productions. A Novello show had become the hallmark of polished excellence in London theatreland, and *Full House* consolidated his reputation as one of the foremost young playwrights in the English theatre.

It was during the run of *Glamorous Night* that one of Novello's proudest moments in the theatre happened—King George V and Queen Mary, the Duke and Duchess of Kent, and Princess Alice all came to a performance at Drury Lane, and enjoyed the play very much indeed. A week later Ivor and his mother received an invitation to the Royal Garden Party, and Ivor was introduced to the King. The following conversation took place:—

H.M.: 'And you write the story and the music and act the principal part yourself! Don't you find it very tiring in this hot weather?'

Novello (trembling but happy): 'Not when *you're* in front, Sir.'

H.M.: 'Well, I can tell you this. We enjoyed ourselves enormously, with one reservation (Ivor's heart sank)—we could have wished a different ending. We found it a little sad, the Queen and I; in fact, you made the Queen cry. (Ivor apologized.) Make the next one with a happy ending, please.' (Ivor said he would.)

As it transpired, Novello took the King's advice, and his next play, *Careless Rapture,* had a happy ending. However, he was still busily acting in *Glamorous Night,* which had become one of London's biggest hits of 1935, taking its place with those other West End successes of that year—Emlyn Williams' *Night Must Fall* at the Duchess; André Obey's *Noah,* with John Gielgud, at the New; *Tovarich,* with Sir Cedric Hardwicke, at the Lyric; Michael Egan's *The Dominant Sex* at the Aldwych; and *This Desirable Residence,* with Marie Ney, at the Criterion. Cedric Belfrage wrote in the *Daily Express* that Novello's play was a greater show than anything Ziegfeld could devise!—praise indeed—and it ran to absolute capacity until the end of November 1935. Then it had to be taken off because, unknown to Novello, Drury Lane had already been let for a Christmas pantomime before he had even started rehearsals. He suspected that, following a series of failures at this great theatre, the management could hardly bring itself to imagine that any new production would run right through Christmas. And, in any case, they judged from previous experience that a Drury Lane pantomime would bring in at least £10,000 profit.

Ivor was exasperated by the whole business. Here they were, packed to capacity every night, with standing room only at every performance, with the most wonderful Press notices that any show could possibly have, with bookings being turned away—and the whole show had to be taken off before Christmas. It was preposterous. It was unfair. It was sheer madness. He was determined to do everything possible to prevent this happening, and even gave the management a written guarantee of £8,000 profit over the Christmas period if they would drop their plans to stage the pantomime. They stuck out for £10,000, however, a figure which it was not economically possible for Novello to reach, but as a measure of consolation they asked him to write the next play for Drury Lane, to follow the pantomime in early 1936. He accepted the commission, and set to work on *Careless Rapture,* completing the script and most of the music four days before *Glamorous Night* was to close. But things were not destined to go smoothly this time. He was in for a setback.

One afternoon in November 1935, Ivor read his completed play to the directorate at Drury Lane in an atmosphere of such gloom that he very nearly gave up after the first scene. Everything seemed to be against him. None of his jokes seemed to come off, and he began to blame himself for having read the script to them at all. Surely, he thought to himself afterwards, they could have trusted me to write another play after the tremendous success of *Glamorous Night*? But it was too late to think of that now. He was not a bit surprised when, two days after the last night of his show, Ivor was telephoned by Harry Tennent, who told him very sadly that the Drury Lane Board had turned down *Careless Rapture.* Harry himself implicitly believed in the play, but he had been overruled.

20. Mary Ellis co-starred with Novello in his first musical romance, *Glamorous Night,* produced at Drury Lane by Leontine Sagan in 1935. It was followed by two further Novello musical successes, *Careless Rapture* (1936) and *Crest of the Wave* (1937).

21. In Clemence Dane's adaptation of Max Beerbohm's *The Happy Hypocrite*, His Majesty's, 1936, Novello played Lord George Hell, a dissolute Regency buck.

22. He undergoes a magical facial transformation under the influence of Jenny Mere, played by Vivien Leigh.

So that was that. Ivor was disappointed but philosophical. He knew his theatre. He knew it was a life of ups and downs, that on the stage you could never really depend on anything, let alone success. So here he was, with an enormous new production on his hands, especially written for the huge Drury Lane stage but rejected by the management. What should he do next?

The last night of *Glamorous Night* was quite amazing. The house was crammed to bursting point with Ivor's admirers. Many of the people in the audience had seen the show thirty or forty times! Hysteria was in the air. The performance went with a swing, and at the end twenty-five curtain calls were taken. The entire audience just stood up in their seats and cheered until Ivor came forward and made a short speech. He was naturally elated by the wonderful and heart-warming reception, but he felt depressed as at no other time since his return from Hollywood. He had an awful instinct that this was to be his last appearance at Drury Lane, the theatre he loved most in all London, and the audience quickly sensed this. As he stood there, stumbling through his few words of thanks, the audience seemed to realize that this was a highly important emotional moment in his life, and a strange, tense quietude descended upon the house. When he had finished speaking the curtain came down very slowly to the tumultuous crash of cheers and applause. Again and again they shouted for Ivor. They just would not leave the theatre. Half an hour later, with the grease-paint removed, Ivor in his street-clothes stepped out through the stage-door, where he literally had to fight to get to his car. He was cheered to the echo by hundreds of enthusiasts, and cries of 'Come back soon, Ivor!' filled his ears. Finally, as he sat back in his car, a great feeling of emotion overwhelmed him. As he drove up through Covent Garden he looked back at that great and wonderful theatre. His eyes were moist. Here he had spent some of the happiest months of his professional career. Here he had enjoyed his greatest personal triumph. Here he had seen the fulfilment of all his dreams, and the combining of all his talents in a stage production which will be remembered as long as there is a Drury Lane Theatre. It was a very sad parting.

★

For the time being *Careless Rapture* was shelved, and Ivor, after a holiday, began to think seriously of his next stage appearance. Several managements offered him starring roles in new plays, but Novello turned them all down—except one. After his string of successes he had decided to be careful about the kind of role he accepted, but, oddly enough, he rejected all the comparatively easy star parts which were offered him in order to make an attempt at an extremely difficult character part—that of the Regency rake, Lord George Hell, in Clemence Dane's dramatic version of Max Beerbohm's story, *The Happy Hypocrite* (with music by Richard Addinsell). That was typical of Ivor. Being blessed with those almost unbelievable good looks, all his life he had been obliged to stand up to criticisms of his acting ability, on the grounds that anybody as handsome as Novello just could not be a good actor. In his own play, *Proscenium,* Ivor had startled even his bitterest critics into admiration by the exquisite performance he gave as the middle-aged army officer in the Prologue. In *The Happy Hypocrite* he took the part of a bloated, fat, dissolute, raucous-voiced rake who, by the miracle of finding true love, becomes in both looks and character a gentle, handsome, and sensitive character. Beerbohm's delicious fantasy was transferred to the stage by director Maurice Colbourne with extreme skill and delicacy, and it proved to be a well-staged, artistic success, which did not, however, achieve at His Majesty's the long run it deserved. Vivien Leigh and Isabel Jeans played opposite Ivor. Isabel, of course, had made her reputation in the first Novello hit, *The Rat,* and had just finished a triumphant season in his *Full House,* while Vivien had just made an overnight sensation as Henriette in *The Mask of Virtue* at the Ambassadors. With that one performance she laid the foundations of a distinguished career. Her next portrayal, Jenny in *The Happy Hypocrite,* was a delicate, exquisite performance, which made it a far greater pity that the play enjoyed only a comparatively short run. For her acting alone it was a production to be seen.

In Novello's career certain well-known plays, films, and songs represent well-defined stepping stones in his journey to world fame. 'Keep the Home Fires Burning' was one, *Call of the Blood* was another. *The Rat* was a third, and *The Truth Game* was fourth. *Glamorous Night* was probably the most important turning-point in his life, and *The Happy Hypocrite* occupies the sixth honoured place. The reason is that Novello was really acclaimed by every single critic for his performance in this play, being praised for his abilities as an actor rather than as a glamorous and gifted personality. Admittedly he had always been well received by the Press. *Enter Kiki* and *The Firebrand* being perhaps notable exceptions, but for his performance as Lord George Hell Novello was hailed with the highest enthusiasm by every one of the dramatic critics. He made a striking personal success. 'Although the play was not a money-maker,' Ivor told me, it was not only a joy to act in and one of my loveliest memories in the theatre, but it was a most remarkable investment in reputation. By that I mean that the critics were so kind that I honestly could hardly believe that they were talking about me.'

In any book about a great stage star a mere listing of well-disposed Press notices is in danger of becoming wearisome, and I have sincerely endeavoured to avoid this wherever possible. Nevertheless, since the play *The Happy Hypocrite* unquestionably marked the first real sign of widespread critical acceptance of Novello as an actor of significance, I beg the reader's indulgence for reprinting a small selection. In the *Sunday Times* James Agate delivered himself as follows: 'Mr. Novello plays Lord George with great sincerity. His make-up for the first act is very effective, and exactly gives the note of Caligula with a touch of Sir John Falstaff. He acts all the latter part of the play with a disarming simplicity; to have such a profile and pretend not to know it would write him down as an artist of enormous sensibility. It is a beautiful performance throughout.'

The *Sunday Graphic* opined: 'I never thought the day would come when Novello would demand serious consideration as an actor. Yet I here and now affirm that he plays Lord George Hell as no other actor could. His is a beautiful, restrained, and sincere performance.' And that was not all. 'The best performance of his career', wrote Herbert Farjeon in the *Sunday Pictorial*. 'This is Mr. Novello's triumph!' commented the critic of *The Times*. 'Novello has never done anything as good', was the opinion of the *News Chronicle*. 'Far and away the best thing he has ever done', stated the *Morning Post*. Ivor was elated—but there was more to come.

In the *Daily Express* Paul Holt gave it as his opinion that 'Novello, now the most considerable personality on the English stage, has scored a theatrical *tour de force*'. The *Daily Mail* summed up the general feeling in an article which included the following passage: 'Ivor Novello broke with his own tradition last night at His Majesty's when he appeared in a make-up as ugly as Lord George Hell was conceived by Max Beerbohm.* Mr. Novello justified his courage, both in that respect and in tackling a role far from his usual field. His performance has a simple sincerity, and is a personal triumph.'

The *Happy Hypocrite* was also notable for the acting of Isabel Jeans, Viola Tree, Charles Lefeaux, Carl Harbord and Marius Goring, as well as for the music of Richard Addinsell. The direction of Maurice Colbourne matched the high quality of the acting, and the whole production was marked by extreme good taste. In spite of that—or perhaps because of it—*The Happy Hypocrite* had only a limited run of a few months.

★

In the meantime, while Novello was establishing a reputation for great acting at His Majesty's, what was happening

* A young scenic designer called Angus McBean designed the mask worn by Novello in the play. He was also an amateur photographer; when Ivor heard this he asked him to photograph the play. The results, McBean's first professional efforts, were published everywhere and started him on a career as one of London's finest stage photographers.

at Drury Lane? The death of King George V had cast a pall over all theatres and cinemas—not unnaturally—and the pantomime at Drury Lane was one of the shows which suffered most. In spite of the excellent comedy performances of Binnie Hale, Shaun Glenville, Douglas Wakefield and Charles Heslop, *Jack and the Beanstalk,* as it was called, instead of making the expected profit of £10,000, suffered a definite loss. It was followed by a new musical called *Rise and Shine.* As W. Macqueen-Pope reported in his book on Drury Lane, 'This show never rose and never shone, and although everything possible was done for it, it did not live up to its title in any way'.

Novello, recalling *Rise and Shine,* told me: 'Although finely produced and with a good cast—Binnie Hale, Jack Whiting, Syd Walker, Grace Lane and Mary Honer—it was a complete flop and ran only for forty-four performances. I wonder if you will think me an inhuman monster if I confess that, apart from the distressing thought that the artists engaged in this production would soon be looking for new jobs, I could not help having a secret feeling of satisfaction?'

When *The Happy Hypocrite* ended its run Ivor took a short holiday, after which he commenced negotiations with a London management for the production of his second musical play, *Careless Rapture,* in the autumn of 1936. Suddenly there came an SOS from Drury Lane. Would he come back and put on the show they had rejected, on his own terms? Would he? Try and keep him away! This time, however, as Ivor said to Barry Jones (the King in *Glamorous Night*), 'I shall definitely be the boss. They will never again take off one of my shows at the height of its success. I have really learned my lesson. I'll go back—but completely on my own terms'. And he did—remaining as King of Drury Lane for the next three years.

On the day that the Drury Lane management signed the contract with Ivor to present *Careless Rapture* in September of that year, Ivor went to a matinée of *Rise and Shine.* All the chorus boys and girls, both dancers and singers, who had been in his *Glamorous Night* were also in *Rise and Shine.*

The notice had been posted up that this was to be the last week, and at that performance Ivor had never seen such a dispirited-looking crowd of chorists. That night, however, when spirits were at their lowest ebb, before the final show, a notice was posted up at the stage door: —

'There will be an audition to-morrow for the new Ivor Novello production.'

Harry Tennent and William Abingdon told Ivor afterwards that the atmosphere back-stage in the theatre was the most electric they had ever experienced. Spirits soared at once, dances were danced with more vigour, songs sounded better than they had all the week, and an atmosphere of true gaiety pervaded the whole stage. This gaiety lasted all through the rehearsals of *Careless Rapture* and right through the ten successful months it ran at Drury Lane (from September 1936 to June 1937).

With Ivor in this production (by Leontine Sagan once more, and with dances by Joan Davis) were Dorothy Dickson, his beloved Zena Dare, Minnie Rayner, Ivan Samson, Peter Graves, Olive Gilbert, Philip Friend, Frederick Peisley, and a talented young American dancer, Walter Crisham, who had first come to England to appear in *Ballyhoo,* followed by *Nymph Errant* and *Spread It Abroad.* In *Careless Rapture* he played the part of Toni, and his delightful sense of humour and wonderful dancing made him a new reputation overnight. Crisham is one of the many stage stars to-day who admit that their first big opportunities arrived in a Novello production. In addition, all those stars and celebrities who knew that I was writing Novello's biography wrote to me or rang me up to give me instances of his generosity and unselfishness. In his shows Ivor never surrounded himself with mediocrities. He always wrote excellent parts for everybody in his plays, and he admired talent. He always showed the greatest delight when one of his fellow-artists received acclaim for their performances in his works. Explaining this, he pointed out, 'Well, in a way, applause and recognition for artists who have secured successes with me in my plays is almost as much a credit to me, who wrote the parts, as the brilliant artists who played them.

There you have an indication of Novello's philosophy. He learned very early in life that kindness, consideration, and generosity could make everything so much easier and happier, both in the theatre and outside. Although fame and fortune had come to him early on (and although he was blessed with the most wonderful mother in the world, one who helped and encouraged him continually in every aspect of his progress in the theatre), Ivor had suffered his setbacks. None of them, however, had made him bitter. None of them had hardened him or changed his character in any way. He knew that life was bound to be uneven, and spent most of his time congratulating himself on the tremendous good fortune which had befallen him since 'Keep the Home Fires Burning'. The setback over Drury Lane's rejection of *Careless Rapture,* for instance, had not soured him. After conquering the first disappointment, Ivor accepted the role of Lord George Hell, and, as it subsequently proved, did more good to his reputation by taking a difficult part in that lovely play than he might have done by following *Glamorous Night* straight away with a second musical.

Here he was, then, with *Careless Rapture,* at Drury Lane, another triumph, a play which had opened to the same excitement and enthusiasm as *Glamorous Night.* Novello had certainly hit upon the recipe for theatrical success. Romance. Music. Colour. Glamour. These were the corner-stones of his formula for creating an entertaining musical play, but where Ivor differed from other writer-composer-producers was in the casting of his production, for he used only the most distinguished actors and actresses, recruits from the 'straight' theatre, many of whom had never before appeared in a musical play. He brought dignity to the English musical stage.

Until the advent of *Glamorous Night* the English musical had been going through occasional periods of depression. There had really been nothing produced in London in the post-war years to take the place of the old Daly's and Gaiety musicals, with the exception of imported American successes such as *No, No, Nanette! Hit the Deck* or the Bobby Howes-Binnie Hale musicals which Jack Waller presented in the 1930's. With his first 'play with music' Ivor Novello revived interest in large-scale musicals. Just as *Oklahoma,* some years later, was to create a popular interest in a new cycle of American musicals, so *Glamorous Night* in 1935 developed a tradition of new-type English musical plays (as apart from operettas, which have, of course, continued spasmodically since the halcyon days of the early 1900's). That tradition, founded by Novello and perpetuated by him in the past fifteen years, has continued triumphantly to this day. At a time when the American musicals of the late 1940's threatened to conquer the London stage, Novello, with *Perchance to Dream* and *King's Rhapsody,* triumphantly held his own; he was the only British writer-composer who had successfully challenged American domination of our musical stage. In the 1940's he succeeded again, just as his *Glamorous Night* in the 1930's successfully routed those tag-ends of mid-European operettas which had been monopolizing our English musical theatre since the decline of the English-style musical play, the sad decline which followed after Daly's had faded out as the centre of all that was finest in stage musicals.

Careless Rapture continued in the *Glamorous Night* tradition; it was lavish, gorgeous, brilliantly staged and acted by a distinguished cast. Paul Holt had written in the *Daily Express* that Novello, 'firm in his endeavour, presided like a genius over a show which contained much that was magnificent and was well in the Drury Lane tradition'. A day or two afterwards Holt was reporting that Novello had pulled off a £100,000 deal with the ticket libraries, which would ensure a run of at least nine months. He had scored another hit. He kept Drury Lane full for almost a year, and it convinced the Drury Lane management that in him they had found their saviour, and that *Glamorous Night* was not just a flash-in-the-pan. During the last weeks of his second musical they were anxiously asking him about a third, and the prolific Novello obliged with *Crest of the Wave,* which opened in September 1937, exactly a year after *Careless Rapture*. Also produced by

Leontine Sagan, it had the same happy cast—Dorothy Dickson, Minnie Rayner, Olive Gilbert, Peter Graves and Walter Crisham, plus such stage favourites as Marie Lohr, Ena Burrill, Finlay Currie, Dorothy Batley and John Palmer (who subsequently played in *Perchance to Dream* and *King's Rhapsody*). Alick Johnstone designed the settings and René Hubert the costumes, while Ralph Reader devised the dances, with the ballet choreography in the hands of Lydia Sokolova and Antony Tudor. Christopher Hassall again composed the lyrics to Ivor's song hits, 'Why Isn't It You' and 'Rose of England'. Like the others, *Crest of the Wave* ran for a year, played to 'Standing Room Only' at every performance. Like the others, it had all London talking. Novello had always been famous and renowned, but now his name was literally on everybody's lips, and his songs whistled by every errand-boy. He had 'taken over' the greatest theatre in the world and changed its recent record of flops and near-misses to one of continuous and triumphant success. To have written, composed, and starred in one big musical was a great enough achievement. To have followed it with an equally successful second production was more than remarkable. But to devise, write, compose, and star (as *both* hero and villain!) in yet another strikingly successful musical play made Ivor Novello truly a phenomenon. An amazing indication of his popularity at that time was the fact that he received 5,000 telegrams of good wishes from friends and admirers on the opening night of *Crest of the Wave*.

Three big hits in a row! Three enormous, colossal, sensational hits! Adjectives are all too few to describe that eventful period in the late 1930's when Novello established himself as the giant of our musical theatre. Superlatives are just not sufficient to describe his personal success, his enviable Press notices, the enthusiasm and excitement of his audiences, his ever-mounting popularity, the loyalty of his company, the near-hysteria which greeted him at the stage door nightly, and all the other exciting, fantastic accoutrements of really astonishing theatrical achievement. The biographer must be forgiven for lapsing into superlatives, but it is with an endeavour to capture for the reader the atmosphere of those stimulating, exciting, momentous, thrilling and prosperous years at Drury Lane under Novello's inspired guidance that I am obliged to have recourse to this string of adjectives. Even so, they cannot really do justice to the personality and achievement of the great figure who bestrode the pre-war London theatre like a colossus.

In the December of 1937, while appearing in *Crest of the Wave,* Ivor played Charles Surface in a scene from *The School for Scandal* at a Winter Garden matineé in aid of the King George Pension Fund, a performance which consolidated the growing impression that he had become a vastly improved actor. For years his perfect profile had counted against him, but his acting in *Proscenium* and *The Happy Hypocrite,* as well as his Romeo and Charles Surface in the charity matinées, finally convinced even his sternest critics. He had become, in spite of some scoffers and critics, one of the most gifted and significant figures of the English stage.

Since *Murder in Mayfair* in 1934, Novello had not written a 'straight' play, being busy with his three musicals, but during the run of *Crest of the Wave* he wrote *Comedienne,* a comedy on his favourite topic—the theatre. The central role, that of Donna Lovelace, a former stage star who had been in retirement for many years, was written with Lilian Braithwaite in mind. Ivor had never forgotten how Lilian had stood by him over *The Truth Game;* since her big success in that play she had starred in those other Novello hits, *Symphony In Two Flats, Party, Fresh Fields* and *Full House.* In *Party* she had played the role of a famous actress—loosely based on Mrs. Patrick Campbell, with a dash of Constance Collier—and Ivor knew that the part of the fading star in his new play was ideally suited to her. As it proved, he was right, and Lilian's Donna became one of her most celebrated roles.

Comedienne began its run on June 16th, 1938, at the illustrious Haymarket Theatre, with his old friend Barry Jones, Kathleen Harrison, Alan Webb, Fabia Drake (who had scored a success in *Proscenium*), Betty Marsden, Ralph Michael, Cecily Byrne, Edgar Norfolk and Mervyn Johns completing the cast. The play was concerned with the efforts of a young newcomer to the theatre, Lord Bayfield, whose one ambition it was, to bring Donna Lovelace back to her rightful position as queen of the West End stage. He knew the stories about how difficult she had been in the past, how she never knew her lines until the dress rehearsal—and sometimes not even then—how she 'up-staged' every member of the company, how she behaved disgracefully throughout the run of every play she had appeared in. He knew all these tales, yet he also knew that Donna had brought magic into the theatre not once but a score of times. He had come under her spell when a very young man, and had worshipped her for years before deciding to go into theatrical management. Could the difficult Donna make a return to the theatre which had forgotten her years before? Novello posed this intriguing question, and *Comedienne* followed it through to an exciting third-act curtain.

If Lilian Braithwaite had been a success as a stage star in Novello's *Party,* she was a riot in his *Comedienne.* Her Donna Lovelace became one of the favourite creations of her entire career. She gave an outstanding study of the egotistical, selfish genius of the theatre, slightly larger than life but deliciously entertaining, in a play which also saw good performances from that wonderful comedienne, Kathleen Harrison, and the excellent Barry Jones, Alan Webb, and Mervyn Johns. *Comedienne* ran until the end of the year, during which time Ivor had taken off *Crest of the Wave* to stage his next momentous production. With it he was to startle theatrical London.

13

'Henry V'

'Everything that sincerity, talent, good looks, experience, intelligence, and sense of the theatre can do, Mr. Novello does in the part of Henry V. He takes the stage well, compensating by his bearing for his lack of inches; he speaks very clearly, commanding the vast auditorium with ease.'—*W. A. Darlington in the 'Daily Telegraph', September 17th, 1938.*

How could Novello follow his three Drury Lane triumphs? Should he create a fourth musical extravaganza for this theatre? Should he 'play safe' and give the public once more what it so obviously wanted? Should he —could he—try to improve on his record-breaking formula of theatrical success? All these questions must have been turning themselves over in Ivor's mind when *Crest of the Wave* was drawing to the end of its year's run. Both he and his cast were tired. Most of them had been playing continuously for two years in that show and in *Careless Rapture*, and Ivor felt that he, and they, needed a rest. But, more than that, he felt that he needed a change.

What would he do? Nobody could have guessed his intention. He decided to break completely from his own tradition. Courageously he decided to attempt what he had always wanted to do—to play a great Shakespearean role under his own management. In his reminiscences, published in the *Sunday Graphic* in 1937, he had written of his ambition to stage a season of Shakespeare or a season of unusual plays at a small theatre like the Arts, but it is doubtful whether many of his readers, with memories of his enormous Drury Lane success still fresh in their minds, ever really took him seriously. Nevertheless, Novello was deadly serious. In the summer of 1938, when his *Comedienne* had settled down to a successful run at the Haymarket, he announced that he would follow *Crest of the Wave* with Shakespeare's *Henry V,* staged at Drury Lane, with himself in the title role. To say that the London theatre world was taken by surprise is something of an understatement. It was astounded. Even Ivor's thousands of admirers were not certain that this was a wise move. Several of his friends advised him against it, but Novello had made up his mind.

His friends reminded him that his previous attempts at 'going highbrow' had resulted in failure, particularly notable in this respect being *The Firebrand,* in which he played Benvenuto Cellini at Wyndham's in 1926, and the title role in *Liliom* at the Duke of York's in the following year. But he had always wanted to act in Shakespeare. His great opportunity came in 1935, when a Shakespearean matinée was staged at Drury Lane, and Ivor played Romeo in a scene from *Romeo and Juliet,* with Jean Forbes-Robertson as Juliet. The other stars taking part in this Shakespearean matinée at Drury Lane (arranged by Sydney Carroll and Ivor Novello in aid of the National Theatre) included Godfrey Tearle as Othello, George Robey as Falstaff, Sybil Thorndike as Emilia, Flora Robson as Lady Macbeth, Jack Hawkins as Orlando, Fabia Drake as Rosalind, Angela Baddeley as Ann Boleyn, Jessica Tandy as Ophelia, Lilian Braithwaite as Queen Katherine, Lyn Harding as Henry VIII, Stephen Haggard as Hamlet, Gwen Ffrangcon-Davies as Cleopatra and Celia Johnson as Viola, with Elisabeth Bergner speaking the epilogue by James Bridie. In a show which simply glittered with distinguished names, Ivor's performance was notable, and he was so thrilled by his reception that his ambition to appear in a Shakespearean production continually increased. And so, three years later, we come to *Henry V.*

For his producer Novello chose that distinguished Shakespearean veteran Lewis Casson. Gwen Ffrangcon-Davies acted the role of the Chorus, with Dorothy Dickson as Katherine, the French Princess, Joan Swinstead as Alice, her attendant, Veronica Brady as Mistress Quickly, Peter Graves as The Dauphin, W. E. Holloway as the Constable of France, Stephen Jack as the French Ambassador, Frank Shelley as Lord Scroop, Lawrence Bascomb as Pistol and Frederick Bennett as Fluellen.

Ivor was tremendously thrilled. As he declared to George W. Bishop: * 'For years my greatest ambition has been to play in Shakespeare. With the exception of appearing in the Balcony Scene from *Romeo and Juliet,* I have never played Shakespeare before, but I have studied the plays all my life. If *Henry V* is successful I hope to appear in some of the other great plays. This will be the first Shakespearean production at Drury Lane since Basil Dean presented *A Midsummer Night's Dream* in 1924, while the last time *Henry V* was played at this theatre was when George Rignold appeared in the title role in 1879. Spranger Barrie played it in 1747, under Garrick's management. And, of course, the great Edmund Kean acted the part of the King in 1830.'

Henry V opened on September 16th, 1938—right in the midst of the 'September Crisis'! The great theatre was packed full, with a vast audience mostly of well-wishers. It went without saying that hundreds of Ivor's admirers packed every part of the theatre, although there were some in the audience who just could not 'see' Novello as Henry V, and who were prepared to criticize his first entry into Shakespeare. The atmosphere was tense.

Ivor was just like an excited schoolboy before the curtain rose. Even after a quarter of a century on the stage he still experienced that enervating feeling of apprehension before every curtain of every performance—but this was a very special night. This was the night on which he was to prove whether a performance as magnificent as his Lord George in *The Happy Hypocrite* could be duplicated in Shakespeare's great drama. He need not have worried.

As the King he gave a brilliant study—much, much better

* *Daily Telegraph,* September 10th, 1938.

[Photo: Angus McBean

23. As King Henry in William Shakespeare's *Henry V,* produced by Sir Lewis Casson at Drury Lane, 1938.

Photo: Angus McBean]

24. In his own musical play *The Dancing Years* Novello played Rudi Kleber, with Roma Beaumont as Grete. Also in the cast were Mary Ellis, Barry Sinclair, Olive Gilbert, Peter Graves, and Anthony Nicholls. It ran intermittently from 1939 to 1949, after being 'bombed out' of its London theatre twice, and was made into a film in 1950.

The first night was, let me repeat, a triumph for all concerned, and Ivor was congratulated by all his friends and fellow-artists. His mother was thrilled, for even she had been as apprehensive as some of his friends when her son had first declared his intention to attempt a large-scale Shakespearean production at Drury Lane. After she had heard his readings at the first few rehearsals her apprehension gave place to joy as she realized the quality of Ivor's interpretation of his great role, and the first night convinced her that he had genius.

The first two weeks at Drury Lane were a resounding success, with packed houses at matinées and evening performances. Theatregoers flocked to see Ivor Novello in Shakespeare, and many of them returned again and again. But real drama was in the air. Drama outside the theatre. The drama of politics and war. This was the period when Mr. Chamberlain was vainly trying to placate Hitler; when Europe was in a turmoil; when England feared that war was any day imminent. The 'September Crisis', with its weeks of shifting fears and uncertainties, dealt a death-blow to the theatre, and even shows which had opened as hits earlier on in the year were suddenly forced to close. Theatre after theatre 'went dark'. Fear was in the air. Newspapers were full of the talk of war, air-raid shelters were dug in Hyde Park, and it became obvious to Novello and his advisers, as the third week opened to hardly any audience at all, that they would have to bring their glorious venture to a close. Thus, at the end of three weeks, this magnificent and heart-warming production of Shakespeare, one of the finest seen on the London stage for twenty years, had to come off. Like so many other plays, *Henry V* could not weather the storm of 'The Crisis', and Ivor himself wrote the notice which was posted up inside the stage door announcing that the play must end. He did so with a heavy heart. Originally it had been planned to present *Henry V* for a ten weeks' season, to be followed by *Much Ado About Nothing, As You Like It,* and possibly *Romeo and Juliet,* but the international situation curtailed the whole project, and more than five hundred people were put out of work.

Novello himself had put £15,000 into the play, which he presented jointly with Tom Arnold, and he lost all of it. Arnold had first been associated with Ivor when Tom presented the tour of *Crest of the Wave* during the spring and summer of 1938. When Ivor told him of his ambition to put on *Henry V*, Arnold immediately offered to finance it with him. For this gesture Novello will always be grateful to Arnold, who has since collaborated with Ivor on the presentation of all his musical plays from *The Dancing Years* right up to *King's Rhapsody* and *Gay's the Word*.

As the *Evening Standard* pointed out: 'This production was successful, houses were good, and bookings extremely encouraging. But with the growth of the fear of war, the public did not want to see a play that dramatized war almost from the start to the finish. The only real applause was given to passages referring to peace.' Undoubtedly hysteria was in the air, and *Henry V* was only one of the casualties of that memorable period in Britain's history.

'I do not regret putting on *Henry V*,' said Ivor. 'I had been wanting to do it for fifteen years, and the fact that I personally lost a good deal of money did not really upset me. I was only sorry that so many people were thrown out of work, and that Drury Lane was forced to "go dark" after only three weeks. But I am glad I did it. I worked night and day for months on my performance as the King, and I am gratified and rather touched that the critics were so kind to me. Perhaps in a year or two I may attempt Shakespeare again, either in London or at Stratford-on-Avon, where I have long wanted to have the opportunity to act.'

Thus ended an historic period in Ivor Novello's truly amazing career.

What would he do next?

14

'The Dancing Years'

'It is difficult to get perspective right at close range. But future stage historians will assign to Ivor Novello a most important position in the theatre of the middle twentieth century. For at a time when, through no fault of its own, inspiration and achievement languished under the drain of two world wars, Ivor Novello was there to keep the flag flying, to keep the home fires burning, and to give distinction, quality, and talent to the stage, and joyous, happy memories to millions of playgoers.'—*W. Macqueen-Pope.*

IVOR NOVELLO's name will always be associated with 'Keep the Home Fires Burning', *The Rat, Glamorous Night* and *The Dancing Years.* The latter, the fourth in his list of hit musical shows, which began with *Glamorous Night* and has continued up to *King's Rhapsody,* is one of the most colossal stage successes in history. Commencing its career in 1939, it ran almost continuously in London and the provincial cities for nearly ten years. And at this moment the film version is continuing to delight millions.

How did he come to create it? Let Ivor speak for himself*:

'I started writing *The Dancing Years* in Liverpool while I was on tour in *Crest of the Wave* in 1938. I had been to Venice, not Vienna, for my holiday, and had been very moved and shocked by a story I had heard from an old friend of mine who had gone into his favourite gramophone shop in Vienna and found himself unable to buy any records of music

* *Radio Times,* December 16th, 1949.

of any of the famous Viennese composers who had Jewish blood. This, of course, was after the Nazis had occupied Vienna, and it occurred to me to wonder what would have happened to me if, as a composer of popular music, I had also been Viennese and of Jewish descent. In this conjecture Rudi Kleber, the composer of *The Dancing Years,* came to life.

'Also in the company of *Crest of the Wave* was an enchanting little girl named Roma Beaumont, playing the Dorothy Dickson part, and I remember asking her suddenly if she could play a girl of twelve. She informed me that she thought she could do it—as long as the lighting was good! The lighting must have been very good at Drury Lane in 1939, because the little girl of twelve came on to the stage, danced her way into the hearts of the first-night audience, and—as they say—stopped the show "cold", twice. Also—and this is a very big also—I had always wanted to follow up Mary Ellis's fine triumph in *Glamorous Night* with another part where she could show her fine range of acting and exceptional singing, and it seemed to me that a Viennese prima-donna in the early 1900's would be ideal for her. I further reflected that it might be a good angle that the public should see a composer playing a composer, and that therefore when they heard my music on the stage they would subconsciously identify it with that of Rudi Kleber, and thus give an air of reality to the play.

'The play ran to big houses until the war broke out, and then there was a very sad Thursday night at Drury Lane when, instead of there being the usual £700 to £800 in the house, there was exactly £35. I remember going down to the footlights at the end of the first act and addressing the scanty audience and saying that I did want the last night of *The Dancing Years* to be a happy occasion, and would the people up in the gallery and in the circles come down to the stalls and cheer us up. But I am afraid that all the cast and most of the audience were in tears at the final curtain because we all felt not only that it was the premature end of a play that looked as though it would run for at least two years at Drury

Lane, but that it was the end of the theatre, the end of us, and, in fact, the end of civilization. As I drove down to the country through the first-time blacked-out streets I felt that I might easily never go through a stage door again. But hope springs eternal, and such is the resilience of the human mind and such was the courage of Mr. Tom Arnold that exactly twelve months later, at the Palace Theatre, Manchester, the full original Drury Lane production of *The Dancing Years,* with nearly all the original members of the cast, started off on—believe it or not—a ten years' career!

'I think it was shock tactics that did the trick. The provincial public were not expecting anything more in their particular theatres than shows with one set and a few characters. Suddenly *The Dancing Years* burst upon them in all its pre-war glory, and hundreds of theatregoers assured me it had made them feel a new hope that things were not quite so bad as they seemed. People flocked to the play in thousands and thousands. After a tour of eighteen months it occurred to Mr. Arnold and myself that we might risk a short season in London. The "short season" proved to be two years and three months at the Adelphi, and only finished when those charming "doodle-bugs" closed practically all the theatres. So back on tour for several months. Then, when *The Dancing Years* company returned to London to play *Perchance To Dream,* Barry Sinclair—just released from the Air Force—took up the part of Rudi Kleber, which he played practically to the end of the tour.

'Of all my plays, *The Dancing Years* has proved to be the one that could go back and back again to the various cities. It has played Manchester, for example, eight times, and I sometimes wonder whether it is not the nostalgia that comes when we remember the time of mutual danger that brings people so often to see it.

'And now it has been made into a film, with Dennis Price playing my part, and with an admirable musical arrangement by Louis Levy. This music will be heard over the air on Christmas Eve, when the play is broadcast with six of the original members of the 1939 cast—Mary Ellis, Roma

Beaumont, Olive Gilbert, Peter Graves, Anthony Nicholls, and myself. It has been a great joy to all of us to be able to feel not only are we still alive and kicking after ten years, but that the broadcast almost cancels out that depressing evening at Drury Lane in the autumn of 1939.'

Yes, indeed, *The Dancing Years* had an incredibly long run. Leontine Sagan again produced, with Joseph Carl as designer, Freddie Carpenter and Suria Magito as choreographers, orchestrations by Charles Prentice and Harry Acres, and lyrics by Christopher Hassall. Ivor, Mary Ellis, Roma Beaumont, Olive Gilbert, Peter Graves and Anthony Nicholls all enjoyed great personal successes. The Press called *The Dancing Years* 'Novello's Greatest Musical'—and the public agreed. In early 1939 it commenced a ten-year career through the ups-and-downs of war to the first turbulent years of peace. From March 1939 until October of that year it was a solid success at Drury Lane. Then the outbreak of war, which closed so many London shows, brought Novello's fourth great musical play to its undeserved conclusion, and shortly afterwards Drury Lane Theatre, that great playhouse of memories, was taken over by Basil Dean as the Headquarters of ENSA. As W. Macqueen-Pope states in his book about Drury Lane: 'Thus ended, for the duration of the war, the history of Drury Lane as a theatre. Its last stage had been one of real glory, thanks to the genius of Ivor Novello. He had proved to be the man the grand old playhouse wanted.'

For more than five years Drury Lane was no longer a part of the active London Theatre; it reopened in 1946 with Noël Coward's ill-fated musical play *Pacific 1860,* which starred Mary Martin and Graham Payn. All the London theatres had closed immediately the war broke out, but one by one they began to reopen, until finally most of the West End playhouses were giving regular performances, commencing rather earlier in the evenings than in pre-war days. With *The Dancing Years* off, Ivor marked time for a short while before producing his new play. On the night that the Palladium reopened with *The Little Dog Laughed* in early October, he went to the show with Beatrice Lillie, Lloyd Williams and Robert Andrews. Flanagan and Allen, the stars of the show, spotted Ivor during one of their numbers, and, amid cheers from an excited audience, Bud persuaded him and Bea Lillie to come up on the stage and sing 'Any Umbrellas', the hit song of the revue.

By the time Drury Lane had taken its important place in the war effort, the ever-active Novello had written a light comedy which he at first called *Second Helping*. He himself played Justin, an impecunious journalist peer who falls in love with the famous Felicity just at the moment when she discovers that, instead of being the richest young woman in the world, she is penniless. In order to help her win back her former husband, Raymond, Justin agrees to pretend to be engaged to her, with the usual amorous complications. It opened at the Lyric on April 10th, 1940, after a few months on tour, under the new title of *Ladies Into Action*. By this time the critics and public had grown rather attached to the Ivor Novello of the big, glamorous musical (it had been more than two years since *Comedienne,* his last 'straight' play), and *Ladies Into Action* was not particularly well received. As Philip Page remarked in the *Daily Mail*: —

'After his recent concern with very-large-scale musical productions at Drury Lane, together with a shot at *Henry V* at that same theatre, this little bedroom comedy must have seemed small beer; to Mr. Ivor Novello it is a pleasant tipple nonetheless. It develops at times into something more exciting than beer, but never, however, becomes champagne.'

Ivor, Lilli Palmer as Felicity (the role played on the tour by lovely Dorothy Dickson), Martin Walker as Raymond, Maidie Andrews, Finlay Currie, Peter Graves and Kenneth Carten all gave excellent performances, though the gem of the evening, as the *Daily Telegraph* pointed out, was Isabel Jeans' scintillating comedy portrayal as Mrs. Venables, which critic W. A. Darlington described as 'a really witty piece of acting'.

Norman Hartnell designed the really ravishing clothes, and Harold French's slick production made this into a brisk, lively show. As a comedy it was not perhaps in the same class as *I Lived With You,* but it had no pretensions, and was merely a pleasant, frivolous piece of light entertainment. As such it was a success.

As usual the last word lies with James Agate. In the *Sunday Times* he gave his opinion: —

'I am a Novello fan. For this reason—that the major works of this entertaining writer-composer-actor satisfy my anti-Goethe complex. Give him a piano, a love affair, and some Dolomites, and here are Gipfeln, but no Ruth. On the other hand, the non-musical or Thackerayan side of Mr. Novello satisfies me less. His *Ladies Into Action* is a long sustained essay in—how shall I put it?—feminine raillery. It is only fair to say that this is relieved by some wit, or by something which under stage pressure passes for wit. The piece has the assistance of Lilli Palmer's platinum incandescence and Miss Isabel Jeans' sense of glittering enormity. I find this actress unfailingly amusing, largely because she is herself enormously amused. Mr. Novello is excellent. The piece itself? It is one of those comedies in which everybody does a great deal of getting into bed, and nobody seems to get out of it!'

By the time the play had settled down into a pleasurably successful run, however, the period of the 'phoney war' was over, and the first shock tactics of the Nazis had had an effect. Holland and Belgium fell to the storm troops, and the remnants of a gallant British army were rescued from Dunkirk in a memorable expedition which will go down in history. The Dunkirk disaster left the English people stunned. Talk of 'invasion' was in the air. England faced her greatest crisis since the time of Napoleon. Nobody went to the theatres or cinemas. Everyone stayed at home by the radio, awaiting the latest news of the movements of Hitler's armies into France.

Just as the outbreak of war had closed *The Dancing Years,* so the events of this depressing period closed *Ladies Into Action.* Understandably, the play began to do badly, and Novello took it off after it had played to half-empty houses.

During the rehearsals of this play Ivor had given several troop concerts at the piano with Olive Gilbert, playing songs from his various shows. He continued to do this after the play was off, while at the same time rehearsing a revival of his best comedy, *I Lived With You.*

In June he went on a very successful three-months' tour of the provincial cities with this play, and repeated his personal triumph as that extraordinary character, Felix, the White Russian prince, in a cast which included Elisabeth Allen, Hilary Allen, Maidie Andrews, Minnie Rayner and Eliot Makeham. (Both Minnie and Eliot, of course, had been members of the original 1932 cast.) Through the fateful summer of 1940 Ivor continued to tour, returning to London just in time to be bombed out in the 'blitz'.

I Lived With You was playing the King's Theatre, Hammersmith, on August 26th, when there was an all-night raid on London. The noise was deafening, and at the end of the performance Ivor told the audience that he and his company would continue until the next morning, if necessary. Most of the audience remained inside the theatre rather than go home during one of the worst raids of 1940, and Ivor and the others played the piano, danced, and sang songs with the theatregoers until the raid had ceased. Novello left the stage at six o'clock in the morning! This was one of many such incidents during the war years. The following week they were due to play at Wimbledon Theatre, but it was hit by a bomb and the performances were cancelled. Disheartened, Novello brought the tour to a close. The war was really on with a vengeance. Only a dozen London theatres remained open, and things began to look very black.

In 1940 Madame Novello Davies published her autobiography, *The Life I Have Loved,* and Ivor contributed an amusing Foreword, written during an all-night raid on London: —

'In writing this Foreword to my Mother's Book—the capital letters are used to emphasize the prominence which her Book has had in all our lives for the past year—I wish to state that I have not read what comes after. By the time the Book is published I shall, of course, have read it, but by then it will be too late—and just as well; for why should I possibly throw the cold water of criticism on something that has been such a labour of love?

'If she has been too indulgent towards me, her son, I can only bless her for it. If she thinks that my plays are the best of all plays, far from allowing my natural modesty to delete those glowing opinions, I can only wish that she were the dramatic critic of every leading newspaper.

'My first recollection of my mother is a glowing face, a mass of black hair, a glittering dress, and an exquisite smell, bending over my cot before going off to conduct one of her innumerable concerts—and, like as not, swishing me out of my cot to go to the concert with her. My present view of her is still a glowing face, with masses of white hair, a glittering dress, and still the same exquisite smell; but the positions are reversed. I bend over her and whisk her off to the theatre where I am acting.

'No! I think it much better that I don't read the book. I might question too much, which is apt to make a moving picture stand still, and reduce emotions to mathematics.

'My father, I know, would have been the ideal collaborator. He went through all her earlier triumphs with her, and didn't mind her calling him, just occasionally, when she wanted to spread her wings too far, 'a wet blanket', so long as the blanket was there to keep her warm.

'Her life has been curiously selfless—she has never saved a penny—and, in addition to having no sense of money at all, she has a sound conviction that what is hers is also somebody else's. Some years ago it was calculated that she had given hundreds of thousands of singing lessons, and I feel quite sure that each lesson—even if it didn't turn the pupil into a Melba or Caruso—sent her or him away with a better knowledge of how to live.

'Any kind of adventurous spirit I have comes direct from her, but I have also a leavening of caution from my father, which I suppose is the reason that I don't contemplate re-building the Crystal Palace and in each corner producing six different plays with a cast of at least six hundred people!

'I know there will be many names mentioned in this book that cannot have any interest for the general public, but if mother were asked to leave one out she would exclaim: "What! Leave out dear old So-and-so?" I might shrewdly reply that her dear "So-and-so" will probably buy the book to see his name in it, and she would then exclaim: "Oh, no! I am giving a copy to him!" which, in a nutshell, explains the character of the authoress of this book, also the authoress of her son who writes this Foreword with trepidation and deep and abiding love.'

★

Summer 1940, with the West End virtually closed down by the raids, was no time to plan a new London production, as Ivor and Tom Arnold both agreed. Consequently they made plans to revive *The Dancing Years* for an extensive tour of Great Britain. Little did they realize what an experience was in store. So eager was the British public to get a glimpse of Novello in the large-scale musical hit from the celebrated Drury Lane that when Arnold began to arrange booking he found that with ease he could book a tour of no less than eighteen months! In the bigger cities, like Manchester, where they had a triumphant opening, Edinburgh, Glasgow, Birmingham, and Leeds, seasons of from four to six weeks were booked, and, even so, the show returned to play these cities as often as six and seven times. Novello's 'Grand Tour', as it became known, swept through the country to riotous receptions everywhere. In his role of Rudi, the half-Jewish composer who finally becomes a victim of Nazi persecution in Austria—a contemporary theme tragically all too familiar—Ivor repeated his Drury Lane success in dozens of towns in the British Isles. He spent a year and a half on tour—and it was an amazing and eventful experience.

The tour was not all glamour, however. Difficulties of transport and accommodation, coupled with the inconveniences of the total black-out, made the lives of the company far from easy. Actors and dancers were suddenly called-up, and understudies played at a few days' notice. It was chaotic—but not one performance was missed. In some towns members of the cast had to sleep on the floors of schools and church halls—and even police stations. In other towns the only accommodation was several miles from the centre of the city, and meant a long and tiring journey in the black-out after the evening's performance. In some cases transport facilities were almost negligible after theatre time, and some of the company had to walk all the way home if they were unlucky enough to miss the last bus. Long train journeys in the black-out, endless hold-ups, the nightmare of Sunday travel, shortage of food, lack of rest in trains and 'digs'—all this made life difficult. But the shows always went on, the company was always fresh and sparkling. Ivor and his cast did a grand war-time job, and thousands upon thousands of people forgot the war for a few hours to sink into the luxury of watching a love story superbly told and sung.

'I have nothing but praise for my company during that long, long tour', Ivor told me. 'And I want you to find some space in your book to mention their patience, their uncomplaining and ever-cheerful attitude throughout all the difficulties of a week-by-week tour through the winter black-out. They made the whole thing seem like an adventure. They really enjoyed all the performances, no matter under what conditions, and as a consequence the audiences simply "ate it up", for this enjoyment was communicated to them. For me it was a great moment when I called the company on to the stage after the performance one night and told them that we were not closing down after the long tour, but were going to present a London revival of *The Dancing Years* at the Adelphi Theatre. How they cheered! How pleased they were to be going back to their home town. And how happy I was to give them the good news. We had been out of London from September 1940 until February 1942. Now our show, which had delighted soldiers and civilians for almost eighteen months, was to have another crack at entertaining London's millions.'

The Dancing Years was the most magnificently-staged and the most lavishly-presented musical play which had ever been produced outside London. It made show business history. It played to packed theatres all over England—became part of the war-time scene. Every soldier took his wife or sweetheart to see it, not only once, but time and time again. It became an institution. It was Novello's war effort. It was a way in which Novello, too old for active service in the Forces, could 'do his bit'. Untiringly he worked through hundreds and hundreds of performances. He did not spare himself, and his company, realizing this, did not spare themselves either. Every night of that spectacular provincial tour was a First Night.

Then came March 1942. Would it run at the Adelphi? Tom Arnold thought so—and the public agreed with him. The Drury Lane show had by that time become a tradition of the theatre, and it opened as a pre-sold 'smash hit'. It ran solidly until June 1944—a thousand performances at the Adelphi alone*—and only came off because of the flying bomb raids on the Metropolis in the summer of that year. Hitler's new 'secret weapon' emptied the London theatres once again, and Ivor's show was one of the thirty or more theatrical casualities.

While on tour in the autumn of 1940 Ivor wrote a light comedy which he called *Breakaway,* with Peter Graves in mind for one of the leading roles. This play was subsequently presented at Windsor by Novello's 'local' repertory theatre in May 1941, with Graves in the cast, and produced by Oliver Gordon and Ivor. Also in *Breakaway* were Olga Lindo, Avice Landone, Frederick Piper, Edward Sinclair, Bruno Barnabe and Frances Rowe. The latter, who played Princess Ottisnno, was considered by Ivor to be one of the most brilliant young comedy actresses he had ever seen, and they became great

* During this period Novello appeared in dozens of troop concerts on Sundays and during the days while he was acting at the Adelphi in the evenings. In June 1943 C. B. Cochran invited him to play his own song, 'Home Fires', in a War Charities Cavalcade called *Seventy Years of Song,* at the Albert Hall; Ivor shared with George Robey and Violet Loraine the personal success of the show.

friends. The play was not produced in London, and thus achieves the distinction of being the only one of Novello's plays which has not yet reached the West End. Ivor occasionally talked of revising it for London presentation, but nothing has ever come of it.

Frances Rowe has since become known as one of the best of our young actresses. She left Windsor to appear in *They Came to a City,* followed by *The Last of Mrs. Cheyney.* After appearing opposite John Clements in *Marriage à la Mode* at the St. James's in 1946, she went to New York and co-starred with Maurice Evans in Shaw's *Man and Superman,* making one of the biggest personal successes ever scored by a British actress on Broadway. Last year she returned to England to play leading roles with the Old Vic. Company at Bristol. 'I've always wanted to play my original part in a new production of Ivor's *Breakaway*', she told me. 'Maybe I will—some day.'

★

Since the outbreak of war Mary Ellis had been engaged in hospital welfare work; thus the role of Maria Ziegler was played on tour and at the Adelphi by Muriel Barron, who had first come to Ivor's attention when she played a small role in *Glamorous Night.* She subsequently toured as Militza in that play, and Novello had always had a high regard for her ability. Muriel received her big opportunity in the Adelphi revival of *The Dancing Years* (and later appeared in Novello's *Perchance to Dream* at the London Hippodrome in 1945). Franzel was played by Peter Graves (and afterwards very successfully by John Wynyard), while the large cast also included Olive Gilbert, Roma Beaumont, Veronica Brady, Dunstan Hart, Victor Boggetti, Grant Tyler, Gordon Duttson, Orest Orloff and Keith Lester.

Another fine singer, Maria Elsner, formerly a well-known star of the Continental musical stage, began by singing for Muriel Barron at matinées and afterwards took over completely. Miss Elsner (now Lady Fisher) told me that she had never had such a wonderful role as Maria, not even back in

Berlin and Vienna, where she had sung in every kind of operetta and musical play.

'Working with Ivor was a great and wonderful experience,' she went on, 'for not only was he amazingly talented, but he was the most charming, kindly, and sympathetic man in the London theatre. I adored him. My two years in *The Dancing Years* are among the happiest I have ever spent on the stage. Ivor was a genius—but, more than that, he was a genius with a heart as big as the stage of Drury Lane.'

All the members of Novello's companies felt a similar affection and loyalty for him—something not often found in the theatre. One such was Dunstan Hart, a magnificent tenor, who had been a well-known concert singer before he gave an audition to Novello in 1939. He was engaged on the spot to play the part of Ceruti in *The Dancing Years,* and did not miss a single one of the 2,000 performances. He then appeared in *Perchance to Dream* during its entire run at the Hippodrome, and also went on the South African tour.

'I have thoroughly enjoyed my long association with Mr. Novello', wrote Hart.* 'He is a most delightful man, accessible to everybody in the company. He knows what he wants, surrounds himself with talented people, and has time to be kind to absolutely everyone.'

In 1943 Mary Ellis, who had been working up in Scotland with her husband, decided she would like to return to the stage again. At the same time Novello, playing nightly at the Adelphi to packed houses, was working on another ambitious musical, devised on Drury Lane lines, with His Majesty's Theatre in mind for its production. That theatre proved not to be available, however, and *Arc de Triomphe* was produced on the much smaller stage of the Phœnix Theatre. As a consequence the production was thrown out of balance. The spectacle and magnificence seemed lost on the small stage, and it did only average business for a few months before the flying-bomb raids on London finally caused it to close.

Arc de Triomphe, the story of a French prima-donna in the 1900's, featured a one-act opera, *Joan of Arc,* which formed

* *Stage and Cinema,* February 20th, 1948.

part of the play. It gave Mary Ellis magnificent opportunities to prove once more what a wonderful singer she was. With Peter Graves and Raymond Lovell as her leading men, and Elizabeth Welch as Josie, the play opened at the Phœnix Theatre in November 1943, and, as Marie Foret, Mary Ellis made another huge success in a strongly dramatic role which revealed her to be not only a first-rate singer but a very fine actress. (Indeed, when *Arc de Triomphe* closed, Mary joined the Old Vic. Company at Liverpool, and distinguished herself in such plays as *John Gabriel Borkman, Point Valaine* and *The School for Scandal,* before returning to London in the summer of 1945 to appear in Peter Daubeny's presentation of *The Gay Pavilion* at the Piccadilly. Since that play Mary Ellis has built up a new reputation as a serious actress, culminating in her vivid performance opposite Eric Portman in Terence Rattigan's *The Browning Version* at the Phœnix Theatre a year or two ago.)

Arc de Triomphe did not share the same success of Novello's other musical plays for a variety of reasons, but mainly due to the fact that it was staged at the wrong theatre just before the flying-bomb raids commenced.

Even though Ivor's music was as tuneful as ever, his opera *Joan of Arc* musically superb, and Mary Ellis's singing still as lovely as it had been in the *Dancing Years, Arc de Triomphe* did not earn high critical praise, nor achieve the lengthy runs of shows like *Glamorous Night, Crest of the Wave* or *The Dancing Years.** Nevertheless, it established Peter Graves as a new star.

In common with Mary Ellis, Fay Compton, Ursula Jeans, Lilian Braithwaite, Isabel Jeans, Robert Andrews, Dorothy Dickson, Zena Dare, Phyllis Monkman and other well-known stage stars, he had achieved his biggest successes in Novello shows. The son of Baron Graves, Peter played a tiny role in *Glamorous Night* in 1935, after which Novello gave him

* Beverley Baxter, in the *Evening Standard,* summed up the general critical reaction when he wrote: 'One is disappointed that this gifted man did not dare more instead of supplying the mixture as before. The English stage is crying out for arrogance and leadership. Mr. Novello should accept the responsibility of his success and gifts.'

a chance by letting him take over Robert Andrews' part for a time in *Full House* at the Haymarket. Again through Ivor's efforts, Graves was given a larger role in *The Happy Hypocrite,* after which he understudied Novello in *Careless Rapture,* and played his part of Michael several times during the run at Drury Lane. In 1937 he had earned a more important role in *Crest of the Wave,* and was highly praised a year later for his performance as the Dauphin in Novello's production of *Henry V*. He created the role of Franzel in *The Dancing Years* at Drury Lane, appeared in *Ladies Into Action* at the Lyric in 1940, and again played Franzel in the Adelphi revival of *The Dancing Years*. By that time Novello had decided that Peter Graves was ready for stardom, and thereupon gave him the leading role of Pierre Bachelet in *Arc de Triomphe,* since which time Graves has been well known as a stage and screen star. In 1947 he took time off from filming to play one of the leading roles in *We Proudly Present,* his tenth part in a Novello production. Peter was one of the many well-known people in the theatrical profession who wanted me, in this book, to acknowledge their gratitude to Novello for his help and kindness and for giving them the opportunities to develop their careers.

'There is no doubt', Graves told me, 'that every success I may have had in the theatre was due entirely to the encouragement and friendship of Ivor, a great showman and a wonderful and very loyal friend.'

Peter Graves is a typical example of a present-day star who has been encouraged and aided in his career by the man described by everybody as 'the most beloved man in the English theatre'.

★

The raids on London in the summer of 1944 completely paralysed entertainment and the arts. Out of the forty theatres usually functioning in the West End only eight managed to remain open. The London theatre encountered its third great war-time crisis, and Ivor was forced to bring down the final curtain not only on *Arc de Triomphe,* but also on *The*

Dancing Years, which had been playing to diminishing houses during the ever-increasing raids. It was with extreme regret that Ivor broke up his loyal five-year-old company, many of the members of which had been in the original production at Drury Lane, but he promised that he would take out another tour of the play in the winter. In the meantime he had an important appointment to keep—with the British Army in France. Before keeping this, however, he arranged with Basil Dean to send out a company for ENSA called 'Stars of *The Dancing Years',* to give troop concerts in England during his three months' absence. The nucleus of his own Adelphi company formed the new unit, with Barry Sinclair, Muriel Barron, Olive Gilbert and Dunstan Hart heading the cast, and with Lloyd Williams as company manager and general factotum. This tour was very popular and very exciting. Every day 'Lloydie' wrote to Ivor, telling him of the day's performances and events, and Ivor wrote back from the war zone with stories of incidents and adventures behind the British lines in France.

At various times during the war years Ivor had played to audiences of soldiers stationed in many parts of the British Isles, and he had also given scores of troop concerts. Immediately D-Day came, and our armies poured into France and Belgium, he telephoned Basil Dean and asked him if he could take a company across to play in France. At this time several stage and screen stars were forming units to tour the war zones, including Rex Harrison and Lilli Palmer, Deborah Kerr and Stewart Granger (in *Gaslight*), and Richard Greene and Patricia Medina (in *Arms and the Man*). Ivor, at first, wanted to take a production of *I Lived With You,* but finally he decided on Frank Vosper's dramatization of Agatha Christie's *Love From A Stranger,* long one of his favourite plays. Daphne Rye produced and also played in it, with Diana Wynyard as the unsuspecting wife, Margaret Rutherford (direct from her three-year run as Madame Arcati in Noël Coward's *Blithe Spirit*), Robert Andrews, whose last appearance in a Novello production had been in the 1940 tour of *Full House,* Esma Cannon and Joan Benham. Ivor played

Bruce Lovell, the handsome, charming, homicidal maniac—a part he revelled in after years of playing the sensitive Austrian composer—and his tour of Normandy and Belgium, which lasted from June to September, was for him a great and satisfying experience. He really 'felt' that he was doing something important, something right on the scene of action as it were. He threw himself into the work of entertaining the troops with renewed vigour.

Lionel Grose, a young West End actor, who was an Entertainments Officer in Normandy during the latter part of 1944, assured me that Novello, who did several shows for his units, made an immense personal success, not only as an actor, but as a person. 'His charm and kindness', he stated, 'made itself felt wherever he went.' Most of Novello's soldier-audiences had seen him during the war years as the conventional handsome hero of *The Dancing Years,* and it came as somewhat of a surprise to some of them to realize that the famous matinée idol was also a gifted and versatile actor, and one who made the part of Bruce Lovell in *Love From A Stranger* a fascinating and blood-chilling creation. *Love From A Stranger* brought pleasure to thousands of soldiers in France, and it also gave Ivor a much-needed break from his five-year run. Everywhere he went he was received with enthusiasm by the troops, and the Novello/Wynyard unit successfully played in dozens of towns and camps behind the lines in France and Belgium. Ivor, looking back on a long period of entertaining the public, declared that his Continental tour of the war-front in the autumn of 1944 was his most deeply satisfying experience. He knew, as did all ENSA performers at that time, that their job of entertaining was in every sense vital, contributing in no small measure to the morale and well-being of the Services.

Within an hour of landing in Normandy they had given a performance on an airfield, to an audience of airmen. Subsequently they played in theatres, barns, town-halls, schools, in the open air, on the stages of bombed-out play-houses, and in the fields and on the beaches, often giving as many as four different performances in one day.

Describing Novello's landing in Normandy, playwright Alan Melville* relates the following: —

'On a Saturday evening, long before Normandy settled down to being the green and pleasant land which it is to-day, an ancient bus rattled and bumped its way up the road from the Allied beach-head to a camp just outside Bayeux. Out of it and into the white dust which was inseparable from all Normandy traffic there stepped Mr. Ivor Novello and a company of mummers who were about to perform *Love From A Stranger* for the edification of the troops. They had had a terrible crossing; they were tired, dirty, and justifiably tetchy; and their tempers were not improved by finding Mr. Arthur Macrae and myself, looking rather spruce in our best uniforms, waiting to greet them and to pinch their cigarettes. They were due to begin, on the following Monday, a long and very arduous tour of the play in the exquisite little municipal theatre in Bayeux (it was, in fact, the only proper theatre they played in—usually their performances were what are known rather loosely as *alfresco*). Novello had hardly got the dust out of his eyes when an R.A.F. officer suggested that it might be a jolly good show to give an extra performance on the Sunday. The Novello smile flashed and the Novello charm dispelled the dust. Certainly, by all means; what an excellent idea; nothing would give him greater pleasure. 'Wizard!' said the officer, and went off thinking what a remarkably nice chap Novello was—an opinion shared by anyone who has either met Novello for a minute or known him for years. On the Monday, and each day thereafter, the company played *Love From A Stranger* at least twice, and frequently thrice, a day. It is not an easy play from the actor's point of view, and it is a tricky piece to put over with aircraft zooming low overhead either through hostile intent or friendly exuberance. At the end of every performance Novello stepped forward, announced that it was high time we had a little music, and settled himself at an upright piano as ancient as the bus, and making much the same kind of noises. There he stayed for an hour or longer; playing his hit of the

* *The Sketch,* September 14th, 1949.

First World War—'Keep the Home Fires Burning'—playing a little thing he'd just written and which had not then been heard in London (its eventual title—you may have heard of it—was 'We'll Gather Lilacs'); playing and singing anything and everything the boys wanted. Ivor has basked in the adoration of audiences for many years; he can never have had a more grateful audience than those in Normandy, nor an audience to whom he gave greater pleasure.'

For eight weeks Novello's company appeared almost non stop, finally landing up in Brussels, where they gave three exciting 'farewell performances' before regretfully setting off for England. Ivor would have stayed there for several months, but for the fact that Tom Arnold had by that time booked yet another tour of *The Dancing Years,* and the company was standing by awaiting Ivor's return from the Continent. The livelihood of hundreds depended upon him and it was necessary for him to don Tyrolean costume once more.

As before, the tour was a huge success, and it obviously could have run quite happily throughout 1945 and 1946, and also enjoyed another lengthy London season. Ivor, however, had been turning over an idea for another musical since *Arc de Triomphe* had come off, and the tour was finally brought to an end so that he could go straight into his new musical play. Titled *Perchance to Dream,* it opened at the London Hippodrome in April 1945 with most of the company from *The Dancing Years* in it.

By the time that the new show had settled down as a hit at the Hippodrome, Tom Arnold, in response to insistent requests, decided to revive *The Dancing Years* yet again. There was life still left in the play. After a long tour it opened in 1947 at the Casino Theatre, produced by Freddie Carpenter, with Barry Sinclair as Rudi, Jessica James and Nicolette Roeg, and stayed there for another successful and lengthy season, while Novello himself was playing to packed houses round the corner, at the Hippodrome.

Sinclair is another protégé of Novello's. After appearing in several West End successes, he played Ivor's role, Anthony Allen, in *Glamorous Night* when it went on tour in 1936. He also played this part in the revival of Novello's first musical play at the Coliseum Theatre in May 1936. During 1937 and 1938 Barry Sinclair toured again in *Glamorous Night,* and afterwards as Michael (Novello's part) in *Careless Rapture.* He built up a big reputation in the provinces as the star of Novello shows. In 1940 he again toured, this time with Ivor himself, in *The Dancing Years*; Ivor played Rudi, of course, with Barry as Franzel. When this play returned to London and opened at the Adelphi in May 1942, Barry shared the role of Rudi with Ivor, first playing for Ivor when he became seriously ill through strain and overwork in June 1942. Afterwards he played it at matinées and for many other performances while Novello was on holiday. In fact, Barry Sinclair has become completely identified with Novello's heroes, and his entire career during the past dozen years—apart from several years in the R.A.F.—has been involved with various of Ivor's plays, culminating in his starring appearance in 1946 as Rudi in the Casino revival of *The Dancing Years.* When that revival ended, Sinclair once more took the play out into the provincial cities, and only ceased playing Rudi in 1949.

Sinclair admits that all his success and stardom is directly responsible to Novello, who encouraged him and aided his career in every possible way since the tour of *Glamorous Night.* A year or so ago Ivor acted as best man at Barry's wedding to actress Nicolette Roeg, who had appeared opposite Sinclair in *The Dancing Years* on tour and at the Casino. Like Peter Graves, Olive Gilbert, Robert Newton, Elisabeth Welch, Vanessa Lee, Walter Crisham, Roma Beaumont, Maria Elsner, Muriel Barron and Jean Webster Brough, among others, Sinclair achieved his initial success in one of Novello's productions. He is only one of the many players on the British stage who are only too anxious to declare that they 'owe our start in the theatre to Ivor'.

15

'Perchance to Dream'

'I agree with Sir Herbert Tree when he said that the whole business of the stage was to create illusion.'—*Ivor Novello.*

COMPLETED on the 1944–45 tour of *The Dancing Years, Perchance to Dream* opened in the fifth year of the war. As the great Hippodrome curtain rose on the opening scene, Ivor turned to Robert Andrews and said quietly: 'With luck, this will be our Victory Production.'

He was lucky enough to be right, for shortly after the wonderfully successful first night came VE Day, followed by VJ Day, both celebrated wildly throughout Britain and the world. On VE Night the packed house at the Hippodrome stood and cheered Novello and his company for a full half-hour when the show was over. London was wild with excitement. This was the end of a long and terrible European war. Here was victory at last!

After that thrilling Victory Night performance Ivor and the rest of his company held a great celebration party in The Flat. As Ivor leaned out of his window high above the Aldwych and looked down on the cheering, excited throngs below in the Strand, his mind must have gone back to the Armistice Night of the First World War, when, as a young man, he had watched another Armistice being celebrated in Stockholm, several hundred miles from home. Twenty-seven years separated those two momentous happenings. This time it was a much happier occasion. This time he was surrounded by all his friends and all the people he loved most dearly (the one exception, of course, being his beloved mother, who had died three years before). Here he was, one of the greatest men on the English stage; he and his plays had somehow survived the terrible war, and, in spite of being 'bombed off' twice, and experiencing several anxious moments, he had come through it all safely. A magnificent new Ivor Novello production was holding the London stage at the moment of the greatest victory of all time, just as a Novello production had been running at Drury Lane when the war had broken out. That was somehow right and proper. His shows had kept going through 'blitz' and black-out, had toured the British Isles from end to end, had been seen and enjoyed by millions —literally millions—and had been an incomparable aid in maintaining morale during those difficult years. His shows had been an integral part of the war effort; now he was thrilled, proud, and happy to know that his new play was part of the Victory Celebrations. That night was one that he long remembered.

Actually, as Ivor once confessed to me, *Perchance to Dream* almost never got produced at all. For some time he had envisaged a romance which took place in and about a stately home of England called 'Hunter's Moon', first in the early days of the nineteenth century, then during the middle of that century, and finally at the present time. In a memorable last scene the ghosts of those who have known it and loved it gather in the great hall of 'Hunter's Moon' while the two star-crossed lovers come together at last. That was the outline of his new work; he had mapped out a first draft, and he himself was to play three parts. First, a Regency Buck, heavily in debt and paying off his bills by being a highwayman on the side. Secondly, a Victorian composer, who marries the wrong woman, and at length falls in love again, only to be parted from his true love. Thirdly, a modern counterpart of both the buck and the musician, who finds happiness with the modern counterpart of the girl he has loved and lost in former generations. This was roughly the basis of the play with which Ivor planned to follow *The Dancing Years*.

James Agate, for many years one of Novello's advisers and admirers, warned him against putting on a lavish musical production, especially a costume play. 'They won't like it', he said. 'You will find that even a first-class cast, charming music, and a good plot won't save the show. What the modern generation apparently wants is plenty of hot music and trans-atlantic rhythm.'

Ivor was a little depressed by Agate's opinion, for it was one which was greatly valued in theatrical circles, and he went home that evening from the Café Royal slightly dispirited. At any rate, he decided he would go away for a week's holiday to the seaside, to work out his plans and think things over. Perhaps Agate was right. And then, again, perhaps he was not. Should he continue with his play—or start on another? The decision needed careful consideration.

Ivor had always liked Brighton, that gay seaside town in Sussex where the Prince Regent once lived, and where the Regency architecture and wonderful old buildings remain as a permanent reminder of Brighton's colourful past. One evening, in the Royal Pavilion, that extraordinary building built by 'Prinny', Ivor went for a walk through the Royal Apartments and into the lovely Royal Banqueting Hall. It was here, in these great rooms, that he first captured the real spirit of the musical play which had already formed itself in his mind. Here, where the former generation of Englishmen had gathered to wine and dine under the hospitable roof of the Prince Regent, he finally decided that his friend Agate was wrong. He made up his mind there and then to risk everything on a costly and spectacular new production linked with the past. A soldier, an ordinary English Tommy on leave was the deciding factor in convincing Novello that he was right.

With his girl friend, the soldier was having a look round the State Apartments. Like Ivor, they were both vastly impressed with the magnificence of the Banqueting Hall, the beautiful paintings, and the notable architecture of a bygone age. 'They don't build wonderful places like this nowadays, do they?' remarked the soldier to his girl.

That decided the playwright—for he was certain that if a Regency building could appeal to a young English soldier and his girl, then a Regency musical production, with a tremendous cast, splendid costumes and an original musical score, would provide entertainment for his family, his friends, and himself.

Straightaway Novello went back to his hotel on the Brighton front, picked up the first few completed pages of the script of *Perchance to Dream,* and went on writing far into the night. He completed the play during the last weeks of the Adelphi run of *The Dancing Years,* revising it while on tour in France with *Love From A Stranger*. The final touches were put to the score while he was touring in *The Dancing Years* again during Christmas, 1944, and complete details of the new production were eventually mapped out in the early part of 1945. When *Perchance to Dream* had been running for nearly two years, James Agate admitted that he had obviously been wrong. The public had made the final decision, and obviously the Novello formula, as indicated by his host of successes from *Glamorous Night* to *Perchance to Dream,* just could not fail.

Novello's sixth musical, produced by Jack Minster, with décor by Joseph Carl and choreography by Frank Staff and Keith Lester, opened at the Hippodrome to a rapturous reception. Not only was it a triumph for Ivor, who gave excellent performances in all three of his roles, but it meant personal success for Roma Beaumont, the famous Grete of *The Dancing Years,* Olive Gilbert, one of the finest contraltos on the English stage, Margaret Rutherford, who had accepted the part while touring with Ivor in *Love From a Stranger,* Zena Dare, Muriel Barron, Robert Andrews and Dunstan Hart. All the dramatic critics and theatre columnists assured their readers that *Perchance to Dream* was obviously set for a record-breaking run—and they were right. It could easily have run as long as *The Dancing Years* if Novello had wanted it to do so, but after it neared its fourth year he began to long for a change, and the prospect of a South African tour, which he had been offered, appealed to him strongly. This, he thought, would give him and his company the break they all deserved, and it would also give him a chance to work on his seventh musical play, which he intended to base—somewhat loosely—on the real-life story of Rumania's Prince Carol and his devoted Madame Lupescu, afterwards Princess Helena.

Perchance to Dream did not have an empty seat at the Hippodrome from April 1945 right until the end of 1947,* when Novello took it off while it was still playing to packed houses. It had become a theatrical byword. Just as *The Dancing Years* had been *the* show of the war years, the *Chu Chin Chow* of the Second World War, so *Perchance to Dream* became *the* post-war musical play. Eager for real relaxation after five long years of war, the British people celebrated the victory by flocking to the Hippodrome in their thousands, but not only did they do so during Victory Year, but they continued to do so during 1946 and 1947. The thousands of soldiers who had had their first contact with a Novello show while on leave during the war, or had seen him at a troop show or concert in Britain or overseas, were anxious to renew acquaintance with the man whose shows had helped to brighten those grim years. *Perchance to Dream,* spectacular, colourful, and tuneful, with its lilting songs like the famous 'We'll Gather Lilacs',† was the ideal mass entertainment for the post-war years of peace and adjustment. It became an institution. One of the best-known theatre stories going the rounds when the play was in its third

* In 1946 Claude Soman presented Novello's production of Somerset Maugham's *Our Betters,* at the Playhouse, with Dorothy Dickson, Nuna Davey, Cathleen Nesbitt, Peter Willes, Lois Maxwell, George Woodbridge, Anthony Hankey, John Allen, Peter Madren and Max Adrian, who also directed. Décor was by Cecil Beaton.

† This song was first suggested to him by his great friends Alfred Lunt and Lynn Fontanne, who so admired his lilac trees while staying at 'Red Roofs' in 1944 (when they were in London to appear in *There Shall Be No Night,* at the Aldwych). Straightaway he sat down and composed the song. During his tour in France and Belgium he 'tried it out' on the troops when giving concerts between performances. They liked it so much that Ivor had Christopher Hassall set lyrics to it for *Perchance to Dream*. It became *the* hit song of the years 1945 and 1946.

year concerned a man whose friends rang him up at Easter and asked him and his wife to join them at a party on the Monday.

'Oh, I'm afraid we cannot do that', he exclaimed. 'You see, we always go to see Ivor Novello in *Perchance to Dream* on Easter Monday!'

Nevertheless, Novello brought it to an end eventually. With African Consolidated Theatres he arranged to take the complete production, bag and baggage, to South Africa for a ten weeks' season. For nine years he had not been out of England, except for the ENSA tour of France and Belgium, and he was longing to travel abroad once more. South Africa and sunshine! He could hardly wait.

★

In the spring of 1947, while Ivor was appearing in *Perchance to Dream,* his new play, *We Proudly Present,* was produced at the Duke of York's, under the management of Peter Daubeny, thus giving Ivor the distinction of having three plays running simultaneously in London, since at that time *The Dancing Years* was also being revived at the Casino. There was an interesting story behind the production of this play. Before the war Daubeny, then a young actor with the Liverpool Repertory Company, was introduced to Novello by William Armstrong, the celebrated producer at Liverpool. Daubeny and Novello became great friends, and their friendship continued through the early years of the war, when Daubeny was serving in the Guards. In September 1943 the young man was wounded in the landing at Salerno, as a result of which he lost his forearm. Novello immediately sent him a telegram of sympathy, and, curiously enough, on Daubeny's first night back on leave from Tripoli he went into the Savoy Grill and bumped straight into Ivor. Over dinner the young officer, shortly to be invalided out, discussed his plans for the future, telling Ivor that he intended to go into theatrical management; with one or two fellow-officers he had formed his company, Peter Daubeny Productions, while in the desert, and a nucleus of capital had been obtained. Ivor, with his lengthy experience of management, thereupon made out a rough balance-sheet for the young man on the back of an envelope, working out that Daubeny would need at least £12,000 in the bank before he could safely go into production in the West End of London. In addition, he promised that he would write a play for the new management, and during the next two or three years Novello was always ready to give help and advice to Daubeny. There was a certain amount of opposition to the young management from the established concerns when it first went into production, but Novello was always, as Daubeny declared, 'one hundred per cent helpful'.

After producing *The Gay Pavilion,* by William Lipscomb, *Jacobowsky and the Colonel,* by S. N. Behrman, *But For the Grace of God,* by Frederick Lonsdale, and *Power Without Glory,* by Michael Clayton Hutton, Peter Daubeny had a year or so later become accepted as a new and enterprising young producer. He reminded Ivor of his promise, and Novello agreed to have his new play ready as quickly as possible. Finally, in late 1946, he rang up Daubeny and told him, 'I have written your play. Come round and we'll celebrate it'.

We Proudly Present, as Novello's new comedy (his twenty-second play) was called, was not only written for Peter Daubeny, but was about him. It told the story of a young ex-officer and a friend who decide to become theatrical managers, in spite of the opposition of the other West End managements and the general antipathy of theatre owners, the leading stars, and so on. Peter Graves played the part of the young man, with Anthony Forwood as his enthusiastic fellow-officer, and Ivor wrote a part specially for his dear friend Phyllis Monkman, that of on 'old pro' who had found it difficult to obtain work as an actress but gladly joined the two young men as a kind of advisor and mother-confessor. This was a deliciously-written role in which Miss Monkman scored a great personal success, as also did Ena Burrill (who had been in *Crest of the Wave* ten years before) as an established, 'difficult' and slightly passé West End star who had to you that the theatre is not dead, but very much "alive and kicking".'

In all his many years on the stage, during which time he had had some wonderful ovations and memorable first nights, Ivor believed that he had never had such a thoroughly *enjoyable* and altogether happy period in his life as the one he spent in South Africa. It was preceded by an exciting trip to New York, accompanied by Olive Gilbert, Robert Andrews, Gordon Duttson and Lloyd Williams. Then they all flew to Jamaica and spent a five week's holiday there. Ivor even found time to buy himself a house in lovely Montego Bay before flying to Johannesburg with his friends. He followed the Cape Town season with a three weeks' holiday at Hermanus, having renewed acquaintance before that with Vivien Leigh and Laurence Olivier, then on their way out to Australia with the Old Vic. Company. Vivien had, of course, been his choice of leading lady in *The Happy Hypocrite,* and she and Olivier, Gwen Ffrangcon-Davies, Marda Vanne, and Ivor spent a very happy period in Cape Town before the Oliviers continued on their journey. Hermanus, a small town eighty miles from Cape Town, was the country retreat of Gwen Ffrangcon-Davies. She had a delightful house there, in which Ivor, Olive, Bobbie, and Gordon stayed until their departure for Jamaica for another restful stay in Ivor's new house. Then it was back to work for Ivor, back to another extensive period of acting in one play while preparing another.

During Ivor's absence Tom Arnold had booked a long tour of *Perchance to Dream,* and from April 1948 to the January of the following year the popular star visited once more the great provincial theatres which had seen him during the war years in *Ladies Into Action, I Lived With You,* and, of course, *The Dancing Years.* Audiences rushed to welcome their idol back in his new musical, and Ivor was glad to *be* back. On this tour he worked hard on the libretto outline and some of the score of his next show, *King's Rhapsody.* It was a long tour, and by the time it was over, after ten months of continuous work, Ivor was ready for a holiday. He decided to fly to the U.S.A. and relax for a few weeks.

25. *Perchance to Dream,* Novello's sixth musical play, opened at the Hippodrome in the fifth year of the war and ran until the end of 1947, with Ivor playing three roles. Above: as Sir Graham Rodney in the Regency sequence.

26. In June, 1944, Novello took a company organized by E.N.S.A. to play to the troops in France and Belgium. He chose Frank Vosper's *Love From a Stranger*, in which he played the homicidal Bruce Lovell. In this group, taken on the day they landed in Normandy, are Diana Wynyard, Joan Benham, producer Daphne Rye, and Robert Andrews, all members of Novello's company.

27. Olive Gilbert, Gordon Duttson, Ivor, and Bobbie Andrews snapped at the foot of Table Mountain during the South African tour of *Perchance to Dream*, 1947-48.

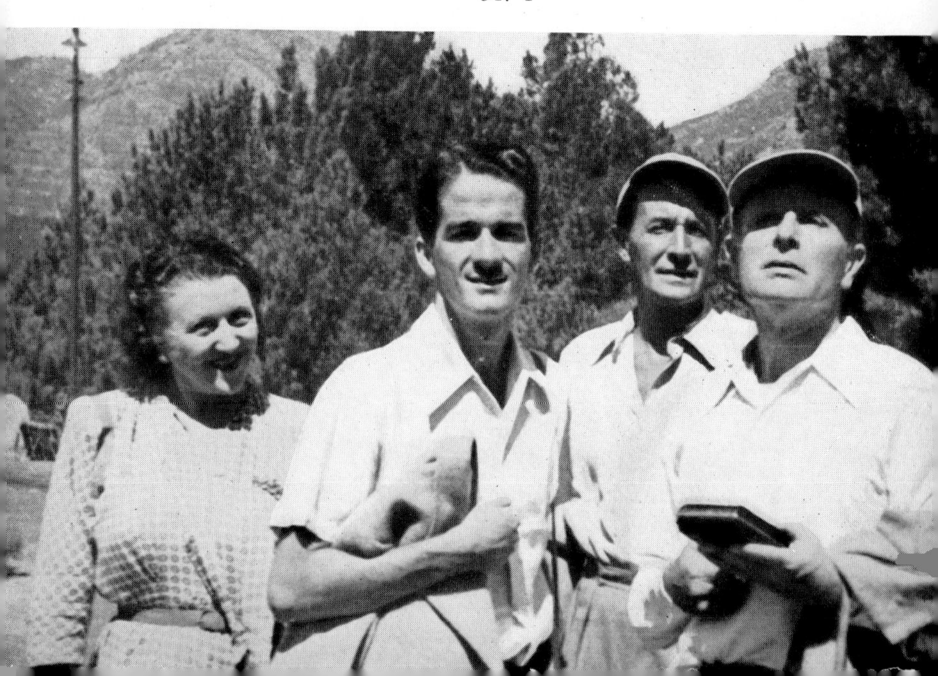

From January to March, Ivor, Bobbie and Zena Dare went to New York for their holiday, followed by several weeks in Montego Bay. (*Perchance to Dream,* however, continued to tour, with Geoffrey Toone taking over Ivor's roles.) 'I just don't know when I'll have a chance to go to my house in Jamaica again', Ivor exclaimed to me. 'It's a wonderful place. The climate is just like California, and the sun-bathing and swimming are superb. I did a lot of work on *King's Rhapsody* during those weeks, and completed it when I was back in London in the summer of 1949.

(Actually Ivor did visit his Jamaica home once more. At Christmas 1950, after fifteen strenuous months in *King's Rhapsody,* he took time off for a holiday at Montego Bay, where he relaxed with his friends in the sunshine. Back in London six weeks later he once more took over his role from Barry Sinclair, who had acted Nikki during his absence. In February Ivor attended the first night of his new musical play, *Gay's the Word,* starring his old friend Cicely Courtneidge, at the Saville. That was to be his last play, his last great hit. Already he was feeling the strain, however. Overwork was beginning to have an effect on his health, and following the performance on March 5th he died after a heart-attack. The news was a terrible shock to millions of people, and his death was felt as a personal blow by everyone in the English Theatre.)

16

'King's Rhapsody'

'Ivor Novello is a creative artist who, despite his vast earnings, delights in self-expression, and does not think in terms of money. That comes to him naturally because he is not only talented but handsome, not only charming but energetic. Six Novellos could stay the American invasion of the London musical stage, because they could automatically pack all the theatres they played in.'—*Hannen Swaffer in 'Illustrated', October 8th, 1949.*

On September 15th, 1949, Ivor Novello's seventh musical play, *King's Rhapsody,* opened at the Palace Theatre, with Ivor, Phyllis and Zena Dare, Vanessa Lee, Robert Andrews, Olive Gilbert, Denis Martin, Victor Boggetti, Gordon Duttson, Michael Anthony and John Palmer. Lyrics were by Christopher Hassall, production by Murray Macdonald, décor by Edward Delaney, costumes by Frederick Dawson, and choreography by Pauline Grant.

'I really think *King's Rhapsody* is the best thing I have ever done,' Novello told me, when he had put the finishing touches to it. 'In my opinion it has the best story, best music, and is the best-constructed of all my musical plays. It is the mixture as before, but I think it is what people want. I hope I am not wrong.'

He need not have worried. The first night of *King's Rhapsody* was an echo of all his other first-nights rolled into one. It had a highly enthusiastic reception, and within twenty-four hours Tom Arnold assured Ivor that advance bookings guaranteed a minimum run of at least a year, with a strong possibility of a two- or three-year run. And his newest musical play proved to be his finest.

Set in Murania (a mythical Central European country) in the latter part of the nineteenth century, *King's Rhapsody* tells the story of Nikki, a young prince, who, as a result of his country's political intrigues, and his disagreements with his mother, the queen, leaves his native city for a life of pleasure in Paris. The years pass, and the prince's father dies. He is now king, and the prime minister and the scheming queen journey to Paris to persuade the new monarch to leave his mistress and return to his country. There they plan to marry him to Christiane, the princess of a neighbouring and highly strategical country. To oblige his advisers, the king does so, but brings his mistress with him. He settles down and makes a real attempt to govern his people, and they learn to love him. Eventually, however, his views prove to be too radical for his Old Guard Cabinet, and he is forced into exile, leaving his wife, whom he married to please his family, but now loves dearly, behind with his infant son and heir. On Nikki's abdication his son becomes king, and the play ends with the ex-monarch (incognito) sadly yet jubilantly watching his son's coronation from the back of the cheering crowds.

Novello's performance as the Left-wing monarch was probably his finest since his Henry V. As the ageing, cynical king who goes into exile rather than allow his reactionary Cabinet to pull the wool over his people's eyes, he had written himself a sympathetic and moving role which he played to the hilt. At the age of fifty-six, the boy-wonder of the First World War and the brilliant and versatile youngster of the 1920's had bridged the gap of the war years to the 1940's, capping his triumphant career with his best musical play.

'Novello's best yet,' declared the *Evening News*. 'Ecstatic applause', reported the *News Chronicle*. 'A better musical than *South Pacific*', was the opinion of Harold Hobson in the *Sunday Times*; while Ivor Brown, in the *Observer*, wrote:—

'Mr. Novello continues to conquer. *King's Rhapsody* is

everything the Novelloites can desire. Mr. Novello, author, composer, and actor, can with his tranquility stand up to all the bounding Oklahomans and Brigadooners in the world. He is far the biggest box-office attraction of our native stage, and he has earned his victories by honest service of the public appetite. Sweet tooth is sweetly served, and, what is more—abundantly. He hands out no trivial fable, but lashings of plot, with plentiful changes of scene. He has a witty part for Zena Dare, who delivers it wittily, and a pretty one for Phyllis Dare, who prettily responds. When Olive Gilbert sings "Fly Home, Little Heart", a myriad little homes will be emptied by hearts flying out to hear her. Vanessa Lee, as the Nordic angel, sings and looks the part admirably, while Ivor Novello himself sadly rules and gladly deserts Murania, looking half Hamlet, half Antony, and wholly the darling of his public.'

Hubert Griffith, in the *Sunday Graphic,* asserted: 'Novello's new play will be a challenge to the dominance of American musicals in London', while even the American *Variety* declared, 'With an unbroken list of winners, both straight and musical, behind him, this seventh mammoth spectacle of Ivor Novello's shows every indication of emulating the phenomenal success of the others'.

That is a brief selection of only some of the truly astonishing Press notices. Once again Ivor had unreservedly conquered the London stage. Even before *King's Rhapsody* opened it had taken £50,000 in advance bookings, something which no other show, either in London or on Broadway, had ever done before. Critic Harold Hobson not only headed his *Sunday Times* column in praise of the new Novello play, but also devoted his entire column in the American *Christian Science Monitor* to a lengthy critical appraisal which contained this passage:—

'The music is quite enchanting, and Novello's performance extraordinarily accomplished and beautifully timed. How superbly he manages to bring off the different aspects of the theatre into a single harmonious whole, *South Pacific,* the current hit of the Broadway stage, requires Rodgers, Michener,

Logan, and Hammerstein to do what Novello achieves single-handed in *King's Rhapsody*; and then, in my opinion, they do not do it so well.'

*

Vanessa Lee, who became an overnight star in *King's Rhapsody*, was another Novello discovery. As 'Ruby Moule' she had sung in several concerts and toured with ENSA during the war. When the third London revival of *The Dancing Years* opened at the Casino Theatre in 1947, Ruby was engaged to understudy the leading lady. One night Jessica James, playing Maria, had a severe sore throat and was unable to go on. Ruby stepped into the breach and was so good that Barry Sinclair sent a message round to the stage door of the Hippodrome, asking Ivor to step into the Casino on his way home as he wanted him to hear a wonderful new girl. Accordingly Ivor, who finished half an hour earlier than the Casino show, stopped by and went into Sinclair's dressing-room. Over the 'inter-com' he could hear the final scenes of the show, and was at once thrilled by the magnificent voice of the unknown girl playing Maria. When the curtain had come down, Ivor immediately called Ruby into the dressing-room, told her how much he admired her voice, and assured her that he would give her a chance to prove whether she had the 'stuff of stardom'.

Muriel Barron, who was appearing with him in *Perchance to Dream*,* would not be coming out to South Africa in his season there at the end of 1947, as she was going out on a provincial tour as the star of *Careless Rapture*. Novello decided to take a chance on this strikingly lovely girl with the remarkable voice. Would Ruby like to join his company and play in *Perchance to Dream* in Johannesburg and Cape Town?

The girl could hardly wait to assent. There was one thing, however—'Ruby Moule' was just not suitable. Would she let Novello choose a new name for her? Again, yes. Out of

* Both Sylvia Cecil and Hilary Allen deputized for Muriel at various times during the run.

the blue Ivor thereupon chose 'Vanessa Lee', mainly because he liked the initials V.L. (the initials of his beloved Vivien Leigh) so much. He had created a new star. Vanessa Lee left England as an unknown girl. After the South African tour she was well on the road to fame, and with her performance and singing in *King's Rhapsody* she was acclaimed. Now she is established.

'She is one of my insurances for the future', he admitted wryly. 'For when I am too old to appear in my own musicals Vanessa will be able to star in them for me, and keep them running for years!'

Also in *King's Rhapsody* were several players who had appeared with Ivor in many of his other shows. Olive Gilbert, whom he adored, and who had a flat right underneath him in the Aldwych, also appeared in *Glamorous Night, Careless Rapture, Crest of the Wave, The Dancing Years* and *Perchance to Dream*. 'No new show of mine would be complete without her', he told me. 'And the same goes for Victor Boggetti and John Palmer, who have been with me since *The Rat* and *Crest of the Wave* respectively, Bobbie Andrews of course, Peter Graves (who has recently been too busy being a film star to appear on the stage), Barry Sinclair, who so gallently plays all my own parts on the various tours, Zena Dare, who brings wit and elegance to every one of the plays lucky enough to have her, Gordon Duttson, who has been in my shows for ten years and is now my invaluable secretary as well as a loyal friend, and Harry Fergusson, who has been with me continuously since *Crest of the Wave*. Then, of course, there is poet and playwright Christopher Hassall, who was first associated with me as my understudy on the tour of *Proscenium* in 1934. He afterwards played the Robert Andrews' part in *Fresh Fields* on tour, and then appeared with me in *Murder in Mayfair* at the Globe. Christopher, one of my most valuable collaborators, first wrote lyrics to my songs for *Glamorous Night,* followed by *Careless Rapture, Crest of the Wave, The Dancing Years, Arc de Triomphe, Perchance to Dream,* and, of course, *King's Rhapsody*.

'Nothing pleases me more than to have old friends around

me. I have had the same business manager, Fred Allen, for thirty years, William Newman my production manager for ten years, Winifred Newman (now the company business manager and stage director) for ten years; and Victor Melleney has been my stage manager for several years. Joseph Carl designed the excellent settings for *The Dancing Years, Arc de Triomphe* and *Perchance to Dream,* while Leontine Sagan directed *Murder in Mayfair* and each of my first three musical plays before returning to South Africa on the outbreak of the war. I prefer to have the same people in all my productions. Once I begin to admire and respect someone's ability, I like to have him or her associated with every new venture. Old friends are best friends, and it gives me the greatest pleasure to know that in all the various companies of mine which are playing in London or in the provinces, the same names occur again and again. They are my own "Stock Company", and I am very proud of them all.'

Just as the hit songs of *Glamorous Night* had been 'Shine Through My Dreams' and 'Fold Your Wings', of *The Dancing Years* 'Waltz of My Heart', 'I Can Give You the Starlight', 'My Life Belongs to You' and 'Wings of Sleep', and the hit of *Perchance to Dream* the celebrated 'We'll Gather Lilacs', so *King's Rhapsody* featured several songs in the score, all of which seemed likely to achieve the phenomenal success of Novello's previous compositions. The most popular was 'Someday My Heart Will Awake', followed closely by 'Fly Home, Little Heart' and 'A Violin Began to Play'. His outstanding setting to Pauline Grant's ballet *Muranian Rhapsody* recalls the lovely score he composed for his one-act opera *Joan of Arc* in *Arc de Triomphe,* and indicated that in the realm of light music and operetta he had no equals in British contemporary music.

★

In an article entitled 'Music from the Heart'* written a month after *King's Rhapsody* opened, Novello gave an outline of his philosophy of success:—

* *Band Wagon,* December 1949.

'Let's have no nonsense about art for art's sake. Art cannot exist in a vacuum. It is essentially communication, the communication of idea of sounds, of pictures. If an artist creates something it becomes sterile if it has a message only for himself. We of the theatre are artists. We write and act to please the public, to 'fill the plush', to convey our emotions across the footlights and share our rhapsodies with the audience. No matter how good a play or an operetta may seem to be, if it fails to draw an audience then, to my mind, it ceases to exist, to have any useful purpose.

'I am not saying this because I have been singularly fortunate with my musicals—we all of us have our flops—but because I have always been a general public-minded man. And I say this in no derogatory sense. I don't despise the public. Quite the contrary. I pay them the compliment of trying to give them the type of music I like myself. And the measure of my ability to do this has been my good fortune in the theatre over the past years.

'I know certain people say: "Oh, Novello just churns the stuff out; it's easy!" Is it? If it were, in fact, so simple, they would do it themselves—and I know that for many of them it is not for want of trying. But it isn't at all easy, not even for me. In the past decade I have written only four musicals, which must certainly take them out of the category of pot boilers. And I wrote these four because I had to. Because the music was bubbling inside me, waiting to come out. I suppose I could have driven myself to write a musical every year, but by this time I would have been written out and, as far as the theatre is concerned, written off, stale and virtually unprofitable. While I am playing in a production it absorbs my entire energies, mental and physical. Then, towards the end of its run—an end, by the way, dictated by my own restlessness, and not lack of public support—I get the desire to work on something else.

'That happened with *Perchance to Dream,* which was withdrawn at the height of its success. A year earlier I had conceived the idea of a Balkan piece, featuring some music of a more Continental character as a change from the purely

English idiom of *Perchance to Dream*. A libretto began to form in my head. That's the way I normally work; I complete the libretto before I start on the score. And in South Africa, while on tour with *Perchance to Dream,* I started on the music of *King's Rhapsody*. It was at the Carleton Hotel in Johannesburg, two years ago. There was no piano in my suite, so I had one sent up and began to form the melodies you can hear at the Palace now.

'It nearly always happens like this. I think of a scene, immerse myself in it completely until its musical content begins to take expression in my mind. Then I go over to the piano and start to improvise. I really don't know for how long I play, or even what I play, but somehow, whenever I am on the right track, I feel I am capturing the mood of the scene. Meanwhile, every note has been taken down on wire by a recording machine, a simple gadget that I manipulate myself. And when I find I am suddenly empty I stop playing, sit back, and turn on the record.

'Very often all that emerges is a jumble of chords and broken melodic lines, a sort of musical shorthand, but just as often a complete embryonic melody comes out, one that I would never have recognized as my own without the evidence of the disc. That makes me excited, gives me something to work on, something to enlarge, to polish, to perfect till it glistens like a jewel. Then I have to play it over to someone, immediately; I feel like a prospector who has struck gold and wants to tell the world about it.

'I am a gregarious individual. I like to have people around me. I am not one of those solitary souls who must bury themselves in a Cumberland cottage, and can woo the Muse only after a long communion with lofty peaks and mirrored lakes and the myriad shy animals that burrow in the woodlands. I can work anywhere so long as I have a piano, my fountain-pen, reams of manuscript paper, and people—people whose opinions I respect. People to whom I can say "Listen, what do you think of this?" and be elated or despondent for days depending on their answers.

'So the score takes shape until finally it is completed. Then follow long sessions with my friend Harry Acres about the orchestration. We chat about each number; I play it over and over again until Harry seems satisfied, and when Harry is satisfied I know his orchestration will be exactly right, with every instrument featured just the way I would do it myself.

'It doesn't end there. By no means. Long before the cast is assembled or the sets designed we have a separate rehearsal for the score. Early this year we engaged members of the Liverpool Philharmonic Orchestra to play over the entire score of *King's Rhapsody* just to prove to Acres and myself that it was up to Palace standards.

'When I say, as I mentioned earlier, I try to give the public the type of music I like myself, I mean precisely that. I suppose I am essentially a romantic, because emotional music appeals to me beyond anything else, and I have been familiar with the best in music from my earliest youth.

'I was brought up on the classics, nurtured as a chorister with dollops of Bach, Beethoven, Haydn, Handel, Mozart, Byrd, Purcell, Gibbons. Now, with the exception of Mozart's opera, I can't bear any of them. To me they are too full of form and lacking in emotion. At this moment I can positively hear gnashing of teeth and bellows of rage from classical music-lovers. "Who does he think *he* is?" I can hear them say.

'Perhaps as a reaction from my severely classical musical boyhood, I swung clean over to the romantics, and my present preferences run from Mendelssohn onwards; with anything before his time, barring a few exceptions, I am out of musical sympathy. Particularly I adore Wagner, and the later Wagner most of all. I never miss the "Ring" cycle when I am in town, and for me Kirsten Flagstad is enshrined beyond compare as the ideal singer. Wagner says something to me emotionally all the time, every musical phrase strikes an answering chord, every *leitmotiv* has all the force and conviction of a living statement that penetrates to the depths of my soul.

'Of course I like the Strauss's, Lehar, Fall, and Kalman. Of English musicians my favourite is Elgar, to whose veneration I have become a late convert. I like Bliss—his piano concerto particularly—William Walton, Addinsell, and Edward German.

'To which school of British musicians my own humble efforts belong is difficult for me to say. Viewed dispassionately, I am sort of betwixt and between; if there was a hymn that was neither ancient nor modern, it would be me.

'I started writing very young. My first song was published when I was only fifteen, and at twenty I wrote "Keep the Home Fires Burning", a song that became a best seller all over the world, and is still remembered. Many moons have passed since that first war marching-song was written, but essentially my music remains the same, simple, emotional, and directed unashamedly towards the heart. I make no apologies for that. I repeat, I like that sort of music, and I am convinced the British public likes it, too.'

★

On January 15th, 1950, *King's Rhapsody* was the new play dealt with in that highly intellectual and intensely critical B.B.C. programme 'The Critics'. Of Novello's latest work that well-known dramatic critic and authority on opera, Philip Hope-Wallace, had this to say:—

'The first question a critic ought to ask himself is this: Is this good of its kind, and exactly what kind is it? Well, *King's Rhapsody* isn't operetta, in which the music must involve all the principal people and play a leading part. It's rather a play decorated with music; so don't let's try and compare it with masterpieces like *Die Fledermaus,* or *Merrie England,* or *The Mikado.* We've got a great tradition of musical comedy and operetta in England, and don't let's think that the Americans invented it all with *Oklahoma.* But it would be unfair to put *King's Rhapsody* into that company. In fact, this isn't Ivor Novello on the level of his *Careless Rapture,* which was often as good as Lehar. But merely as a musical play is it good? Has it wit, pithiness, originality, suspense, and drive? I think the answer has to be "No" in each case. But with triumphant assurance it does what it sets out to do—that is to tell a Ruritanian tarradiddle with brilliant people to play in them! It might be different if I were a different sort of a playwright. If one was writing a heaven-sent play with a "great message" to give the world, that would be another thing altogether. But, as I repeat, my business is to entertain, and I make no secret of that fact. I always try to get two or three stars for each of my plays if possible, and in most cases I have already written the roles with various star personalities in mind. To show you that I have had good fortune with this method, I would remind readers that the average length of run of the plays that I have been managerially concerned with, spread over ten years, is 292 performances each play.'

That statement was typical of Novello. It was not false modesty. It was genuine, it was real, and it was rather disarming.

The great French painter Degas one said a very wise thing: 'It is easy to have talent at twenty, but what *is* difficult is to have talent at fifty!' The point about Novello is that he had talent at twenty, at thirty, at forty, at fifty—and right until his sudden death at fifty-eight. Bernard Shaw was young in heart, and so was Novello, and, like that great old man, he created some of his best work while in his fifties. There, of course, the comparison ends. Shaw's plays are primarily plays of ideas; with him, dramatic entertainment, though it is often there, comes decidedly second. Novello's plays are not plays of ideas. Their main job is, as Ivor put it, 'to fill the plush'. They are frothy comedies, entertaining frolics, witty comedies of manners, or large-scale, splendiferous musicals designed to appeal to the greatest possible number of people. Novello's work was, as someone put it, 'designed for happiness'. That was always his object—and the world knows how he succeeded.

'I am not a highbrow', he asserted. 'I am an entertainer. Empty seats and good opinions mean nothing to me. I have always striven to give the theatre the best that is within me. I have no pretensions. What is the use of "good" repertory on the Yorkshire moors if nobody comes to see you? I am an unrepentant sentimentalist. I have always tried in every-

28. Constance Collier.

29. Sir Edward Marsh.

30. Robert Andrews.

31. Noël Coward.

[Photo: Anthony Buc

32. With *King's Rhapsody,* his finest work in this sphere, Novello reached maturity as a composer of operetta. Produced at the Palace, in 1949, it served to introduce a new star in Vanessa Lee, who played opposite him. In this play Novello made his last appearance, on March 5th, 1951, dying three hours after the fall of the curtain.

thing I have written to appeal first to the heart. Rightly or wrongly I believe that the theatre is primarily a place of make-believe. I don't believe in using the theatre for moralizing lectures on social behaviour; other playwrights do that far better than I ever could. I remain firmly within my *metier*. I repeat: I am unrepentant.

'I'd like very much to write an opera. Music is still my first love. Maybe I'll get time to try my hand at this in a year or two.' Unhappily Novello's opera was never composed.

★

And what of Novello the man? Every personality has a dozen faces. The version as to a person's character as heard from one of his friends will generally differ greatly from that supplied by an enemy. With Novello a rather curious situation arose, for one could never find anything unkind, unpleasant, or even highly critical to record. Even those other playwrights, actors, and composers who were inclined to be jealous of his continued successes, could not but agree that he was a most charming and kindly man. Not a breath of unpleasantness besmirched his name, and the entire world of music and the theatre subscribed to the opinion that he 'was a very fine person'. Indeed, those are the words used by Sir Michael Balcon, who was associated with Novello for many years, and who cannot speak too highly of him both professionally and personally.

Adrian Brunel, who knew him for over thirty years, has a theory that although Ivor's personal magnetism and charm developed greatly through the years, it was first inspired by the *desire* to be liked for himself as a person, as well as for the handsome son of a famous woman. Brunel propounds the theory that Ivor, a celebrity at the age of twenty-one because of 'Keep the Home Fires Burning', and film star by the time he was twenty-five, developed a technique of *appearing* to be charming, friendly, and interested in the other person and his point of view, as well as in the fans who crowded stage doors to see him, and who sent him hundreds of letters every week. From making a real effort to be kind and gracious, something most people in public life have to develop, Brunel contends that Ivor, naturally a very friendly soul, found himself actually *being* the kind and gracious human being which he was endeavouring to be.

This may sound a little involved, and is, of course, merely Brunel's pet theory, but it holds water. Novello had learned early in life that kindness creates happiness. He had forced himself to be patient and approachable; he had realized that his entire success depended upon the way his personality 'came across', both on the screen and in private life. He took enormous trouble to get to know all the people in the various plays and films in which he appeared, right down to the smallest small-part actor. He began to be known for this, for the way he was loyal to his friends, and for the unexpected generosities with which he was always surprising members of the company.

Over the years the stories of Ivor's lovable nature have grown into a legend. Whether or not he deliberately cultivated a kind of charm in his very early days, which soon developed into his own natural charm of personality, one cannot say. All one can record is that he was the most beloved man in the modern English theatre.

Everyone who worked with him will affirm that he was a most astonishing and wonderful man in every way. In the theatre he was an excellent employer, faithful to all his old friends. There was nothing so dear to his heart as an old friend. One of these is Collie Knox, the well-known author and critic, who wrote*: —

'I have known Ivor since we were both very young men, and I wrote lyrics to his music for four songs in the revue by name *A to Z,* including 'Night May Have Its Sadness', still, I believe, Ivor's favourite finale number. As I was at that time an innocent subaltern in the Regular Army, the ways of theatrical management were a mystery to me. They are still a mystery, but I am not innocent any more. The revue ran for two and a half years, and when I remember that I sold my lyrics outright for £15 apiece I feel faint. Ivor was

* In *The Queen,* November 23rd, 1949.

wiser. He is a keen businessman, and as a dramatist-composer has an extraordinary talent for hitting on the Only Formula to enthuse his multitudinous followers.

'At the beginning of the Second World War Ivor said to me, "What about writing a war song, like my 'Keep the Home Fires Burning'?" So we wrote one, called it "We'll Remember", and waited for everyone to go mad about it. They didn't. I heard it played on a scratchy record last week and all is now clear to me!

'Ivor is a friendly soul, beloved by all who work for him, entirely unspoiled, and though he is, unbelievably, fifty-six, his profile still thrills romantic hearts. His lately produced *King's Rhapsody* at the Palace Theatre has everything in full measure—melody, romance, gorgeous costumes, considerable sentimentality, and Novello's miraculous formula to excelsis.'

Another typical comment came from Phyllis Monkman, who appeared with Ivor in *Downhill,* and in *The Gate Crasher* at the Palladium in 1928, as well as in his more recent play *We Proudly Present.*

'Ivor was a love and a lamb, and terribly kind,' declared Phyllis. 'I never heard him be catty about anyone, and he never forgot anyone or anything. You could not help but adore him.'

When a theatrical magazine (*Play Pictorial*) interviewed him after his big success in *The Rat* twenty-five years ago, Ivor answered the questions as follows: —

Favourite play? - - -	Barrie's *Mary Rose.*
Favourite hobby? - -	Redecorating my flat.
Favourite dish? - - -	Lobster Newburg.
Greatest ambition? - -	To own an island.
Favourite motto? - -	If you want to be a success—look it.
Pet aversion? - - - -	Meeting new people.
What, if you were not connected with the stage, would you prefer to be? - - -	Dead.

In 1951 Ivor would probably have answered almost exactly the same way. Fundamentally he never changed.

He still occupied the same flat which he had when he first came to London, and he would live in no other. He still had the same country house at Maidenhead—and again he would never change this. It is, of course, called 'Red Roofs', and is certainly one of the loveliest houses I have ever seen. Ivor bought it in 1926, and redecorated it several times, adding new wings, building a swimming pool, and making it into an ideal country home. It reflected his warm personality.

Until 1926 he had lived completely in London, though he had always had an ambition to possess a cottage in the country. While searching for a cottage he had looked over 'Red Roofs', which was secluded behind white-washed walls in a corner of Littlewick Green, a small village a mile or two from Maidenhead. The price, however, was £4,000, and he had no hope at all of obtaining this amount at that time. A few weeks later Basil Dean asked him if he would star as Lewis Dodd in the film version of *The Constant Nymph,* and Ivor refused. He was a little nettled that he had never been approached to act this part when Basil Dean produced the play on the stage—but after a few days he began to relent. On an impulse he sent a wire to Dean telling him that he would star in the film for a lump sum of £4,000—the price of the house. To Ivor's surprise, Dean agreed at once, and when Ivor returned from Austria he was able to start work on the rebuilding of his beautiful new home to his own specifications. He almost named it 'The Constant Nymph' in memory of the film which had virtually bought the house for him, but finally decided on 'Red Roofs'—and 'Red Roofs' it has remained to this day.

When working in one of his plays, Ivor usually spent the week days in his Aldwych flat, but every Saturday night the faithful Morgan drove him down to Maidenhead, where he remained all day Sunday and Monday before driving up to town on Monday evening for the performance. Those week-ends at 'Red Roofs' were what he looked forward to all the week. They were the perfect end to six days of hard work in the theatre, and Ivor was continually grateful to Basil Dean and Gainsborough Pictures for making this lovely home possible.

Novello would tell you that he was not particularly prolific, but this was by no means true. He was never content to settle down into a long run of one of his plays until he had also started work on at least another play, or the score for a new musical. He usually went to bed quite late, for he often took a few friends back to his flat after the show for a late night session of coffee and drinks, chat, card games, and reminiscences. He adored cards, and was one of the best bridge and canasta players in London. He breakfasted on pints of coffee, with plain toast, and always started the day by doing—or, at least, attempting—*The Times* crossword. He did not like getting up early, and would usually lounge in bed until at least mid-day, dictating replies to business and fan letters to his secretary, Gordon Duttson, the young actor, who helped him with his correspondence after the death of the famous 'Lloydie'. A light luncheon cooked by Ellen Ashman, who had been with Ivor for many years, was followed by a session at the piano, perhaps, or at the writing-desk. He recorded his ideas for compositions on to a recording machine, which he played back continuously until he obtained his theme to his satisfaction.

If he was not composing songs or ballet music for his forthcoming shows, he was working out ideas for new plays. Once having sketched out the idea in rough form, Novello usually dictated the entire play, scene by scene, to a stenographer, revising and revising again as he went along. In this way *Glamorous Night,* for example, was drafted in twenty-four hours and written in two weeks, though Novello did not recommend this method. Certain of his plays were growing at the back of his mind for years before he finally transferred them on to paper. The actual physical business of writing dialogue and thinking up effective scenes and curtains for his plays came easily to him. He had a fertile imagination, and was a naturally witty man, with a highly developed sense of humour.

By tea-time Novello had a short nap, which refreshed him for his evening performance. Then he was whisked off in his large and shiny Rolls Royce to the theatre, where he carefully made up and prepared to give another performance of the kind which had earned him praise and admiration since *The Rat* in 1924.

Even during the show, however, his brain was constantly active. When sitting in his dressing-room, waiting to be called for a scene, he put down ideas for plays, or notes of music which entered his brain. He was an energetic person, although he knew the value of relaxation. All his work was done carefully, checked and double-checked, rewritten and rewritten again until it was dramatically foolproof. He was a perfectionist, although that was not always so. At one time he used to dash off a play in a few days, but later he took more time and trouble with everything he did. This care was reflected in the rising quality of his work, in the added strength of his plays, and in the glorious tunes of his recent scores.

An example of how Ivor worked on a new show while appearing in another one was given to me by Gordon Duttson:—

During a performance of *Perchance to Dream,* where Ivor used to sit at a piano idly playing with the keys, while the lights dimmed to indicate the passing of time, he once began to formulate a tune on the keyboard. Duttson then had to enter, as Thomas, and tell Ivor that a lady (Roma Beaumont) had come to see him. On this particular night he gave his message, and Novello, who was involved in scribbling down notes as he improvised on the piano, absent-mindedly answered, 'Please ask her to wait. I won't be a minute.'

That line was not in the play, but, obediently, Duttson turned on his heel and walked into the wings, where he and Roma waited to see what Ivor's next move would be. Victor Melleney, the stage manager, was going frantic. For what seemed like an eternity Ivor quietly played the tune over and over on the piano, and the audience, who knew nothing of any deviation in the plot, listened spell-bound to this lovely new melody, thinking it was in the play. At last Ivor finished noting down the song on a scrap of paper and motioned to Gordon to bring Roma on. With a sigh of relief Gordon obediently did so, and the play proceeded.

That song was 'Some Day My Heart Will Awake', which subsequently became the rage of London and the hit of Novello's next musical, *King's Rhapsody*.

★

W. Macqueen-Pope once asserted*: —

'The truth about Ivor Novello is that he is an incurable Romantic. And it is well that he *is* incurable, for Romantics are valuable people and there are not nearly enough to go round. Ivor Novello, on and off the stage, much prefers life as he would like it to be to life as it is, and he succeeds in making it so, both in and out of the theatre. Like another great Romantic, the late Sir Herbert Tree, he is acutely aware of the present, and misses nothing of it, but he manages to live his life in the Past, the Past of his own fashioning. He is able to do so because, to Novello, life is the Theatre. What goes on outside does not concern him very much. He detaches himself from it, and in his plays, especially his musical plays, he does that very thing which the old poet Omar so desired to do—he recreates Life according to his heart's desire. His great sweeping musical shows are not musical comedies, nor musical plays—they are Musical Romances. In them he puts the life in which he believes, the life he adores. But he shows his grip on real life, too. He never gives his audience the conventional happy ending. His hero and heroine never bring down the curtain clasped in each other's arms, doomed to live happily ever afterwards. Ivor the Realist does not believe in that. But then Ivor the Romantic steps in. Up goes the curtain once again, mystery fills the stage, the orchestra swells, the strings (he believes in strings, not saxophones) send great waves of emotion across the hushed auditorium—and there, in a Vision, are the two lovers, meeting, clasping, and dancing away to eternity,

* *Everybody's*, November 1949.

living romantically as Memories in each other's hearts. It is a great stage trick by a man who understands stage trickery which is, of course, Romance—and the audience acclaim his play—and him—and leave the theatre misty-eyed with joy.

'He is able to do this, he is able to take the double view because he is in himself two persons. There is David Ivor Davies, which is his real name, and Ivor Novello, who is largely his own creation. There is nothing of the Jekyll and Hyde in this dual personality, and you have to know him very well indeed before you catch a glimpse of David Ivor Davies. But he is always there—a steadying influence, a tough, sturdy Welsh character, full of Celtic fire, and yet, strangely enough, with a very strong dash of Saxon tenacity. When trouble comes, as it has come from time to time, it is David who deals with it, who takes it on the chin and stiffens up, to fight back to victory. David Ivor Davies is not a Romantic—he is real flesh and blood and very human. It is he who makes Ivor Novello believe that life is not all happiness and roses, but he always lets Ivor Novello have the last word. David is just as sterling a fellow as Ivor. He is the power behind the throne, and largely responsible for Ivor's success.

'For Ivor Novello is the most successful man in the theatre to-day, and the most popular. Everyone calls him by his Christian name. That does not betoken familiarity, but affection. For that is the quality he extracts from everyone with whom he comes into contact. He gets it because he is intensely human, and also because, with all his vast and cumulative success, he has never become in the least conceited or swollen-headed. He does not know what it means.

'One of his secrets is that he never takes anything for granted. He never says, "Oh, that will do; it's good enough". It has to be his best. For he believes in Quality. He has his own standard, and he never lets it down. He adores praise, but flattery passes him by. He knows all about that. He has the heaven-sent gift—in a man of the Theatre—of listening to what those of experience say to him, and he will take advice. Sometimes he takes a good deal of convincing, and wants much proof of the criticisms offered. But he weighs it up—and he acts on it. He knows that the looker-on sees quite a lot of the game.'

As to his being an incurable Romantic, Macqueen-Pope was probably right, though with regard to his personal romantic life Novello was noticeably reticent. In past years the newspapers have linked his name with various of his leading ladies, like Benita Hume, Gladys Cooper and others, but, as Ivor himself once confided to me:—

'I cannot speak of this part of my life without embarrassing certain people. It would be a little tactless, for instance, if I went into a perfectly true story of a deep romance which happened years ago, when everybody knows that the adored one is married to someone else and has a large family of children! Naturally, loves and deep affections have played an enormous part in my life, and any account of my life without revelation of these inner things is bound to have gaps. For the biographer reticence obviously has its disadvantages. Yet it must suffice for me to say that all my life, from the age of six, when I adored a nurse who came to look after my father when he had pneumonia, I have loved somebody—sometimes it has been imaginary, sometimes it has been real. When it has been real, it has lasted. Otherwise—not. If only one could be certain that love—that something which makes it impossible for you to be away from the loved one—would gradually deepen into a lasting and very wonderful friendship, then perhaps one would take love more seriously. All I know is that I have suffered deeply from love, and had my greatest joy from friendship. One of the things that I enjoy most in life is to look round when I am having a little party at my flat and see that out of the forty people present there are at least thirty whom I have known for more than twenty years. Maybe to outsiders we all look middle-aged, but in each other we see no change, and any lines that are there are lines of laughter and expression. My one regret is that I have never married, for I would love to have a family. Now I am too set in my ways to attempt marriage and much too difficult to live with.'

Ivor's 'family', nevertheless, existed, consisting of his friends, the members of his many companies extending over the past thirty years, his business and artistic associates, and his domestic entourage. And what a family it was! Until his death in 1948 Lloyd Williams had been his secretary and friend since 1918. On Lloydie's death, Gordon Duttson, who had been an original member of the Adelphi company of *The Dancing Years,* took over the work, and became Ivor's close associate and private secretary, a position he had for six years. Then there were several old friends. Ivor's business manager, Fred Allen, had been with him for thirty years; Winifred Newman, his stage director, since *Perchance to Dream*; Arthur Morgan, his chauffeur, for thirty years. At one time Morgan combined his work as chauffeur with playing small parts in Novello plays like *The Rat,* but in the last fifteen years he deserted the 'boards' to concentrate on the Rolls-Royce.

Bill Wright, Ivor's valet and dresser, first joined him in 1934 for *Murder in Mayfair.* He remained with Novello ever since, and would not dream of seeking other employment, although he had many offers from rival stage stars, intrigued and impressed by his efficiency and remarkable personality.

In his Aldwych flat Ivor had Ellen Ashman, his cook for several years, while at 'Red Roofs' Mabel Almond had been his maid for more than fifteen years. When Ivor was touring France and Belgium in 1944 he met John Crawford, a Welfare Officer for ENSA. He looked after Ivor's company so efficiently that Ivor asked him if he would care to be his butler at 'Red Roofs' when the war was over. John eagerly assented, and for more than five years he was 'general factotum' at Ivor's country home.

The jolly chef at 'Red Roofs', Tommy Almond, one of Ivor's 'show-pieces', is brother-in-law to Mabel, the maid. Tommy is a superlative chef, and a wonderfully humorous personality. Nothing disturbs him. He has met literally scores of the most famous stars in Europe and the U.S.A. He knows what kind of food they all like, and is always ready to bring them a special dish as a surprise. He is master of the kitchen, and a more devoted man Ivor could not have wished to have. He remembered only one occasion when Tommy's usual *sang-froid* deserted him. That was a year or two ago, when Ivor's good friend Greta Garbo stayed at 'Red Roofs' while on a visit to England. She is a noted gourmet and loves to cook. One of the first things she asked to see was the kitchen, and Ivor, unannounced, took her into Tommy's sacred quarters. The chef was quietly stirring a delectable soup for lunch when he heard Ivor entering the kitchen. He turned with a smile, at once recognized Greta Garbo, dropped his ladle, ejaculated 'Oh, Gorblimey!' and fled into his room to change into a clean uniform!

All of Ivor's friends and associates were of long standing. During the 1930's he was associated managerially with a young American, Richard Rose, whom he had met in New York while he was appearing in *The Truth Game* on Broadway. Rose became a great admirer of Ivor's. He had had some experience in theatrical management in the U.S.A., and in 1932 he came to England and joined up with Ivor to present *I Lived With You.* He subsequently presented several other Novello plays, including *Fresh Fields, Sunshine Sisters, Murder in Mayfair, The Happy Hypocrite* and *Comedienne,* before returning to the U.S.A. just before the war.

Since that time Ivor was associated with Tom Arnold, the man who took a chance with Ivor's *Henry V,* and had his confidence repaid a thousandfold with all the successes accumulating from Novello's musicals of the past fifteen years.

★

Ivor loved to read, adored music, went to the theatre as often as possible, was never inactive, and had a wonderful zest for life. Sir Laurence Olivier once remarked, 'Ivor has an infinite capacity for enjoyment', and this exactly hit the nail on the head.

Of Olivier Ivor stated, 'He is the greatest actor of our time. It is exciting just living at the same time that he is!' Of contemporary playwrights Ivor admired Christopher Fry and Terence Rattigan. Fry, in particular, he considered to be the most talented young playwright we have had on the English stage for years. 'He has brought to the modern theatre not merely poetry but pure enchantment', he declared. When Ivor was not working on a new play or composing a new score, or arranging for the various tours of his productions, or supervising a new film, radio, or television version of one of his plays, or doing the other hundred and one things which kept him continually busy, he was at the theatre. He went to matinées of every show he could possibly find time to attend while his own plays were running. During breaks or rehearsals he spent every night at a different theatre. He saw hundreds of plays every year, and learned something, he assured me, from every one of them.

'The only way to learn more and more about drama and dramatic technique is to keep going to the theatre and studying new plays and new productions', he said. 'All I know about writing plays and music and acting has been taught to me from watching other people's successes and failures in the theatre. I am the perfect theatregoer. I am the first to laugh at any signs of comedy, and always the first to fumble for my handkerchief in the death scenes. The worst actors in the most mediocre productions can grip my imagination, keep my attention, and wring my emotions. Even to-day, with all my years of experience in the theatre, I have not lost the capacity of being frightened or moved by a plot on the stage. I have been in love with the theatre since the age of five, and I know I always shall be.'

The theatre was his great love—the cinema only secondary, although he was always an avid filmgoer.

In 1950 a version of *The Dancing Years* was successfully produced by Associated British Pictures, with Dennis Price as Rudi, Gisele Preville as Maria, Patricia Dainton as Grete, Grey Blake as Franzel, and Anthony Nicholls playing the part he originally created at Drury Lane. The director was Harold French, who had produced Ivor in *Ladies Into Action* in 1940; the producer, Warwick Ward, had planned to make a film version of this play ever since he first saw it at Drury Lane in 1939, although war-time conditions had prevented him going ahead with the production of a large-scale musical film. *The Dancing Years* emulated the enormous success of the stage production, and film versions of *Perchance to Dream* and *King's Rhapsody* will no doubt be made at some time in the future.

Ivor had very little to do with film production latterly. He was not particularly pleased with the movie version of *Glamorous Night,* nor with the film of *The Rat,* but had no time to take an active part in the production of films from his plays. As to screen acting, he did not regret having kept the promise he made to himself not to make a movie after *Autumn Crocus.*

This is what Novello once said to me about films:—

'I am often asked what I think is the fundamental difference between film acting and stage acting. I would say that inside the mind and the heart there is no difference at all, but that the mechanics need complete readjustment. Everything on the screen has to be minimized. You must feel your emotions just as deeply, but you must reduce your facial expression and the tone of your voice by ninety per cent of what you would use on the stage. I think that is why, when stage actors first go on the screen, they are apt to over-play; and when they have been on the screen for some time, and return to the speaking stage, their methods have automatically become so intimate and their effects so small that they do not get past the first few rows of stalls. I, personally, am very thankful that all through my career I have done films and plays alternately, because I have never had time to forget the technique of the one while I was doing the other.

'I will make a frank confession. I love seeing films, but I hate doing them. I believe I always have; anyhow, after the first novelty of seeing myself on the screen wore off. I hate the hours one has to keep. I have never been able to get up early in the morning without a feeling of impending death. I don't like going to bed early. And both these things are essentials if you are filming, though why there should not be some adjustment, such as starting work at noon and working until midnight, when all one's acting qualities would be shown at their best, and also one's face would have settled down into its customary routine, I cannot imagine. That first shot at nine o'clock in the morning, usually in evening clothes, with the memory of a nice warm bed almost too close, is my idea of one of the lesser-known forms of Chinese torture.

'Please do not think that I am not grateful for the chances I have had to film. Of course I am grateful. I should be a fool and a liar if I said I was not. But to me there is no comparison between the two arts. On the stage every performance is an event, because you have a living, breathing audience to conquer. You *know* immediately whether you are doing something that pleases or offends, and you can adjust yourself accordingly. But the camera, which is never supposed to lie, makes no response whatever, and, even if the director seems pleased, he is only one man. Just compare that reaction with a Saturday night at Drury Lane with two thousand five hundred people showing their interest by their laughter, their silence, and their deeply appreciated applause! Also, there is something so final about performing for the screen. Once it is—as they say—'in the can', that is the end of *that*. You have no opportunity to perfect or alter. It is there for good and all, whereas on the stage every performance means spiritual and mental growth of some kind. Oh, yes, give me the stage every time.'

Commenting on the film of *The Dancing Years,* Leonard Mosley, the film critic, compared Novello with Danny Kaye, whose new film, *The Inspector General,* was also being shown in the West End that week.*

'Novello has the great man's knack', he wrote, 'of turning the trite into the terrific. I have a feeling that he can write a musical with a mouse-trap as its setting, and still make a million people come in and want to see it. It is thirty-four years since he wrote 'Keep the Home Fires Burning', and it is still a good tune. He writes as a sincere romantic, and

* *Daily Express,* April 6th, 1950.

the notes sound that way. So long as he can go on producing songs like the ones in this film—and he does not seem to have lost the flair yet—Ivor Novello will stay at the top. Those who sneer at him are just envious fools.

'Novello takes his place with Danny Kaye as a great figure and a great tradition. Sniping at either of them is just a waste of time. As they stand at the moment, their decriers might find a more profitable occupation loosing off their pop-guns at all these flying saucers.'

★

Novello was essentially a modest man. He saw himself in true perspective. He was proud of the acclaim his works received over the past decade; he delighted in the knowledge that he brought pleasure to millions; he was thrilled at the continuance of his quite extraordinary popularity. But he had no false illusions about himself, or about his plays and his music. 'Whenever I was tempted to sit back and regard myself as really quite a remarkable fellow,' Ivor confessed to me, 'I think back to the day, a dozen years ago, when I was starring in *Careless Rapture*, the biggest success in London at that time. I met an old friend who first of all looked surprised that after five years I was not going about with a stick. He greeted me warmly.

' "Hullo, Ivor, how have you been all this time?"

' "Fine," I replied.

' "What are you doing now?" he inquired.

' "Acting."

' "Acting! I say! Are you in a play?"

' "Yes, I am in a play."

' "Called what?"

' "*Careless Rapture*."

' "*Careless Rapture!* I say, that sounds a bit highbrow to me."

' "It isn't at all highbrow. It's a musical comedy. It was written by me to please the public, and I'm glad to say it has."

' "Oh, I must pop along and see it one night. Where are you at?"

' "Drury Lane."

' "Oh, pantomime?"

' "No, Charles, it is not a pantomime. I wrote it myself."

' "I didn't know you had taken up writing."

'By this time we had reached the corner of the Strand, and, risking life and limb, I dashed across the road in spite of the red lights being against me, and left my poor bewildered friend wondering what he had said that caused my "flight into Egypt".

'This conversation, mark you, took place after I had been acting for sixteen years, had had fourteen of my own plays produced, had played the leading part in most of them, and generally was beginning to regard myself as an established fact. But I am not an established fact. I wasn't then—and I'm not to-day. I don't believe anybody is, and I think the first time a person forgets this marks the birth of conceit and the death of accomplishment.'

He never stopped working. While checking the manuscript of this book he was at the same time completing the novelization of *King's Rhapsody* for *Woman's Pictorial,* completing a series of articles on 'How to Write a Musical Play' for *Woman,* checking the proofs of the Foreword he had written to his friend Billie Burke's autobiography, *With A Feather On My Nose,* working on the book and lyrics of two new shows, and appearing nightly at the Palace Theatre. His energy was prodigious. So was his enthusiasm. He bubbled over with it. He had a zest for work and a zest for life which were infectious.

His plays are continually being broadcast and televised; he appeared in most radio versions of his works. He listened a great deal to the radio, mainly to the symphony concerts, and had one of the largest collections of gramophone records of orchestral music in the country. His favourite composers were Debussy, Ravel, Delius, Elgar, Puccini—and especially Wagner. One of his favourite stories, told to him by his mother, concerned a performance of Wagner's *Lohengrin* in Vienna.

'As you know,' he recounted 'in this opera Lohengrin, clad

in shining medieval armour, is drawn off the stage towards the end in a boat propelled by white swans. On this particular night Leo Slezak, the tenor, who was singing Lohengrin, somehow missed his step, with the result that the swan boat vanished without him, out of sight into the wings . . . A horrified hush fell on cast and audience, but Slezak, a notable joker, was equal to the occasion. He strolled down to the footlights, jerked off his mail gauntlet, and consulted an imaginary wrist-watch.

' "Excuse me, conductor," he said calmly. "What time does the next swan go?" '

Ivor's sense of humour was one of his most predominant characteristics. In such of his plays as *I Lived With You, Party, Comedienne* and *We Proudly Present,* his pretty turn of wit is notably displayed, and his light comedies, especially *I Lived With You,* must be the best plays of their kind in modern English drama. Even his musical plays, like *King's Rhapsody,* reveal a particularly well-developed dry sense of humour. He was without doubt one of the acknowledged masters of our lighter stage, often under-rated by dramatic critics.

Ivor loved London, but he also liked touring the provincial cities. Since *The Rat* he appeared on tour in all his successes, and numbered thousands of his most faithful followers outside London.

'I love the hustle and bustle of a tour', Ivor asserted. 'Why—every Monday night is a First Night! It's exciting. Sometimes I hear people on the stage saying "Oh, my dear, I wouldn't *dream* of going on tour. Could anything be more *deadly*?" How wrong they are! Touring to me is an absolute delight. It is like one continuous house-party, with a nice fat cheque at the end of the week; it is a wonderful way of making new friends and keeping old ones, and it does definitely build up a public that remains faithful. And my first advice to anyone who wants to make a position on the stage is—*don't* neglect the provinces. Also, I have never been on tour without writing at least one play. There is something about London that is stultifying to work, and unless I get away from the ever-ringing telephone and attractive invitations to luncheon or a matinée or a film, I cannot get my work done.'

There has hardly been a period during the past twenty years when a Novello production has not been on tour somewhere in the British Isles, and often two or more of his plays are touring at the same time. At one historic period in 1949 four of Novello's plays were touring Britain, while he was starring in a fifth at the Palace.

When he returned from his Jamaican holiday, after the South African season, Ivor toured in *Perchance to Dream* from April 1948 until January of the following year, when Geoffrey Toone took over the star part until the end of 1949. While Ivor worked on the completion of the libretto and score of *King's Rhapsody* during the summer of that year, *Careless Rapture* was also touring, with Barry Sinclair, Muriel Barron and Nicolette Roeg. All three had previously been touring in *The Dancing Years* since the end of its revival at the Casino in 1947; when they went into *Careless Rapture* their places were taken by Max Oldaker, Victoria Campbell and Julie David, who continued the tour of that perennial success. In 1948 Ralph Reader (Ivor's dance director at Drury Lane) presented a tour of *Glamorous Night,* which became an immediate hit, with Barry Mackay playing Anthony Allen, the part he had taken in the film version, Sylvia Cecil (and afterwards Victoria Campbell) as Militza, and John McHugh.

Thus when Novello opened in *King's Rhapsody* in September 1949, *Perchance to Dream, Careless Rapture, The Dancing Years* and *Glamorous Night* were all on tour in various provincial cities—a record not equalled in the entire history of the English theatre. It must not be forgotten also that during this period several of Novello's plays were produced in various repertory theatres all over the British Isles (and *The Dancing Years* film was being completed at Elstree Studios). Even his own twice-attained record of three productions running simultaneously on the London stage—*Fresh Fields, Proscenium* and *Sunshine Sisters* in 1933, and *Perchance to Dream, The Dancing Years* and *We Proudly*

Present in 1947—take second place to his fivefold achievement in 1949, his peak year.

★

Ivor, of course, had his faults, and he was aware of most of them. His worst fault was his inability to say 'No'. He was sometimes over-enthusiastic, and had a vein of obstinacy which could prevent him from admitting a mistake when he had made it. Like Nelson, he sometimes put the telescope to his blind eye and saw in people only what he wanted to see. But he had no jealousy, malice, or meanness in his make-up. Nobody had ever heard him speak a bad word about anyone on the stage, or off it. He never lost his temper, and his natural charm helped him to get things done where tears and temperament would lead to chaos. He inspired loyalty because he was himself loyal.

Essentially a happy man, he had always done the things he wanted to do—and this, he said, was the secret of happiness. He was always busy, but he knew how to relax. (He could go to sleep on a couch in a roomful of people.) He was gregarious, friendly. He liked to have people around him, but he was no 'gay dog'. He rarely went to parties, but liked to have his friends with him at his own flat or in his country home. He loved good food, but had a sparing appetite. He dined out rarely; his favourite restaurants were the Ivy, the Savoy Grill, and the Caprice. The latter is, of course, famous for its wonderful food, and all the stars of the London stage are to be seen there nightly. The proprietor, Mario Gallati, was at the Ivy for more than twenty years; he has made the Caprice deservedly world famous, and Ivor was one of his greatest friends. Mario even named a delectable ice-cream dessert after him—'The Ivor Novello Bomb'. Ivor hardly drank at all, though he smoked continuously—enormous boxes of cigarettes were scattered on every table in every room of his house. He was a keen tennis player and swimmer, but his greatest joy was to sit at the piano and compose new melodies.

To Ivor work was life. He worked right up to the last few

hours, and had commenced his next musical play, on a Welsh theme. Discussing this project with his partner, Tom Arnold, over supper at his flat on the night of March 6th, he complained of feeling tired, and of pains in his legs, retiring to bed in the early hours of the morning. At 2-30 a.m. he passed away peacefully, with the echo of applause still ringing in his ears.

That was the way Ivor wished to die. To Elizabeth Frank, who wrote his life story for *Woman's Pictorial,* he confessed how he would like to end his career: 'I should like to make an enchanting curtain speech at the end of a wildly successful first night, and to the sound of cheers and applause—drop gracefully dead. If possible, *before* the curtain falls!'

In one lifetime Ivor had accomplished enough for a dozen men. He lived as he wanted, and he died the way he wanted to. That was, at least, some small consolation for the millions who mourned him. And, as long as there are men and women to sing his glorious melodies, Ivor Novello, the man who made the people sing, will never be forgotten.

THE END

Postscript

WELL, this is the first book that has ever been written about me, and now, having read it, I'm still wondering if it is about me—the 'me' I've known intimately all my life! Has all this happened? It must have, I suppose, because there it is in not altogether cold print.

It is very difficult to assess one's value as an artist; more difficult still to calculate how much permanent impression one has made on the contemporary theatre; and almost impossible to say 'Yes, that's me' (or is it 'I'—I never know) because one feels quite different to oneself from what one appears to one's biographer, however sympathetic or prejudiced he may be. I cannot help being profoundly grateful to Peter Noble for this most painstaking and generous biography, partly because it is always pleasant to read nice things about oneself and partly because it has saved me the trouble of doing it myself, and having therefore to leave half the praise out and increasing the blame by at least one hundred per cent.

February, 1951

Index

INDEX

INDEX

INDEX

INDEX

INDEX

INDEX

INDEX